GIANT STEPS

DEREK SHULMAN

WITH JON WIEDERHORN

MY IMPROBABLE JOURNEY
FROM STAGE LIGHTS
TO EXECUTIVE HEIGHTS

FOREWORD BY TONY VISCONTI

GIANT STEPS

MY IMPROBABLE JOURNEY FROM STAGE LIGHTS TO EXECUTIVE HEIGHTS

DEREK SHULMAN WITH JON WIEDERHORN

A Jawbone book
First edition 2025
Published in the UK and the USA by
Jawbone Press
7 Orlando Road
London SW4 0LE
England
www.jawbonepress.com
books@jawbonepress.com

ISBN 978-1-916829-24-4

Printed by PBtisk

2 3 4 5 30 29 28 27

CONTENTS

FOREWORD
BY TONY VISCONTI

Wherever I go, I'm always surprised when someone will recognize me in the street, approach me, and say, 'I love Gentle Giant.'

And really, I'm so pleased when that happens, because their self-titled debut was, on every level, one of the best albums I was ever involved with. There were several progressive rock bands emerging at the time, but my inspiration for doing what I do came from the most progressive rock group the world has known, The Beatles. Fully knowing I wouldn't knock their producer George Martin off his throne, I said to myself that there must be more Beatles in the UK to discover. By 1970, I had found what I was looking for. They were Gentle Giant.

I needed to work with musicians of that caliber because I studied classical music, I trained hard, and this was very, very challenging. We were working with analog tape and they were doing things that, honestly, you would have required Pro Tools to pull off. And Pro Tools hadn't been invented. So we did some tricks that were akin to what George Martin and The Beatles were doing with analogue tape, and made a fantastic work of art.

Here's how it all happened. There was a meeting with the group in my flat in Putney, London. It was congenial, and plans were made to get into a studio ASAP. I can't remember if we had actual rehearsals, but the group was super 'ready to rock.' Derek has told me that the group learned a lot from me, and I'm flattered. This wasn't going to be the kind of session work the band members were used to from their former group, the easygoing

Simon Dupree. This was going to be intense, and it was! All my musical training would be challenged.

With analogue tape you could fix a mistake by 'dropping in' in tight spaces. Because we were a group of perfectionists, we 'dropped in' all over the place. For one song, I had to drop in at the beginning of a 15/16 bar and drop out before erasing the music immediately afterward. I rehearsed it a few times by tapping my index finger in the space next to the record button, got the feel, and then it had to be done. As the band were all virtuosi, we got it right the very first time.

When we turned in the record, the label was quite disappointed because it was art rock. The album eventually did sell, but the initial sales were very disappointing, maybe only a few hundred. But when I believed in something, I thought, *To hell with the sales, to hell with the A&R department, these just had to be done*, because, culturally speaking, they were very important.

I love that album, and album two, *Acquiring The Taste*, which was in many ways better than the first one. But *Gentle Giant*, the first one, was my favorite because we broke so much fresh ground. It was so innovative. I was also working on David Bowie's *The Man Who Sold The World* at that time, which I would say was the pop-rock version of Gentle Giant. These were pioneering days.

Despite the amount of time that passed since we recorded the albums, listening to the music, as most of us know, unlocks memories, and when it comes to Gentle Giant, mine are fond ones.

TONY VISCONTI, NEW YORK CITY, 2025

PROLOGUE
THE TRAUMA

Every night, my father, Lewis Shulman, would come home in the wee hours from his jazz gigs. He was a bandleader, trumpet player, and an extremely hard worker. He also played hard. A heavy drinker, smoker, and gambler, my dad thought life should be a celebration, and when he was having a good time, he didn't think about money. Fortunately, he was an excellent horn player who somehow (considering his vices) was never out of breath when he was onstage, and he was good enough at band business and self-promotion to support the family with a meager living wage even after his hedonistic indulgences.

Despite the long hours, which didn't always end after the gig, my father always got up early in the morning to start the coal fire in the house, so even when the air was chilly, the house was warm. I often woke at 6am to the sound of my dad's coughing—the result, I suppose, of drinking his poison of choice for decades and smoking up to sixty cigarettes a day. At age sixteen, I knew he had bad habits, but he was lively, exuberant, and funny. Everyone loved him, and I figured he would live to a ripe old age. I was never concerned about his morning cough; that's just the way it was. I was just glad he set an alarm to make sure the fire was lit by the time my mom, my brothers Ray and Terry, and I woke up, so we were relatively comfortable in our drafty house in Portsmouth, England, where it was often raining and bitterly cold from fall to the late winter or early spring.

On the morning of May 14, 1965, I woke up with a start. My dad's coughing was worse than ever—loud, wet, and raspy. I groggily thought he must have caught a nasty cold, and I hoped he wouldn't pass it on to the rest of us. The more awake I became, the worse my dad sounded. This didn't seem like a cold or the flu. He was wheezing, gasping. My mom abruptly opened the bedroom door, which startled me.

'Dad's not feeling well, so he's gone back to bed,' she said. Her voice sounded strained, which was unusual, so I got dressed and went downstairs. The raspy coughing continued. Then it got louder.

'Derek, something's really wrong!' Mom said. 'Go get Phil!'

My brother Phil, who is ten years older than I am, lived next door with his wife, Roberta, and their young son, Calvin. We didn't have a phone, so I ran outside and jumped over the wall between our two houses. I didn't want to lose time running around and opening the gate. I banged on the door and Phil opened it.

'Dad's really sick!' I exclaimed. 'We need your help!'

Phil was a teacher, so he was already dressed for work. He ran back to the house with me, and we both charged upstairs. My father was in bed, half-asleep, his breath shallow between weak coughs.

'Dad. Dad! Can you hear me? Everything's going to be okay,' Phil said.

Dad didn't respond. We were losing him.

'Goddammit,' Phil was yelling. 'Derek, go get the doctor!'

The doctor lived about a hundred yards down the street. I was a good runner, but I think I broke speed records that morning. I banged on the door and, even though it was before 7am, the doc opened it.

'Please, help us!' I shouted. 'My father's really sick! He can hardly breathe!'

The doctor told us he'd grab what he needed and come right over. I turned around and was sprinting back to the house before he'd closed the door. By the time I got back upstairs, my father was in bed, gurgling. Phlegm and foamy spit dripped from his mouth down his chin. I couldn't believe my active, smiling father, who was rich with love and kindness, had turned into this shell of a man. Any previous resentment that we never had enough money or that he dipped into the emergency money jar to go drinking with his mates or pay off gambling debts immediately vaporized. He had flaws, but his zeal and oversized personality usually overcame his weaknesses.

I looked over at my dad, whose breath had slowed to a mechanical rattle. His eyes rolled up and he shat himself.

The doctor arrived a couple of minutes later. Dad had stopped breathing. Phil had been holding him up in bed. He laid him back down and the doctor wiped off my father's mouth and performed CPR twice, but he was way too late. Dad was already blue and had no pulse. He had suffered a massive heart attack while he was setting the coal fire and was already dying by the time he got into bed. Even if the doctor had been there when it happened, he probably wouldn't have been able to help.

'What can we do?' I asked. 'Should we get him to hospital?'

The doctor looked me in the eyes. 'Your father's dead,' he said matter-of-factly. 'There's nothing anyone can do.'

We were all in shock. Dad had seemed perfectly fine the night before. And this morning when he came downstairs, he wasn't clutching his chest or anything. He was just coughing. I thought he might have pneumonia or bronchitis. I never imagined he was having a heart attack, or that, not ten minutes later, I would watch him die just inches from where I stood.

I ran out back to the garden, where my mother had planted tulips, and shouted at the top of my lungs. All the sorrow, pain, and fear in my heart echoed in that scream. Then I screamed again. Rivulets of tears ran down my cheeks and watered the flowers. The screaming calmed me a bit and relieved some of the terror. Soon, the raw, seething anger was replaced with a cold emptiness. I could still feel and think, but my body was numb.

Mom was crying when I got back in. Terry and Ray sat like statues. Phil stayed in the house, comforting our mom. We didn't have a phone, so the doctor reported the death, and the local morgue sent a hearse to the house to remove Dad's body. About an hour or so after his heart attack, reality sank in. My father was gone, and we had to move on.

Jewish law requires corpses to be buried within twenty-four hours, since they can't be embalmed or otherwise preserved. The rule comes from the Torah—the first five books of Moses—which states, 'You shall bury him the same day. … His body should not remain all night.' These days, most Jewish burials take place within three days of death. Autopsies are allowed but are discouraged unless the death is suspicious or the procedure could help protect the lives of others. There was nothing suspicious about my dad's death, so he didn't need an autopsy.

The Jewish community in Portsmouth was very small—about two hundred families in a town of a quarter of a million people—so we sought what comfort we could from them and tried to do everything according to principle. A select group of Jews, the Chevra Kadisha, washed my dad's body in a process called *Tahara* and then dressed him in a plain burial shroud. When he was alive, my dad had been a member of that group and had helped prepare other people for burial. He didn't buy into Judaism as a religion, but he believed in the traditions. I have followed his lead and still consider myself a cultural Jew. I often went to Shabbat services as a kid, and I learned Hebrew. That was part of the tradition of being a Jew. As an adult, I have rarely gone to religious services aside from bar and bat mitzvahs, weddings, and funerals.

My mother was devastated by my father's death. Even though he was often away from the house with his band and drank, smoked, and was a bit of a philanderer, she loved him. Odd though it was, their partnership was real. My mother took care of us, cooked for us, and made sure we went to school and did our homework. My dad went out with the band and made enough money for us to survive. Now, she was alone, and while she was always a pillar of strength, she suddenly had a far greater weight to support. She was a single mother in a home full of kids. My sister Evelyn (who we called Eve) was living with her husband, John King, in Portsmouth, but she came back to the house for a while to help out. Still, my mom did most of the heavy lifting. She wouldn't have it any other way.

Before the funeral, my mom's brother, Chaim, the one who had introduced my parents decades earlier, came over to help with the preparations and be there for the family. He had been my dad's best friend since childhood, when they both lived in Glasgow. He and my dad both left school when they were eleven years old to work and help support their families. They had a long history and had endured plenty of hardships together, so Uncle Chaim was crushed when we told him Dad had died. Even though Chaim wasn't part of our community's Chevra Kadisha, he insisted on taking part in washing my father's body and wrapping him in burial cloths. The community welcomed his help, and being with my father in his last moments before burial provided Chaim with some comfort and closure.

Since we didn't have much money for the service, the coffin, or the burial, the community rallied around us and paid for everything they felt a good Jewish man should be entitled to after he dies, whether or not he had money. Even in my numb state, I thought that was nice. The synagogue was small and the congregation orthodox, so the men all sat together on one side of the temple, and the women sat separated from their husbands and sons. The rabbi gave the sermon and talked a little bit about my father. After the service, we went to the cemetery, which was half a mile away. Since Phil was the oldest son, the rabbi asked him to say the Kaddish, which is the Jewish prayer for the dead.

Before my father was buried, Chaim and some of Dad's friends spoke to the small crowd. As my dad's best friend, my uncle knew that out of his four sons, I had the most contact with him, so he asked me to say the Kaddish at temple every week for a year. I half-sleepwalked through the funeral. I went through the motions and even scooped a shovelful of dirt from a pile and dumped it on my dad's coffin, where it fell with a muffled thump. I felt like all the air had been sucked from my lungs and I hoped I would wake up at any moment, breathless from the nightmare and I would hear my dad softly coughing downstairs. But I knew I was awake. I could speak; I just didn't want to. Nothing I could say would have any meaning after what had happened. Nonetheless, my mother sent us all to school the next morning.

'Staying around the house won't change anything, and you'll fall behind in your studies,' she said. 'That's not what your father would have wanted.'

Being back in school was strange. No one knew or seemed to care why I was absent for two days. It was almost like nothing had happened. None of the students or faculty said anything to me, and as I drifted from class to class, I kept to myself and remained silent. On some level, I think I was embarrassed to be a kid who suddenly had no father. I already felt weird because we were poor, and I played this strange music with my brother. Now, I felt like even more of an outcast.

When I got back from school, people started coming over to sit shiva with us. After someone Jewish dies, friends and community members visit the family every day for between three days and a week. They bring food and drink and keep the bereaved company, which was comforting but also confusing. I'd go to school and pretend everything was normal, then come home to people who wanted to help mourn my father's death. Some of them told funny stories about my dad, which was amusing but bittersweet, since my father wouldn't be telling any more stories or playing any more gigs. After shiva, the house was empty, and entering the front door was like walking into a hole.

Everyone tried to go on with their daily lives. It was hard, and my mom was the glue that kept us together. When there were melancholy lulls, Phil and my sister, the eldest siblings, tried to keep the conversation flowing. To me, it seemed like we were all putting on a play. I tried to march along through my normal routine, but my steps had no grounding. There was no floor under my feet.

The terrible dreams began within a week after Dad's death. Night after night, I'd relive that horrid morning in vivid Technicolor, starting from the sound of my father coughing right up until the moment the doctor told us he was dead. But then, at the end of the dream, my father would always wake up and say something like, 'No, it's okay. I'm fine. Let's go make some music.' And he'd get out of bed. The dream recurred every night for nine months. Despite the happy ending, it was terrifying.

Ray also had trouble sleeping through the night. That didn't stop us from practicing music as hard as ever. We were determined to continue the band we had formed. It gave us something to focus on, so we weren't always thinking about Dad being gone. And it made us feel good. We were getting better, and we knew it. Even before Phil joined and brought his musical abilities into our group, we were finally playing songs that moved well. They were soulful and catchy. We were learning how to combine the sounds of our biggest influences—The Beatles, Chuck Berry, Little Richard, Muddy Waters, and B.B. King—with the romantic fervor of English pop, without sounding like anyone else.

We wished Dad was alive to see us improve, become popular, ascend the national charts, and play *Top Of The Pops* as Simon Dupree & The Big Sound a few years later. But at least he saw us perform at a small soul and blues club. We were nowhere near ready for the big time, but whenever I looked over at Dad during the show, he was smiling. He was so proud of us for carrying on the Shulman music tradition.

For a good year after he died, I went to Saturday morning Shabbat services as often as I could to honor my father, just as Uncle Chaim had asked me to do. Sometimes that meant rushing home from Friday night gigs so I could get enough sleep to get up early the next day and be awake enough not to fall asleep at temple. During a service, the rabbi repeatedly instructs the congregation to stand up and sit back down, so it's glaringly obvious if you're deep in slumber. As Simon Dupree & The Big Sound started playing more shows outside of Portsmouth, it became harder to make it to services, and eventually I stopped going. But even now, on the rare times I'm in a synagogue, I say the mourner's Kaddish for my dad and other loved ones I've lost over the years.

Losing our father at such a young age had a profound effect on all of us. None of us thought we were going to live past the age of fifty, which was one reason we progressed and performed like we had the proverbial noose of time around our necks. During the fifteen years or so between the nascent days of Simon Dupree & The Big Sound and the end of Gentle Giant, we drove in fifth gear at double the speed limit. We knew we couldn't do this forever, so we were non-stop as if our lives depended on it. We were determined to succeed. Failure wasn't an option, and if it took working twice as hard as any of our peers, that was what we would do.

At the very least, we wanted to prove to ourselves that we were making music that we loved and that would have impressed our dad and made him proud; for most people, that was a tall order, since he was a natural and could play any instrument five minutes after picking it up. More importantly, we wanted—no, needed—to succeed on a national and international level. In Dad's absence, we had to help our mom so she didn't have to work so hard. She gave up everything for years to support us. It was our turn to give back. We didn't want to spend money on cars, girls, and materialistic indulgences. We wanted to take care of her and the rest of the family. When I reached the point with Simon Dupree where I had a solid income, I bought my mom a house, and I was happy to do it. We lived there with her for a while, but I made all the payments, and, after all she had done to support me, I was proud to be able to provide something tangible for her.

In my late teens and early twenties, I felt like my experience proved I needed to stay clean, run like the wind, and grab every opportunity by the balls just to remain in control and not wind up like my dad. It took some intensive therapy as an adult to realize I had been suffering from post-traumatic stress that whole time, and long after my dad died. Aside from the nightmares and the relative certainty that I wasn't going to live past fifty, I've had various psychological issues, some of which are still with me to this day.

I could never call my dad's death a mixed blessing. It was a horrible tragedy, yet some of the fallout from that tragedy was positive. I knew Dad's lifestyle had contributed to his heart attack, and I vowed to take care of myself and avoid dangerous indulgences. I wasn't opposed to the idea of sin, and I didn't fear eternal damnation. I just didn't want to die before I made a significant mark on the world. So, I've tried to eat healthily, exercise regularly, and avoid the temptations that brought down my father, because I didn't know how much of his undoing was in his genes—and mine—and how much was due to his smoking and drinking.

I've never smoked a cigarette. I've only done hashish a couple of times, and I didn't enjoy the brain fog. I've never been drunk (although I do enjoy a nice glass of wine with dinner). I've never tried quaaludes, meth, cocaine, or heroin, and I've only done LSD once, when I was dosed (more on that later). Seeing my father transform from living to dead in a mere thirty minutes scared the hell out of me and scarred me for life. Knowing that I could start coughing, suffer cardiac arrest, and become as inactive as a wound-down cymbal-clanging toy monkey shook me to the core.

All my siblings were affected by my dad's death in their own way. Phil and Eve smoked at the time my dad died—almost everyone did—but they quit immediately after. Strangely, while I've rushed to the doctor whenever my stomach's hurt or I've had a headache, my sister refused to see a doctor until her dying day. Phil has flat-out refused to talk about the day my dad died. If you ask him about it, he'll change the subject. And I'm sure it contributed to his negativity and cynicism. And Ray dealt with his own psychological torment, though he was still young enough when our dad passed that he wasn't as affected as the rest of us. Ah, the resilience of naïve youth.

I just know the inoperable mental shrapnel that struck me that day was indelible. I've suffered several panic attacks, some of which were understandable and signaled something that desperately needed to be changed about my current circumstances. Others were sparked by nerves, paranoia, and the memory of my father's last thirty minutes on earth. In Gentle Giant, I was always overly concerned about my health, which I always felt explained my need to be in top form as a singer in a perfectionist band. My therapist later convinced me there was more to it than that.

When you're in your seventies, you expect to have some health problems, and I'm no exception. I'm approaching twenty-five years of active life past fifty, and none of my current ailments are going to send me into a rapid spiral to the hospital. I might live another year. I might go on for a decade or more. It's impossible to know until you receive that diagnosis you've feared your entire life. That recently happened to my brother and lifelong best friend, Ray. He died in 2023 at the age of seventy-three, and I'll always miss him. In my heart, I understand that death is a natural, obviously unavoidable part of the human condition. Nonexistence is inevitable. And after that, who knows?

I'd rather not dwell on it, as I have found doing so to be terrifying, so I continue to stay active and involved with projects that stimulate me and enjoy the rewards with which I've been blessed. But when activity slows, I know all the life-affirming moments aren't going to stop me from worrying every time I have a sore throat or a stomach ache. And maybe that's what keeps me going.

GIANT STEPS

PART ONE

FINDING MY FEET

GIANT STEPS

CHAPTER ONE

POOR BUT RICH

I was born in a tenement building in Glasgow, and we moved to Portsmouth soon after, so I don't remember much from my earliest days. As established as my dad was in the jazz scene, we never had any money. Living in a tiny rental flat on Fawcett Road in Portsmouth was colorful, but it wasn't glamorous. At the age of ten, I slept in a small room on a single mattress with my younger brothers Terry, who was a year my junior, and Ray, who was two years younger than me. At least it made the room seem bigger than it would have had we each had our own bed. My older sister, Evelyn, had a small room to herself, and my parents slept in a room that wasn't much bigger. Eve moved in with her future husband, John, when she finished school, and the rest of us moved to another rental, this one on Eastney Road, which was right next door to the house where Phil and his wife lived.

My parents' new house was old and drafty, and none of the furniture matched. Not only did we share a single toilet, but we had to go outdoors to use it. Using an outhouse—whether it was the middle of winter or the heart of the summer—and having to wait if someone was ahead of me in line, colored the rest of my life. I was determined to be successful when I was older and to have enough money to buy a house with as many bathrooms as I needed. As it was, we barely had enough money for groceries.

Poverty was not fun. It was shameful to me, and it was in my roots, wrapping around the angular limbs of my family tree and threatening to suffocate us. My grandparents came from peasant villages in Poland and struggled to survive. They were chased out of Poland during the pogroms—violent village raids by gangs from local communities that felt threatened or intimidated by the area Jews. My grandfather on my mother's side fled with his wife and boarded the closest ship out of the country. When they landed in England, he thought he was in America. He didn't speak a word of English, and he had to accept any menial job he could find—sometimes three at a time—to support the family. I'm not even sure how long he spent in Glasgow before he realized he wasn't in the United States.

Growing up, we all had a bath on Friday night—once a week—and since we couldn't afford to waste anything, we used the same bathwater. Phil and Eve didn't bathe at the house anymore, so I got the clear, warm water; Terry got the slightly murky water, which was disgusting enough; poor Ray, who was two years my junior, got cold, gray sludge. Having to scrimp and save colored everything I did when I was older—how I worked hard, the way I saved money, why I always kept pushing ahead for fear that if I paused, I would lose something I had achieved. From the time I was old enough to work, I hustled. I watched the shops for local storeowners, dug up ragworms to sell to fishing shops for bait, and, when I was fourteen, got a job working at a pork butcher at six in the morning on Saturday. Only later could I appreciate the irony of working on Saturday, the Sabbath, hanging up sides of pork, the one food that many Jews who don't even keep kosher won't eat. It was utterly disgusting, but it paid me a few pounds, so I was able to help out the family when my dad couldn't.

I was always a bit confused that we were poor and Jewish. There were not many Jews in our town, but those that there were had a family business, or the father was a lawyer or architect. They had money. We didn't. We were outsiders in a community of outsiders. But at least my parents were cultured. They loved to read, my mom enjoyed having long discussions with us at the dinner table, and we all listened to music. My parents started Ray on violin when he was seven, and he took to it right away. They valued the arts and education and were convinced that good schooling was the key to success.

Phil worked as an English and art teacher. My mother expected me to do something similar, and I started out on the right track. At the time, nearly all eleven-year-old children in England took an exam called the 11-Plus, and the students who did extremely well—about three percent of those who took the test—were sent to a grammar school instead of the regular local schools, which had a lower standard of education and were geared toward students from working-class homes. I came from good genes and was a smart kid, so I scored very well on the exam. I was accepted to Portsmouth Southern Grammar School, which wasn't specifically for rich kids but didn't really cater to students from poor families (who, it was assumed, would wind up at a lower-tier school). Most of the students at Portsmouth Southern Grammar School were from middle-class families. We all wore uniforms and looked the same, but when they weren't in class, the other students wore new clothes while Ray and I had on our brothers' hand-me-downs. None of my classmates had an outhouse at their homes either, so I never invited friends over because I didn't want them to see how poor we were.

I was never bullied or physically attacked for being Jewish. The prejudice was more subtle and institutional. My school was very strict and structured. The teachers all wore mortarboards and cloaks, and the place was run with the precision of a German railway. We started the day with all two thousand students attending the morning assembly. There was a dais with a headmaster standing there. A teacher spoke about how all the school teams did in sports, and that was followed by a morning service for the Christian students. While they prayed, two other Jews and I, and three Jehovah's Witnesses, had to leave the room. The school didn't intentionally ostracize us, but they made it clear that we didn't belong there while they prayed. They weren't the only ignorant people in Portsmouth. Some of my friends who I played football and cricket with asked me if the rumors they heard about Jews were true.

'Why did the Jews kill Jesus?' was a popular question. Here's a less accusatory but more hurtful one: 'Is it true that when you turn thirteen, you get £10,000 and you're taken care of for life?'

The latter was upsetting to me because I wasn't from a family of Jews that could afford to buy fancy cars, and I didn't even grow up in a nice house, and since I felt out of place, I imagined all the kids staring at me and thinking I was part of a cult that drank baby's blood as I was ushered out of the assembly hall. I have no idea why they didn't let the non-Christians stay with the other students during the service.

To encourage me to be social, my parents sent me to something called Jewish Youth Club but I had nothing in common with those kids. They honored the Sabbath and went to synagogue every week. That wasn't for me.

I was very good at football, and for a while Ray and I hung out with the other kids who played sports. But we soon gravitated more to music and spent a lot of time at home, listening to music. One day, I took some of the money I had saved up from working crappy jobs and went to the local record store. I wanted to buy a single I had heard on the radio. I didn't know who it was by, but the chorus sounded to me like 'Sharp And Round.'

'Do you have "Sharp And Round"?' I asked hopefully. 'I don't know who it's by.' The sales had no idea what I was talking about. He looked it up and couldn't find it, so he told me they didn't have it in stock. But it might be out there somewhere.

I went to another shop and asked if they had the song. 'I don't know anything by that name,' replied the guy at the counter. He pursed his lips, creased his brow, and looked thoughtful for a moment. Then his eyes lit up. 'Is it possible you're thinking of "Shop Around" by the American band The Miracles?' He dug it out from the shelves and put it on.

'Yeah, that's the one!' I enthused. I bought it, took it home, and played it until the grooves wore out.

There was always music in the house. When I was very young, Phil and his friends used to listen to Stan Getz, Shorty Rogers, and Charlie Parker. My dad listened to jazz records, too, but he also liked classical. So, Ray and I heard a lot of interesting music from an early age. We were especially inspired by radio programming in the mid-60s, including Radio Luxembourg and American Forces Radio Network, which we'd listen to at our friends' houses. The audience for American Forces was largely black, so we'd hear soul music and R&B and say, 'Wow, what the hell is this about? This is amazing!'

That was really how the British Invasion was born. Kids didn't want to listen to the lightweight programming of the BBC and buy these silly, shitty records that were coming out. We loved Motown and Stax Records, but we wanted something more gritty and real, and we heard that in black blues music by Muddy Waters, Howlin' Wolf, Sonny Boy Williamson, and other Chess Records stuff they played on American Forces Network. In addition to sounding great, it was simple; a lot of it was composed of three chords. We thought, *Man, we could do something like this.*

My sister, Evelyn, should have been right there with us. She wanted to be a professional singer when she was young, and she had a gorgeous voice. She would sing and I would harmonize with her. I discovered I had a natural talent for harmonies when she was singing the black spiritual 'Down By The Riverside.' I joined in and, without thinking, locked into the vocal harmony as if I had rehearsed with her for weeks. From then on, any time she sang a melody to a song I knew, I'd harmonize with her, and we'd sound great.

Evelyn was married to a BBC producer named John King, who could have helped her with a singing career. Maybe he could have helped all of us. Ray sang amazing harmonies as well. We would have made a great professional singing trio, but in the final years of his life, my father decided his daughter should not undertake a career singing onstage, and he forbade her from singing professionally on any level—not even in local clubs.

She was crushed, but Dad has his reasons. He had played jazz in different cities and seen the way young women performers were treated and taken advantage of. As angry as she was, Evelyn obeyed my father and didn't perform ever again. Instead of spitting sour grapes, she was supportive of all three of her brothers and even convinced her husband to manage Simon Dupree & The Big Sound. After we got a record deal, she co-wrote songs that became B-sides of some of our hit records. And, before all that, she gave me my first guitar—a Spanish acoustic that set me on my path to writing songs.

I learned a few chords and created progressions, which was as easy for me as connecting dots. I had a good ear, so once I learned those five basic open chords, I listened closely to my records and tried to play along. I turned to Ray, who was already a damned good violinist.

'Yeah, that's just E, A, and B on guitar,' he confirmed.

'Okay, let's do that,' I said, and in no time, we were jamming together. To me, E, A, and B are still the most important chords in the world. The key was to interpret them in your own way—to inject your own emotions and experiences into them and own them. Everyone who joined a band did that, and the good ones could use the same chord as everyone else—sometimes in the same basic patterns—and turn them into completely different songs that reflected their personality and aesthetic. That was the start of the British rock movement.

I always loved music, but that's not the only thing that made me want to be a pop star. Life in Portsmouth was predictable. It was boring. I thought being in a popular band would be different and exciting. At that point, it wasn't what everyone else wanted to do. Maybe in America kids were living in awe of Elvis Presley and idolized this wave of early rock'n'roll, which was obviously stolen from the black blues. Elvis, Bill Haley & The Comets, The Big Bopper, Ritchie Valens… none of that moved me. It sounded like white bread compared to the stuff on Chess Records. It was anemic and boring, and it didn't catch on in the UK the way it did in America.

Then everything changed. On October 5, 1962, Parlophone released The Beatles' first single, 'Love Me Do.' Two days later, UK radio started playing the song for the first time, and my life was never the same; it went from black-and-white to full color. That rumbling guitar rhythm was the passenger seat for the glorious vocals. The bass and drums anchored the sound, and it took us several listens to realize that soulful howl was a harmonica. Everything fit. The pieces connected. I was fifteen, and I knew what I wanted to do for the rest of my life.

I continued to be at or near the top of the class, but when I got home I was no longer interested in playing sports or even bunking off from school. I wanted to write music and get it played on the radio—like The Beatles. Ray was the perfect partner, a musical genius. He was fourteen, and he was being coached by a special tutor to join the National Youth Orchestra of Great Britain.

'Hey Ray,' I said to him one day after school. 'I'm putting a group together. You gotta join.'

Part of the reason I wanted him in the band was because he was my brother and we were tight. I also knew he was a great musician, and he'd be able to help write great songs and play them with unmatched skill. At first, my parents were upset that Ray wanted to be a pop musician instead of a classical violinist, but they liked the idea that we were in it together and they supported us unconditionally.

Ray helped me put together chord patterns that provided a musical bed for his melodies. Then he bought a bass for ten pounds at a pawn shop and mastered rhythmic counterpoint immediately, and we were able to work on songs in a more conventional format. It was a clunky old thing made by the English company Grimshaw, but it did the trick until we could upgrade our gear. Ray could have been a great and probably well-respected violinist, but he saw more upside in playing with a rock band, and he brought his musical training with him. We immediately had a leg up on our contemporaries. Ray could play two instruments well, and, unlike a lot of signed artists, he could read and compose music. Our initial batch of songs was hardly radio-ready, but I'm sure Robert Browning's first poems weren't earth-shattering either.

My parents knew that Ray and I were bright and could have gone in any number of directions, but unlike many kids from enlightened Jewish families, we weren't pushed in a certain vocational direction. My mom always worried about my dad's late-night activities and was anxious about whether we'd have enough money to put food on the table or buy presents for Chanukkah. She was a worrier, I guess. That was part of her genetics, some of which I inherited. I'm sure she would have been more at ease knowing that I was a doctor and Ray was, say, a lawyer, and we'd be able to make good money in stable job fields. But she saw how much we loved music, and—even after my father's chosen path led to his early death—she wasn't going to dissuade us and destroy our dreams, as Dad had done with Evelyn. It wouldn't have helped, anyway. Ray and I were determined to take after our father (only without the hedonistic indulgences), and we were well aware of the insecurity that could come from that line of work. We also saw how exciting and creatively rewarding it could be.

On many nights at 6pm, we listened to music on the radio as we watched

Dad iron his shirt to get ready for his 7:30 gig. It was the dance band era, so he didn't tour, but he was a bandleader and played around the area in different jazz groups. He'd return home at midnight or later and often bring musicians back to the house and into the front room of the house. I knew that this was his private time with his mates, but one time I felt bold and snuck downstairs in pajamas to watch him and his friends play.

'Go back to bed,' Dad slurred when he saw me.

'I don't want to,' I snapped back, as only a precocious youngster can. 'Besides, you woke me up and now I can't sleep. Can I watch?'

He shrugged, and I watched them play jazz for hours. I never had to ask again. I'd watch their routine countless times. At around two in the morning, they'd stop playing. Then they'd smoke and play cards until sunrise. Dad was only paid for the gigs, but he loved the jazz life so much that he took it home with him. Sometimes they'd all smoke weed, so I grew to know the smell, though I never liked it. For a while, my dad brought some black jazzers from America back with him who seemed far more distant than his jovial, animated friends. Phil, who as a young adult was wiser to the ways of the world than I was, told me the Americans were heroin addicts. I had no idea what he meant. I just knew they were a little different, but this was the way those guys lived. They weren't like regular folks. They were musicians, and what they did together (aside from drinking and taking drugs) was magical.

In some ways, I inherited the artist's lifestyle, just without the smoking, drinking, and drugging. The obsession my dad had with jazz was like the love I developed for rock'n'roll. Having watched him and his friends, I understood that being a musician came with sacrifices. I knew that if I ever had kids there would be long stretches when I was on the road and wouldn't see them. I accepted that—the drawbacks would come with the benefits. My dad was a natural musician, and Evelyn, Phil, Ray, and I inherited that gift. It would be a crime to throw it away. If I did that, I felt like I would be missing out on all the happiness that being a pop star would provide. I also honestly felt like I would be robbing thousands and thousands—maybe millions—of listeners of the great music Ray and I would someday make and that the public would enjoy.

From the time Ray and I announced our plans to our parents, we were totally upfront about our goals and what we were doing to meet them. And we promised that our school grades wouldn't slip. I had great respect for my mother, so I always let her know what was going on in my life, even after I became a pop star. I never consciously defied her. That said, I wasn't a momma's boy per se, because I wasn't utterly reliant on her. I loved her, of course, but I wasn't helpless without her. I had been working hard since long before I made a penny from music, so I would always have records and whatever I needed for the band. And I pitched in to buy food or pay the bills when my dad was short.

Once Ray and I started throwing together musical ideas, we soon gelled as players. However, I was limited to playing at a low volume because I was still using the Spanish acoustic without amplification. I was playing all the basic open chords—C, G, D, E, and A—and doing what I could with that. I still hadn't fully developed calluses on my fingertips, so the F and B barre chords, which required covering all the strings with the index finger, playing three other notes, and pushing hard on all the strings, were damn near impossible on Spanish guitar. I found a workaround for the F by playing it on only the highest four strings, but I couldn't do that as easily with the B because it required sliding my hand seven frets up the neck.

When my dad saw how serious I was about playing guitar, he bought me my first electric for £20. It was a Red Vox Shadow three-pickup solid-body with a tremolo arm. He bought it on hire purchase, which was like a layaway plan that cost him £1 a week with interest. He couldn't afford it, but he was a musician, and he knew I needed decent equipment to reach the next rung up the music ladder, so he didn't hesitate. I saved up money from my job as a pork butcher and did jobs on Saturday mornings to buy my first amplifier, a triangular-shaped 15-watt tube amp called the Watkins Dominator. I think it was about £15.

There was no such thing as distortion. The only way of overdriving your amp was by turning it up all the way, strumming as hard as you could, and having sensitive pickups. Every unusual amp sound had to be coaxed and lured out of the guitar and amp by the way you set the tone knobs and the way you plucked or attacked the strings. You had to earn everything, and, because of that, a lot of musicians spent endless hours focusing on how to get the best, most unique sounds from their primitive equipment. There were no shortcuts. The only way to sound good was to be good. Having a guitar with an amp was a major step in my progression as a musician since better-sounding guitar tones inspired us to write better melodies.

Ray and I were fortunate that our father was able to attend a small variety show we played, and afterward he was happier than I'd seen him in ages. I felt like I was walking on air. I wanted to recreate that feeling on a regular basis for a long, long time and have him there as a part of it. Dad died when I was sixteen, and dealing with that at such a young age forced me to get serious, be determined, and work hard to provide. We all chipped in and supported my mother and the household, not the other way around. Mom was devastated. She was warm, sensitive, and emotional, and I don't think she ever got over Dad's death. She was in mourning for a long time, and when she finally was able to look outside herself and consider her options, there were few opportunities. She wasn't young anymore, and she had no professional training, so she wasn't qualified to hold a job.

That's the point in my life where I became the COO of the family and earned my de facto business degree. I was always interested in business, and whenever I worked a menial job, I would take mental notes as I watched how my boss would run the shop: *Was he taking constructive steps to make the place successful or not? Was he charging too much or too little for his services?* That kind of attention to money matters helped set me up for negotiating contracts, maintaining efficiency, and setting reachable goals for myself and my family. I was the middle child, but in the absence of my father, I played the role of the patriarch. That approach continued when my brothers and I formed a band and got signed—which I felt we were destined to do—and Ray and I were well on our way to making music far more than a hobby. We got together with friends and rehearsed every day. We were writing our own songs, and we felt good. We got shivers down our necks every time we played something that sounded professional. It felt like a sign of the future.

When I turned seventeen and my classmates and I were working on our A-levels, the schoolmaster, Mr. Rogers, wanted to provide some incentives. Before we cracked open our English textbooks, he went around the room and asked everyone what they wanted to do when they finished their studies. Some of the boys said they wanted to go to college to become lawyers or doctors. Another said he wanted to do something in math like accounting or engineering. There were aspiring scientists and pharmacists.

'How about you, Derek?' the teacher asked when he reached me. 'What do you want to do?'

'I'm going to write music and be a pop star.'

I don't know what I was expecting. Maybe some support or validation that my aspiration was valid—noble even. That's not what I got. My classmates erupted in laughter.

'No, Derek,' said the teacher. 'That will never happen. Choose something else you're good at.'

I stuck to my guns. 'I'm in a band with my brother now, and I want to keep writing music and be famous,' I continued.

'You'll never be a pop star. For everyone that makes it in music, there are ten thousand who wind up working in factories—especially here in Portsmouth. Is that what you want?'

'I'm not going to work in a factory. I'm going to make music and record albums and tour. You'll see.'

Two years later, my band, Simon Dupree & The Big Sound, were signed to Parlophone Records, the same label as The Beatles, and a year after that we had a hit single and performed on the legendary TV show *Top Of The Pops*. Many of the kids that had laughed at me and even Mr. Rogers watched along with a million other viewers as we jammed on our biggest hit, 'Kites.' Strange how life works sometimes.

CHAPTER TWO

THE BIG BREAK

The Beatles released 'Love Me Do' in 1962, and the Stones honed their early sound at their first gigs. It was the beginning of the British beat era, and the air was charged with a new youth movement.

'Man, we need to be a part of this,' I said to my closest school friend, Eric Hine. So, we pulled kids people from our peer group together and convinced them to get whatever instruments they needed and join us. Ray was already on board, and since he was one of the only great violinists playing pop music, he stood out. We were on our way. I realized we needed two guitarists, so I went up to another friend, Ray Feast.

'Why don't you come and join the band my brother and I are making?' I asked Ray. He was my brother's age, and he could play basic chords. Better still, he had a Fender Stratocaster way before anyone else had one. At the time, Fender was facing a trade embargo and was unable to send guitars to England. (It wasn't until Eric Clapton got hold of a bunch of Stratocasters and brought them back to England to sell to his friends—including Jeff Beck, Jimmy Page, and David Gilmour—that British bands started playing Fender guitars.)

I was pretty good at playing simple, melodic solos, so I was the lead guitarist and the singer. I even learned how to play those pain-inducing barre chords, pressing the strings until they cut into my fingers, and persisting until I could wrangle ringing chords out of them. They were much easier to master on an electric than an acoustic. Eric wanted to play guitar as well, but there was no room for three guitarists in an R&B

pop band. What we needed was a keyboardist. I convinced Eric to buy a keyboard, and for someone who wasn't a natural musician, he wasn't half bad. He stayed with us right through to the end of Simon Dupree & The Big Sound.

Our first drummer was Andy Meade. He didn't have a set of drums, and he wouldn't buy one, so we had him bang on pots and pans. That was bad enough. He also couldn't keep time, but neither could some of the other guys we'd brought on board. My brother and I were naturally better musicians than our friends. We would start to play music and they would struggle to keep up. They were good friends, but they weren't good bandmates. It was okay when we had just started out and we were all struggling and making an awful row—trying to play in the same key with the same timing—but once we started to become musical, we had to make some tough decisions.

Andy was the first to go. We needed someone who had drums. Ray Feast didn't make the cut either. The one good thing that came out of that was that, when he left, he decided he was done playing guitar and agreed to sell us his Fender. That was great, but after he left we were no longer friends, which was upsetting but a necessary misfortune. If we wanted to get better and play in front of a lot of people, we had to get our act together. We needed the right players, the right songs, and the right name.

The first name we came up with was The Howling Wolves, after the Chicago electric blues guitarist Howlin' Wolf. That didn't stick for long. Soon we'd changed to The Roadrunners, because of the 1960 Bo Diddley song, 'Roadrunner Blues.' No one loved the name, but we all agreed it would work.

It was around this time that my brother Phil joined us. There were two reasons I wanted Phil in the band. First, he was gainfully employed as a schoolteacher, which meant he had some money to spend on the gear. More importantly, I was able to convince him to play saxophone. He was a trumpeter like our dad and had never played sax in his life, but I thought it would be good for us because everyone was trying to emulate the music on the American soul label Stax, and all those groups had sax players. 'C'mon Phil,' I said. 'You already play trumpet. How different could it be?'

I added that if he joined the group, he would have to supply a van, since none of us had money to transport our gear. Phil had grown tired of teaching and wanted to be a star musician as well, so he agreed. I hoped he would be the star saxophonist I thought we needed, and he really tried, but he wasn't as good as we thought he would be—not good enough to hang with the more talented sax players in the scene. We realized he should probably stick to the trumpet and only play a little sax.

A few moments of introspection later, I realized I was no John Lennon. I could only sing and play guitar to the simplest progressions. Beyond that, I couldn't coordinate my hands to work with my mouth, and my guitar skills only went so far. So, Ray picked up my guitar, and in no time he'd learned all the open chords. Soon after, he was figuring out how to play leads. He was a natural. Just like my father, he could pick up any instrument and learn to play it within two hours.

Once he was in the band for real, Phil made it clear he didn't like the name The Roadrunners. He wasn't the only one. Some friends of ours and a guy who was working as our agent agreed, and, as we found out, there were other bands named Roadrunners. Back then it wasn't like today, where every name is taken and trademarked by somebody so you have to pick something obscure, often by combining two unrelated words—like 'Elemental Gourds' or something equally ridiculous. But Roadrunners… yeah, I guess we should have figured there were probably another dozen of them out there. We told our agent we were changing our name.

'Okay, what you got?' he said. It was more of a command than a question.

'Uhh… Simon Dupree!'

'I can't remember who blurted it out, but we all liked it. Simon Dupree was the first Lord Mayor of Portsmouth, so we were paying homage to our roots. Only, it wasn't quite enough. In a review of one of our early shows, a journalist wrote that we had a 'very big sound.' We liked that, so we threw it on at the end: Simon Dupree & The Big Sound. The name was long, but it floated off the tongue and made a statement.

Calling ourselves Simon Dupree & The Big Sound was an epiphany for me because it gave me a role to play. I've always been opinionated, but

I've never been naturally extroverted. My brother-in-law, John King, was our manager by then, and he wanted me to be the charismatic presence and pretty face in the front of the band. I never considered myself a looker or a natural leader, but with our new name, I didn't have to be Derek Shulman, working-class kid from Portsmouth. I was Simon Dupree, which enabled me to put together a suave, sexy alter ego that took me away from my humble roots and allowed me to become a rock star and put on a dramatic, entertaining show. We were a sweaty, bluesy R&B band, and I loved interacting with the crowd, banging on the stage to encourage them to come closer, reaching out to shake hands with the guys, and touching the arms or tousle the hair of the girls.

We poached our rhythm section—bassist Peter O'Flaherty and drummer Tony Ransley—from a Southampton group with a pretty solid following. I'm not sure why they wanted to leave except they said they liked playing with us better. They brought a jazzy swing to the band that upped our game. We were tight but not stiff, and we played with groove and attitude. We were happening. Mostly we played covers of songs by artists like Howlin' Wolf, Bo Diddley, Otis Redding, Don Covay, and Wilson Pickett, and we became a top touring band on the South Coast of England. We practiced all the time and were on a nearly professional level by the time we played our first batch of gigs at established clubs. We worked our asses off because we had to.

John was a great manager for a new, developing band, and he had experience pitching ideas at the BBC and acquiring and cultivating successful TV programming. At his corporate job, he was clever and inventive. At one point, he proposed an idea for a program where people would bring in old artifacts they had around the house and have them appraised by a panel of experts. He called it *Going For A Song*. Years later, the idea became the hugely popular BBC show *Antiques Roadshow*, which branched into an even more successful US version on PBS. There's another show in England called *Gogglebox* that features people watching TV and offering their opinions of what they're seeing. That was John's idea, too, and it predated all those huge YouTube gamer videos by 50 years. For some reason, he never received the credit he deserved for his innovation.

Fortunately for us, John saw a lot of potential in Simon Dupree & The Big Sound. He eagerly took the promotional helm, pitching us to his media and record label contacts and calling up venues to get us gigs, all while holding down his job at the BBC. There were two choices for new bands. You either became very good very quickly and developed a fanbase, or you became very not-so-good and looked for another line of work. We became very good, and with our manager working his contacts, we made a big splash.

John had a plan to get us national attention. We booked some studio time in Bristol, where he and Evelyn lived, and did some demos. Then John took the recordings to his contacts at the BBC and convinced them we were the next big thing. He told them they should keep their options open for covering us so they would be ahead of the curve because, pretty soon, we were going to be everywhere. Then he appealed to his DJ friends, which might have had something to do with getting us an audition for Parlophone at Abbey Road Studios. We knew we were lucky to have the opportunity to play in front of such a high-profile company, and we made sure we were well-rehearsed. Even so, we had no idea about the kind of high-level scrutiny we were facing.

We plugged in and looked up. Staring back at us, expressionless, were all these major-league music executives in their snazzy day suits. There was Beatles producer George Martin, pioneering studio engineer and producer Geoff Emerick (who also worked with The Beatles), award-winning sound engineer (and Alan Parsons Project founder) Alan Parsons, Dave Paramor (our assigned producer), and about twelve other EMI staffers. It looked like they were obliged to be there, and they couldn't wait to leave and move on to their next appointment. It was nerve-racking, yet we were relentlessly determined to overcome any adversity. And this wasn't adversity. This was an *opportunity*—our entry into the world of rock stardom. There was no way we were gonna fuck this up. It was bizarre and exciting, and we were full of energy.

Strangely, the Parlophone staff didn't ask us to play one or two songs. They had us do our entire set—a full concert for corporate royalty. I picked up the mic. 'Whenever you're ready,' said someone I didn't recognize. Tony did a four-count, and we were off. Despite (or maybe because of) our audience, we weren't stiff or tentative. We were bouncing off the walls, playing like we were in front of a packed crowd at our hometown pub. I always loved performing at any time, any place, so the audition was fun. I struck poses for the executives and made rock'n'roll faces, some of which were practiced but most of which came naturally. We killed it. We were tuned in, in tune, and we sounded great.

It was tight. It was amazing. And I had no idea if we made any sort of impression on anyone. Most of them had their arms folded the whole time. I thought I saw a few smiles here and there, but even those seemed like accidental slip-ups. It was like these guys had been specifically instructed not to clap, bob their heads, or grin. We got offstage and we were introduced to George, Geoff, Alan, and the other suits, who all said hello and shook our hands in a very British, businesslike way. No one told us they liked our performance. No one told us they didn't.

I *knew* we were great, but my confidence was dissolving into a puddle of doubt. One thing I've discovered about myself is whenever there's a pause in the action and I have enough time for introspection, I start to second-guess myself. I guess it's just a symptom of being a neurotic Jew, but over the past sixty years it's literally given my ulcers.

'Maybe we weren't what they were looking for,' I said to Ray when we were back home. 'Maybe they didn't like the songs.'

'You think?' Ray said. 'I don't know. Maybe you're right.'

Ray had always looked up to me and generally trusted my opinion. He was the eternal peacemaker, never wanting to contradict me and even less interested in being at the receiving end of my frustration.

I wasn't depressed about maybe not getting the gig. But I was confused.

'We don't need to worry,' I said, as if Ray was also riding my rollercoaster of self-doubt. 'Even if they don't sign us, someone else will.'

The next few days lasted forever. In the early evening of the fourth day, John King knocked on the door. 'Congratulations. You got a record deal,' he said matter-of-factly, as if he was telling us we'd got a job peeling potatoes in a soup kitchen. 'You're booked to go into Abbey Road studios next week for three hours.'

When John said three hours, he meant it. Abbey Road was strict about schedules. Back then, there was no such thing as 'rock'n'roll time' (meaning *however long it took*). You did your three hours and you got out. Those were the rules, and if you wanted to make another record with the label, you obeyed them. The music business ran like clockwork, and at Abbey Road, there was good reason for that. You never knew who was coming in after you. It could be Cliff Richard. It could even be The Beatles. Naturally, The Beatles were the darlings of the studio. It was like they owned the place, though they never did. They used to leave a lot of their instruments there, and when they weren't around, we were able to borrow their gear and play it without them knowing. It was better than being left alone in a music store without a salesman. Ray's eyes bulged when he picked up George Harrison's 1957 Gretsch Duo Jet, and though I wasn't playing guitar anymore, I couldn't stop myself from strumming a few chords on John Lennon's Rickenbacker 325. It was terrifying and electrifying. They also had a Mellotron, which we used a number of times. We used a lot of their gear, though we handled it as carefully as delicate Waterford crystal.

The Fabulous Four held dominion over Abbey Road—the three-hour rule didn't apply to them. At one point, John and Yoko moved a bed into the studio, and when we saw it there after one of our sessions, we did what kids do: we started jumping up and down on it. Maybe we were a little old to be jumping on other people's beds, but I think we subconsciously knew we'd never have another opportunity to play on the trampoline where a Beatle sleeps, so we went for it.

We each tried to jump higher than the other, and then … in walked John and Yoko.

Uh-oh.

'Jesus Christ, what kind of bullshit is this?' said John in a surprised Liverpudlian lilt.

Yoko was more direct. 'Get the fuck off the bed!'

'Sorry, we didn't know,' I stammered. Since I didn't want to take the blame, I pointed to Phil. 'It was his idea!' I sputtered. We were whisked away before Phil had a chance to tell his side of the story. Good thing they never knew we spent way more time with their instruments than we did on their bed.

Around the time Parlophone was scheduling us to come into the studio to record our first single, our manager pitched the BBC in Bristol a thirty-minute documentary program about us called *The Big Break*, and they green-lit it. John presented it to them as a documentary about up-and-coming bands, and we were scheduled to be one of the bands on the show. A crew followed us around with huge movie cameras, filming us at home, out and about, and in the studio recording our first single, 'I See The Light,' a song we liked by the Texas band The Five Americans. (Their version was most famously released on the *Nuggets* album curated by Patti Smith Group guitarist Lenny Kaye.)

For the behind-the-scenes footage in *The Big Break*, the producers talked to our friends and filmed some humbling personal stuff. The idea was to show viewers what new bands endured and experienced during their quest for success, leaving the audience to try to guess whether or not the groups would become famous or if they'd get that big break. We hoped to come across as an ambitious but likable little band with big dreams and great songs, and the show offered some pretty good insight into our first days on the road outside of the local community. Sure, we were already playing shows, but from the public's perspective we were a brand-new pop group, and seeing us loading into clubs and talking backstage about the show we were about to play was supposed to make viewers feel like they were getting to know us and, hopefully, make them root for us to succeed.

The Big Break was shot with heart and a certain earnestness, focusing on our vitality and naïve optimism. There was footage of us jumping up and down when we heard 'I See The Light' on the radio for the first time. John told us it was going to be played on the BBC on a program hosted by Alan Freeman that counted down new singles, so we were listening to the show waiting for it, anticipating it. With every song, my stomach tightened a little more, and my excitement grew. Then, BOOM! Our song was on the radio. We weren't even paying attention to the film crew that was there to capture the moment. It was a magical moment. A voice in my head screamed, *Hey! You're not playing in the front room of your house, banging on pots and pans. You're not in band rehearsal, learning to play. You're on the radio and millions of people are listening!*

Phil came over from next door and was smiling like a Cheshire Cat, even if he wasn't bouncing like Ray and me. Our other brother, Terry, cheered us on, and Mom kept telling us how proud she was. It was a beautiful family moment. The only one missing was our father. To think that we were this poor Jewish family with a bohemian background, and there we were, listening to our first single on the radio, knowing every kid in the UK dreamed of hearing themselves on the radio, but they never got there. We did, and I knew there was a lot more to come. It was a complete joy for everyone who was there, and that moment burned itself into my memory.

The B-side of 'I See The Light' was 'Is It Finished,' an original by our sister Evelyn and songwriter Paul Smith, with whom we would collaborate for the duration of Simon Dupree & The Big Sound. Our episode of *The Big Break* aired in early 1967, and viewers loved the footage of us hearing ourselves on the radio for the first time—just not enough to buy the number of singles that would have landed us on the charts. But while 'I See The Light' didn't blow up, it got our foot in the door. The Parlophone staff realized we were a talented band, and the executives at the label began to strategize ways to help make us more popular.

GIANT STEPS

CHAPTER THREE

THE RAVERS

By early 1967, we still weren't making any money, and I was still digging worms up at the pier. That was discouraging, but it was still an incredible time to be in a band, and every time we went to Abbey Road was a tremendous learning experience. For a future music industry executive, it was invaluable to see how everything operated at the company and what the different departments (radio promotions, marketing, publicity) did to push the label's acts. But for music fans, going to the studio to record was even more incredible. Not only were we interacting with the top producers and engineers of the day—and some of the best of all time—we got to meet many of the company's top acts. There was a canteen downstairs, and everyone who had a session that day hung out there before and sometimes after they recorded. We'd see Eric Clapton, Jack Bruce, and Ginger Baker from Cream. Cliff Richard might be snacking on egg and chips, and even pop artists of the day like Engelbert Humperdinck could be spotted chatting up the ladies at the registers and the minders behind the stalls.

As much as we loved most of these guys, it was impossible to be a starstruck fan because the place had such a comfortable, congenial vibe. We were all there for the same reason. Sure, the established bands were further along in their careers, but we were all musicians, playing and recording our new songs in the studio. There was no bitterness, no jealousy, and no snide jabs. Everyone there treated us with respect, and there was great camaraderie.

'Have you recorded today? How'd your session go?' were some of the most commonly heard questions between artists. Even the stars said things like, 'When will I get to hear the single? I can't wait.' EMI's artists competed with one another on the charts and in the music papers, but not in the canteen. It was more than a no man's land or a safe haven. As recording artists, we were all under varying degrees of pressure. The canteen was a laid-back, stress-free zone—a place to unwind and temporarily escape the pressure of being in the studio.

When we were in the studio, we worked with George Martin, Geoff Emerick, Alan Parsons, and David Paramor. Having George Martin behind the board might seem mind-blowing or terrifying, but it wasn't the great George Martin of 1969 or '78. It was the guy who worked with The Beatles on great songs like 'Love Me Do' and 'She Loves You,' which were big hits, of course, but George wasn't a *legend* quite yet. He was a producer who was there to work with you to make sure you'd sound great. He didn't have any attitude, and he certainly wasn't jaded.

Following the success of *The Big Break*, John got the BBC to feature us on a show about groupies that was racy and controversial. It was called *Man Alive: The Ravers*. Producers of the show interviewed young girls who were sexually charged and directing their libidos at pop stars, many of whom were perfectly happy with the companionship. It was a little strange for us to be looked at like that because we were never specifically in a band for the girls. We were more intently focused on the music. We didn't party; we didn't hire minders to pick pretty girls out of the crowd for us to hang out with after the show. Yet our pop energy, melodies, and charisma somehow magnetized these young women, who hunted us down and, on more than a few occasions, had their way with us (except Phil, who was married).

It was a golden time—an age of sexual exploration spearheaded by the mass availability of the birth control pill. Many of these girls were raised to be prim and proper, and their parents were convinced their daughters wouldn't have sex until they were married. One popped pill later, they were ditching their boyfriends (who they hadn't yet had sex with yet, because they didn't want to develop a bad reputation) and hooking up with pop stars for the night. All this pent-up sexual frustration flooded out of them, and they gave into their urges because they didn't have to worry about getting pregnant or making anyone in their town think they were easy.

It was like a bonus for all of our hard work—a fringe benefit that turned me and lots of other pop stars who had never been natural Casanovas into sex objects, for lack of a better term. As long as they were of legal age and I wasn't seriously dating anyone, I was open to exploring that world. It was the 60s. No one shamed these girls or warned them to tone down their sex drives. It was fun, exciting, rebellious, and largely harmless. And there were no consequences.

Our first major tour was an odd bill with seven bands, including The Beach Boys. It was in early 1967, and Helen Shapiro, The Nite People, The Marionettes, Terry Reid, and Peter Jay's Jaywalkers were also on the tour. We were third in the lineup—not the co-headliners, but a respectable spot for a band who had only had a handful of songs on the radio.

We were excited to meet The Beach Boys, whose heavily harmonized surf-pop was unlike anything else. 'God Only Knows' and 'Good Vibrations' are still in my personal top ten all-time musical masterpieces. But man, for a bunch of guys from sunny California who made upbeat, positive-sounding music they were miserable and mean. They disliked us right away. I later found out they disliked everyone, and the few times we saw them offstage they were fighting with one another. I couldn't imagine why they were unhappy. They were huge stars. They could have been friendly to us, but they ignored us the whole tour. Why? We were no threat. We were schlubs compared to them. We couldn't even afford hotels. Even worse, they could hardly play their instruments. Apparently, the backing musicians who played on their albums had been denied entry to the UK, so The Beach Boys had to play like a real band. They sounded like beginners, and Dennis Wilson in particular hardly knew how to play drums. It reminded me of my old school friend Andy Mead playing with pots and pans. What a letdown it was to see your idols fall in front of your face!

Sometimes we spent the night at bed-and-breakfasts in northern English cities like Manchester and Newcastle. Unlike hotels, you couldn't book ahead. You'd have to go there after the gig and knock on the door at one or two in the morning to see if they had any rooms. When one was full, you'd move on to the next until either you found somewhere to spend the night or you resigned yourself to sleeping in the van—which on cold, rainy days was practically a guarantee of a restless night. Sometimes there was a 'vacancy/no vacancy' sign in the window, which usually meant either you had a place to stay or you didn't need to bother knocking. Even when they weren't full, it wasn't always easy to get in. There was never a front desk, so you had to keep knocking until you woke up the owner of the house and she came to the door.

'Do you have any rooms?' I'd ask whoever opened the door. Even if there was a vacancy sign, sometimes the caretaker would look at our long hair and scraggly appearance and tell us to move on.

'But your sign says…'

SLAM! The front door would shut hard in our faces, threatening to shave the scruff off our chins.

Some of these bed-and-breakfasts were worse than pay-by-the-hour motels. When we stayed in Salford, Greater Manchester, we asked the woman there if she had any rooms. 'I have three doubles and one single,' she said. There were seven of us, so it seemed like it would work out even though the doubles had double beds, which two smelly guys would have to squeeze into.

Before anyone had the chance to say anything, I jumped in and said, 'I'll have the single.'

Phil shook his head, annoyed, and resigned himself to sharing a room with Ray, and everyone else was too tired to argue with me. Besides, I was the singer. I deserved it. And boy, I got what I deserved. When I got to the room, I found out that it was a single, all right, but there was a drunk sailor in the bed, snoring loud enough to make the windows rattle. I went back to the front door and knocked again until the woman returned. 'You gave me a single and there's already someone in the bed,' I sputtered.

'Yeah,' she said. 'That's what I told you. There are three doubles and a single, and I gave you the single. There are no other rooms.'

There was no arguing with her. I had to sleep next to this bloke. It was either that or sleep on the floor. Good thing he didn't wake up, or he might have belted me for getting in bed with him.

In that specific situation, I took the mistreatment lying down. More often, though, we stood up for ourselves. And we had a way of getting revenge on landladies who slighted us. Most of these places served breakfast in the morning, so when we got up, we scoped out the dining area to figure out what kinds of shenanigans we could pull.

'What do you want for breakfast, eggs or kippers?' was something these women often asked us. If they weren't friendly, well, you could make a good mess with eggs if you rubbed them into the fibers of a rug or stirred them into your coffee and then spilled the concoction over the tablecloth. But kippers, which are bits of smoked herring, made for better ammunition when there was a good place to hide them. We especially liked wall artwork, and our favorite move was for one person to lift the picture a little bit from the wall so that someone else could slide some kippers into the space between the wall and the frame. Then we'd push the painting back the way it was. No one knew there was smoked fish underneath but us.

A couple of times we came back two or three weeks later and told someone on the staff that there was a horrible smell in the dining room and they should call an exterminator. They'd acknowledge something smelled horrible but never figured out what it was. Not once did any of them think of looking under the picture, because by the time the kippers began to rot, the smell permeated the entire room. We'd keep a straight face and act irritated and disgusted, and then when we got back to our room or the van we'd laugh until we almost peed ourselves.

In our defense, we only pulled pranks when we weren't treated well, and not all landladies were harpies. There was a lovely lady in Edinburgh, Scotland, named Mrs. Williams, who had a soft spot for musicians and treated them all—the biggest and the smallest—like VIPs. Some of these acts became big stars, but most of them were still unknown, which is why they were staying in a small-town B&B. Mrs. Williams didn't care. She loved music and respected the musicians, so she talked to the bands and learned everyone's likes and dislikes. She'd let bands sleep until three in the afternoon and then take special orders for breakfast—eggs, baked beans, scones, bacon, juice—and make everything fresh to match your schedule.

The more orders, the merrier. One time we stayed there at the same time as Pink Floyd and The Move, and she made us all breakfast at different times in the afternoon. We were always grateful for her hospitality, and we never pulled any silly antics. I can't promise that other bands weren't more mischievous, but if they were, she never told us.

When it came to Simon Dupree & The Big Sound, I got the most attention because, well, I was Simon Dupree. I was the first one people came to for autographs and interviews. Some of the guys in the band were annoyed by that, but not Ray. He was never disappointed or angry that I was the center of attention. He saw the value in having a representative for the band, and he didn't want to be the spokesperson.

I can't say the same for Phil. Since Phil was considerably older than Ray and me, he thought he deserved to be the head of our musical family. He was older, and as a teenager he'd often taken care of Ray and me. He was our big brother, and we looked up to him. When we played cricket together, he coached me to up my game. 'C'mon, bowl harder!' he'd say. 'You can give me more than that.' So, I kept working at it, got stronger, learned to bowl faster, and made the county team. When I heard the news, it seemed like Phil was as proud as I was. When he became a teacher, he was equally supportive and assertive with his students. But he was used to being in control, and he had trouble accepting that our ideas regarding music and the band were just as valid as his, if not more so.

Phil couldn't change the way things were. I was the frontman. Everyone was looking at me onstage, and when we weren't under the spotlight, I still got most of the attention. Even people at management or the label would ask me how and when things were done. That Phil was unable to reverse the natural order of band hierarchy was frustrating to him. You can't very well go up to a journalist or a radio interviewer and say, 'Hold on, I'm older, and I bought the van. Ask *me* all the questions.' But Phil got increasingly frustrated, to the point where he started to hate the press.

The sibling rivalry that began with Simon Dupree & The Big Sound continued for years and would be part of the reason why Phil eventually left Gentle Giant. I've been called a perfectionist, and there may be some truth to that, but I've never been a control freak. In the band, we tended to do things my way because my way usually seemed to work. While Ray accepted this, Phil always wanted to argue when he didn't agree with me. And when we argued, we went at it. We share a gene for stubbornness, and we rarely compromised without a fight. Maybe Ray was the smartest of the three of us. He wanted us all to get along and for the band to benefit from the kinship, even if we agreed to disagree. Our brother Terry was wise enough to stay away from the fraternal fray and made his living as a sculptor and artist. He was possibly the most genuine artist of the Shulman clan.

As everyone from Ray Davies to Noel Gallagher will tell you, it's very hard to be in a band with your brother. I had two, and that made everything confusing as hell. On the one hand, I still instinctively saw Phil as my mentor, but he was also a rival when we didn't want the same thing. I was the head of the band, and I wanted my way. And Ray wanted us to do whatever would stop us from arguing.

I could be wrong, but I think Phil was jealous. Before Simon Dupree, Phil had been at the top of the brotherly hierarchy, and I accepted him as such. Now, I was the young cub taking over the older lion's role in the pack. So, naturally, Phil fought back. We both loved the band, and we both thought we knew best how to steer it. I can't say I always made the right decisions, but I always believed in whatever choices I made, and I usually got my way. Sometimes that made Phil resentful, so he dug in his heels. He would yell at me about missing a line in a song or holding a note too long, which threw off his tempo. He gave the other players equal time. He shouted at Ray on the rare occasions Ray goofed, and the same went for Kerry and Gary in Gentle Giant. And vice versa. We all scrutinized every element of our playing, and, after gigs, we each pointed out every tiny mistake that was made in an effort to improve. The funny thing is, in both Simon Dupree and Gentle Giant, ninety-nine times out of a hundred, we would bicker about onstage mistakes that only we noticed. No one in the crowd could. We rarely made major mistakes. We were all talented and experienced, and we had great chemistry.

Whenever the volume of our rows got loud enough to bleed through locked dressing room doors, the rest of the band would cower in the corner.

Ray always waited out the storm, knowing Phil and I would eventually stop fighting. I can only imagine what the other guys were thinking.

Oh shit, they're going to break up the band. They're going to start punching each other, and that will be the end.

We never did, though. We wouldn't ever have resorted to blows, because physical violence was off-limits for the Shulmans. Ray knew that, but the other guys in the band were always ready for a bloodbath, and we freaked out more than a few musicians along the way.

Maybe Phil's angst and irascibility stemmed from his youth. He and Evelyn were born in pre-war Glasgow and grew up in the Jewish ghetto with my parents before Ray and I were born. During the war, Dad enlisted in the military, so, at a critical stage of his development, Phil lacked a father figure. Meanwhile, Dad was assigned to be a paratrooper, and the whole family had to move out of Glasgow and live with scores of other military families in the slums of England. They weren't just living in squalid conditions; they were living in fear and desperation. They were constantly under threat of bombing from the Germans, and frequently there wasn't enough food to go around.

When Dad came back from the war, he probably had post-traumatic stress disorder, which might have contributed to his excessive drinking, late nights out, and early death. Regardless, Phil was subjected to an absent parent far longer than I was, and when Dad died, Phil was robbed of whatever connection he had with our father. He was already a natural cynic and had this existential Jean-Paul Sartre attitude: *Nothing matters because we're all dust in the end.* That only fueled his pessimism when our father died. We were all shocked and saddened. More than the rest of us, Phil was also angered, and his anger always simmered under the surface, which might be why he had a shorter fuse.

In his defense—and maybe to his detriment—Phil was also intellectually brilliant, and he questioned everything. He was an academic who found his way into the rock life, and those two worlds don't always mesh. There are plenty of smart musicians, but most rock stars are guys from working-class roots, and their education comes from making music, touring, and performing. Primarily, they focus on what they're good at, and they don't always ask questions.

At the same time, you have to give credit to bands like Cream, Zeppelin, Black Sabbath, and so on, because regardless of how much they drank, how many drugs they did, or how many girls they slept with, they were brilliant musicians. Had they not written great songs and played together really well, they wouldn't have lasted. You can fluke your way to fame, but you can't stay successful without talent. The best bands all got their chops down back in the day, long before they were playing for sold-out crowds and trashing hotel rooms. They had to because image and outrageousness meant nothing on their own. Without serious talent, you went on to become a pallbearer or a plumber's assistant.

Ozzy Osbourne worked in a slaughterhouse and Tony Iommi worked in a sheet-metal factory before I met them. That was a miserable existence, but that's what most people did in post-war Britain. Being a musician wasn't glamorous until you were a star, and it was damn hard work. Most musicians were looked down on by the upper class. Fortunately, the working-class people who worked at factories and other blue-collar jobs loved rock'n'roll because it spoke to them—as long as it was fucking good.

Today, there's somewhat less separation between the upper class and the middle class. When I grew up, England was a place of 'haves' and 'have nots,' and most people had very little. Ninety percent of society in the 60s and 70s was working class, and only about ten percent came from the upper class and had money. Another five percent of the population was middle class, which meant they were maybe college-educated or owned businesses and didn't have to work menial jobs. Hardly any popular musicians were from the upper class and very few were middle class. And for the working class, it was either make a living as a musician, play professional football, or work in a factory. Because of my upbringing and schooling, I think I would have gone to university and become an academic like Phil, but fortunately, rock'n'roll saved our lives.

Like our dad, Phil was in the military, which was somewhere he didn't belong. He wasn't a soldier. He hated blindly following orders, and he asked questions. He was drafted into the National Service by the British

Air Force, and when he reported for duty, the officers immediately disliked him. The sergeant he reported to could tell Phil didn't synchronize with the regimented military mentality. Before everyone in Phil's training group was told where to report for duty, the sergeant called Phil into his office and closed the door.

'Shulman, I've got *great* news for you,' he said with glee. 'You're going to be stationed at Thorny Island.'

The condescending sergeant thought Thorny Island was a dangerous place somewhere in the Pacific, but Phil knew better. And, for him, it was great news. Thorny Island is a little island right near Portsmouth, a half-mile from where we lived. Phil wouldn't see combat, and he didn't have to go anywhere. He served there shuffling papers and was home every night in time for dinner. It was the best news a soldier who wasn't keen about going into combat could get. He even met some girls around town who were turned on by men in uniform, and when he wasn't working or at home, he spent much of his time with them. He was a good-looking guy and a soldier, so he always had a date and sometimes more than one girlfriend at a time.

One night, we were all home and there was a knock on the door. Mom opened the door and saw a girl standing there waiting to be let in. Phil was in the back room when she arrived. He gasped and loudly whispered, 'Tell her I'm not here. I'm not here.'

'I'm sorry, darling,' Mom replied. 'Phil's not here.'

The girl didn't believe her. 'I think you better tell Phil that I'm here and I want to talk to him. Right away.'

Phil, who overheard the brief exchange, came out of hiding and greeted her warmly. She was brassy, petite, and pretty, like a young Sandra Bullock. Her name was Roberta, and while Phil might have wanted to avoid her at first so he could continue to date, he never regretted his decision to talk to her that night. From the start, it was clear the two of them had strong chemistry, and from that moment on, Phil was smitten. Their love for one another grew over the months that followed, and in no time it was obvious that Phil would be with her for the rest of his life. He proposed, she accepted, and they got married in a civil ceremony. Ray and I were happy for him. We had a great time at the wedding, and, at least for a while, Phil's affection for Roberta dulled his cynical edge somewhat.

About a year after they were married, they had their first child. As I now fully understand, having children changed Phil's life. Nothing was more important to him than being a doting husband and father—maybe because our dad was MIA so often. To date, Phil and Bobbi have been married for sixty-plus years, which is impressive for any couple. They're the kind of couple who are constantly together and complete each other's sentences. Had Bobbi not come to the door that night and demanded Phil's attention, his life might have turned out very differently, especially his young adulthood. Phil was twenty years old when he got married, and, as much as he cared for Roberta, it must have been a shock to go from being a bit of a playboy to being entirely committed to one person. Like the rest of the Shulman brothers, though, he had a strong moral compass, and he never dated anyone else, despite numerous opportunities. At the same time, being the only married member of Gentle Giant made him a bit of an outsider. He had no interest in drinking or taking drugs, and without girls to hang around with, he had too much spare time and didn't know what to do with it besides sulk. He wasn't with Roberta, so he was lonely, and he couldn't hang out with Ray and me, who were having a great time playing the field with no strings attached. Phil never complained about being married, but when Ray and I went into secluded areas with attractive girls, I could see the frustration in Phil's eyes.

As much as I will always be a faithful, dedicated family man as well, the one time it was good for me to not have a wife or be in a committed relationship was in the mid-to-late 60s, when our audiences grew from several hundred to several thousand kids a night. Our fans sang along with me and deified my every word and move, and I loved it. Teenage girls were especially excited by my stage persona, and it was satisfying to be desired. They were generous to us too, and when we didn't have any place to go after a gig, these girls would often take us home and spend the night with us. It was frivolous, it was fun, and it was sometimes mind-blowing. But there was an innocence to it all. No one worried about catching AIDS or even the clap; in a worst-case scenario, someone would contract crabs, and the condition was embarrassing for sure, but it was easily cured with topical medication. Fortunately, that never happened to me.

Being surrounded by pretty girls was a welcome fringe benefit, but it was never a priority. Music always came first, and I would never sacrifice missing a rehearsal, band meeting, or—God forbid—a gig to get frisky with a female fan. I knew many, many musicians who were blinded by that side of the rock world, gave in to their libidos, and blew off numerous business appointments. But after a while I had had enough meaningless flings and no longer found them as stimulating as I once had. I had pretty much had my fill. I wasn't exactly like a kid in a candy store who was suddenly tired of sweets, but let's say I was suffering a bit of tooth decay, and my moral compass suddenly kicked in. I decided I would much rather be with someone that I could talk to, take out to dinner, and even take her home to meet the family. In a volatile industry, I craved stability. There was even a point in Simon Dupree when I had marriage on my mind.

I started seeing a girl named Jennie when I was seventeen. She was also from the Portsmouth area and came from a wealthy family. She was pretty in a wholesome kind of way—a poster child for the attractive Sephardic Jew. She had long black hair and a vivaciousness that was contagious. We enjoyed being together, and we were compatible in many ways. She was intelligent, chatty, and good in bed. Everyone in my family liked her, and lots of people thought she could be 'the one.' I certainly could have done a whole lot worse. She wasn't short-tempered, selfish, or impolite. I guess you could say she was good marriage material. And yet, there were times when we were together and she wouldn't stop talking, and I got irritated. I wanted to relax and be at peace, and she had to jabber away about something as if a moment of silence between us would indicate that we weren't right for each other.

Whenever I had doubts about her, I shook them off. *She's great*, I'd think to myself. *She's sexy and smart. Why wouldn't you want to be with her for years? Why shouldn't she be the mother of your children?*

I had another incentive to marry Jennie. Her father, Harry Garcia, owned a big casino and bingo parlor. He and his wife liked me, and he wanted to look out for his little girl. At one point, he took me aside and we sat down on the living room couch.

'Derek, if this music thing doesn't work out for you, you know, as far as your livelihood goes, it'll be okay.' He said this as if he was striking a business deal, which, in effect, was his intent. 'You know, when you're in the family, you'll always have the casinos to back you up. I'd be happy to help you and your family out, so, you know, you'll never have to worry. That's all I'm saying.'

I sat still and squirmed inside like a snake preparing to molt.

Harry patted me on the arm, and I thanked him, shook his hand, and left the room as quickly as possible. I had already made some money by that point, but I knew how unstable being in a band could be. As much as I wanted complete independence and didn't care for a backup plan, being offered financial security from my potential in-laws was somewhat comforting.

I continued to date Jennie as Simon Dupree rose in popularity, which made Phil happy too, since I stopped hanging out with groupies and spent much of my downtime drinking tea, working on my voice, and making band plans with him. Phil liked Jennie. He liked her father even more. He didn't want to go back to teaching, and he loved the idea of having something to fall back on, financially, if the band ended. I was a little less excited by the offer, though I have to admit the thought of never being poor again was enticing, and it was always in the back of my mind—even though I knew I was going to make it on my own.

CHAPTER FOUR

LETTERS OF GOLD

Everything happened so fast. On May 5, 1967, six months after 'I See The Light' went to radio, Parlophone released two more singles. 'Reservations' was originally by Albert Hammond, and our version reached #39 on the single charts. Still not Top 20, but we could see that our mainstream exposure was giving us momentum. The title inspired the name of our only album *No Reservations*, which came out at the end of the year. The B-side for 'Reservations' was 'You Need A Man,' which Evelyn wrote with Paul Smith. We all thought it was nice to have our sister writing for us, especially since our dad had kept her from being a performer. Our third single, 'Day Time, Night Time,' was by Manfred Mann member Mike Hugg, and that came out on May 5, 1967. Our fans loved it. Ray wrote the B-Side, 'I've Seen It All Before,' which was the first hint of what a great songwriter he would become.

It's worth pointing out that we never got paid a penny for any of the singles we recorded at Abbey Road. We didn't care—and not just because my girlfriend's father volunteered to float us. We were being paid for gigs, but we didn't see any real money until after we released our hit, 'Kites' (more on that later). Even if we *had* any money, we would probably have paid for the staffers at the label to record us. We loved being at the studio and using the top-of-the-line equipment. We felt special working with these big-name engineers and producers, and we enjoyed hanging out at the café with other musicians. Most of the groups were friendly with each other, and we also loved hanging out with the symphonic musicians who were always recording in Studio One.

One of the bands we saw down there from time to time was Pink Floyd. I wouldn't say we were rivals; they just weren't our favorite musicians to talk to. Simon Dupree & The Big Sound got solid attention from the mainstream by working our asses off and promoting ourselves like politicians at election time. The Floyd were more tapped into the counterculture elitists and had only played a few shows when they started generating a buzz. They hadn't paid their dues, officially released anything, or developed much of a following. But because they were unpredictable, weird, and irreverent, critics came to their little shows and gushed in the papers about how incredibly cool they were. Journalists interviewed Syd Barrett and Roger Waters about drugs, the counterculture, and revolution. It made for good press, regardless of how shitty their music was at the time, and the producers at the studio read the papers and saw all the hype. The band didn't have to audition for a panel of Abbey Road producers like everyone else. Not only that, they believed their own hype, and they decided they were above recording for free. They demanded a £5,000 advance from Parlophone to record their 1967 single 'See Emily Play,' and they got it. To show how incredibly cool they were, they went out and bought insanely loud Selmer amplifiers.

When the song came out on Columbia in 1967, it generated a cult following but didn't sell many copies. That didn't matter. As long as the press was good, EMI loved them and wanted to keep them happy. We played on the same bill as Pink Floyd a couple of times and, well, they weren't terribly good. They were incredibly loud. Not loud in the good kind of way that makes your knees buckle and loosens your bowels. They were just *bad* loud. Even though they were playing a small club, they turned their amps up as loud as they could go, just to be subversive. Being in the audience when they played was physically and sonically painful. No one could hear what they were playing, and everything blurred into a flaming cloud of noise.

Syd Barrett was a real oddball and said crazy shit to perpetuate the rumors that he was an insane genius like Brian Wilson. In reality, he was merely drug-addled and mentally unbalanced. I don't know how much they practiced, but when we played with them, they were sloppy and out of sync. The psychedelic thing they did sounded good when played at a normal volume, but I thought The Beatles did that kind of stuff way better. Syd was limited as a musician—too limited to be as dismissive toward us as he was when we saw him in the café. Of course, they became much more interesting and creative after he left. After David Gilmour took on a major role in the band, Pink Floyd grew into a great, psychedelic rock machine.

I've got to admit, their timing was good. The psychedelic wave flourished in the UK and around the world, and everyone wanted to take a trip and find themselves. Everyone was influenced by The Beatles' *Revolver* album, and by the time they did *Sgt. Pepper's Lonely Hearts Club Band* and *Magical Mystery Tour*, those who weren't already on the acid train were searching for ways to expand their consciousness and make their music more interesting. So, in a way, we have The Beatles to thank for Simon Dupree's biggest hit single, 'Kites,' which broke us through into the living rooms and entertainment centers of millions of families in the UK and across Europe

The songwriters responsible for the novelty hit 'Itsy Bitsy Teeny Weeny Yellow Polka Dot Bikini,' Hal Hackaday and Lee Pockriss, wrote 'Kites' and gave it to Robbins Music head Ian Ralfini to place. When John contacted Ian (who eventually became the head of Anchor Records), Ian said he thought it could be a hit for Simon Dupree. Since the writers of the song had a track record, some people in positions of power were banking on 'Kites,' and they promised to grease the right wheels to get us on the charts. If we recorded it, we would be guaranteed airplay on Radio One in the off-prime-time hours, and maybe more. John played us an acoustic arrangement of 'Kites,' which sounded strange. It was colored with electric psychedelic embellishments and sound effects and was far from mesmerizing. It was just odd, and at first we didn't know what to say. There was this repetitive piano, sweeping strings, and adult contemporary vocals that might as well have been Neil Diamond.

'You've got to be kidding me,' were my first words to John. 'This doesn't sound like a pop song to me.' The hooks didn't seem strong enough, and I couldn't picture myself singing about 'Letters of gold on a snow white kite' without bursting out laughing.

The problem—which turned out to be a blessing—was that we hadn't written much, so we weren't offered any other songs we liked any better. Phil didn't want to do it. 'Does someone suddenly think we want to be Pink Floyd?' he blurted.

Ray was more diplomatic. 'You know, if the label has connections, and the song is going to take us to where we want to go, why don't we give it a shot?' I agreed with Ray, but I still didn't love the idea of recording this weird song as Simon Dupree.

'Well, what do you think?' John said.

'I don't know,' I replied. 'This doesn't really fit with what we do onstage. I mean, this is not who we are. But we'll give it a shot and see what we can do with it.'

We worked on 'Kites' with Geoff Emerick, Alan Parsons, and Dave Paramor, who produced it. We changed the arrangement and injected the song with the psychedelic flair we loved in Beatles songs like 'Tomorrow Never Knows' and 'Lucy In The Sky With Diamonds.' We put some swirly effects on the guitar, added xylophone, wood blocks, and some sound effects, and recorded the whole thing a few days later in a three-hour session. We all worked hard to make it the best we could and create something that was better than what was originally handed to us, but when we were done, we weren't exactly sure what we had created.

Phil used to tell the press that we didn't like the song and were just fucking around with it. That wasn't true. We thought it had promise, and we tried to put our stamp on it. It was my idea to have a middle-eight that featured someone speaking. I thought of doing that because Traffic had a song called 'Hole In The Ground' that included a part with a little girl speaking. I felt like the same approach would work with 'Kites.' Only, I thought we should get a middle-aged woman who spoke Chinese, since there was a gong at the beginning, and some parts of the song had an Eastern feel.

John King said having a fairly well-known guest performer would make people pay more attention to the song, so he suggested Jacqui Chan, with whom he had a loose connection. She was a sexy Chinese Trinidadian actress, dancer, and singer, and John thought her involvement would attract the tabloids and gossip hounds. She agreed to be involved, and someone asked her to say something poetic in Chinese. What she cooed translated to 'I love you I love you. My love is very strong. It flies high like a kite before the wind. Please do not let go of the string.'

Right after we finished, we recorded the B-side, 'Like The Sun, Like The Fire,' which, as was our custom, was by Paul and Evelyn. Then we went home and figured that, at the very least, doing such a strange, psychedelic pop song would get some people talking.

A few days after we recorded the track, David Paramor called me at the venue we were scheduled to play that night.

'Derek, I'm glad I got you,' he said.

'Is everyone okay?' I asked.

'We've got a bit of a problem. The vocals don't sound right. We need you to come back to the studio after the show and record another take so we can double them.'

'Okay, do I have to do it tonight? We've got another show tomorrow night.'

'Yeah, I'm sorry, but "Kites" is going to radio in two weeks. We have to get them copies.'

I was a little frazzled by the news, but it didn't affect my performance that night. Afterward, we hopped back in the van and drove 285 miles from Newcastle to London. The next morning, I went back to EMI Studios and spent fifteen minutes in the studio doubling the vocals. Then I met the rest of the guys and we headed back on the road to play more shows up north. In less than a week, we were scheduled to take a ferry to Gothenburg, Sweden, to play some concerts in Europe, and I hoped nothing else would go wrong before then.

We were taking a ferry to our first major shows in Scandinavia, so we were excited when we stepped onto the boat, even though the ride was thirty-six hours long. We hoped to get comfortable and relax, maybe kill some time by having some lunch and getting some sleep. The weather was cold and rainy, and we were sailing on the North Sea, which is notoriously rocky, even on a sunny day. It felt like we were driving a car with no shock absorbers through a highway filled with potholes. Shortly into the journey, my stomach was lurching with every wave that crashed against the hull. In no time, we were all violently throwing up. So much for lunch and sleep.

When the boat finally arrived in Sweden, I was shaking and exhausted. I had nothing left in my stomach, and I had stopped dry heaving a few hours earlier, but I still felt like I had Bubonic plague. We had to do press shortly after we arrived, so we bucked up, pried our eyes open, and plastered smiles on our faces. No one vomited during the interviews, and somehow none of the journalists commented in their articles about how green our complexions were. Maybe they figured that's just the natural pallor of the English. The Swedes loved us and danced throughout our sets.

A week later, the tour was done, and we had to take the boat back to England, which none of us were looking forward to. Thank God it was a beautiful day, and while the ferry rocked back and forth during the journey, our stomachs remained settled as long as the motor was running and we were moving.

About six hours into the trip, a man with a hat, glasses, and a white beard came up to me.

'Are you Derek Shulman?' he asked.

He didn't look like a fan, and he sure didn't look like someone from EMI. 'I'm the captain, and you've got an urgent message. Follow me.'

Suddenly, I felt seasick again.

The captain led me to what looked like a first-class cabin and pointed to a phone. 'You've got a call,' he said.

I warily picked up the phone imagining the worst: a death in the family, news that our house had been burglarized, a report that 'Kites' flopped and the label was dropping us.

'Hello, this is Derek,' I said.

It was a publicist at EMI. 'Derek, I hope I didn't worry you, love, but I had to call and congratulate you!'

'Uh, okay. Why?'

'Didn't you hear? "Kites" is a huge hit. You're in the Top 20 on the national charts.'

I'll never forget the sound of her voice or those magical words. The enthusiasm, the joy of telling me we had made it. It's one of those few memories in life that gets frozen in time and can be accessed anytime, as if by the click of a switch. I felt elated, vindicated, as whimsical as a kite in the wind. This was a milestone. This was what I had worked for and dreamed of from the moment I heard the Beatles on the radio. And now I *was* a rock star. As validation of that, Simon Dupree & Big Sound were booked to perform on the biggest national music TV show, *Top Of The Pops*, the next week.

Despite my excitement, I was suddenly calm, completely at ease, and sure I was exactly where I was supposed to be. Getting booked for *Top Of The Pops* was as big as being on *The Ed Sullivan Show*, but it was only for music. Millions of people tuned in every week to watch the top-charting bands play their latest hits. Being on the show was on every group's bucket list, and playing it was unfathomable for a young group from Portsmouth who hadn't even recorded a full album. We were scheduled to perform on the show the same week Status Quo played 'Pictures Of Matchstick Men' and The Move did 'See The Grass Grow,' so we were in great company.

We had less than a week to decompress from our tour of Sweden and play the TV show. On the day of filming, we made sure we had all of our gear and then rushed to the studio. We set everything up and placed the xylophone on the stage, but we couldn't find the mallets. We looked everywhere. Finally, we had to give up and borrow some little sticks with fuzzy heads on them. We played them as though they were mallets. It's a good thing *Top Of The Pops* used only live vocals. The rest of the music came from the original recordings, and everyone in the band would only pretend to hear what they were playing, so even though the fuzzy sticks sounded way different than mallets, no one knew the difference. The crowd loved us and cheered like we were rock stars.

Our appearance on *Top Of The Pops* boosted both our public profile and our market value. Before 'Kites,' we'd had minor hits with 'I See The Light,' 'Reservations,' and 'Daytime Nighttime.' That Thursday evening, we were already a pretty well-known pop band to lots of young people. By the same time on Friday, after we'd played 'Kites' for millions, we were recognized by everyone's moms, dads, and grandparents as well.

We didn't write the song, only arranged it, so we didn't see any of the publishing revenue, but the performance royalties were solid and our tour fees jumped considerably overnight. Viewers went out and bought the single in droves, and the song entered the Top 10. I visited the high school I had just graduated from, where students lined up for my autograph. They weren't the only ones. Some of the kids I'd graduated with, who had laughed at me years earlier when I stated unequivocally that I was going to be a pop star—and the teacher who told me with great glee and sarcasm that it would never happen—waited for me to sign their copies of 'Kites.' Some of other my teachers who surely would have joined in the ridicule, had they been in the same room when I declared my future occupation, saw me on TV and were excited to meet hometown hero Simon Dupree.

There's a wonderful German word, *Schadenfreude*, which means experiencing happiness or vindication from someone else's pain, trouble, or humiliation. There was an element of that in my ascension to stardom. I didn't take joy in anyone else's failure, but as people who had once belittled me clamored to shake my hand and have me sign something, maybe a part of me took some joy in knowing that they were still common people in Portsmouth. I'm not exactly proud of that today, but when I look back, I still feel a strong sense of accomplishment knowing that our hard work and refusal to give up paid off. We were Top 10 pop stars. It was glorious. It was the end of the beginning of the beginning of the end for Simon Dupree.

GIANT STEPS

CHAPTER FIVE

WE ARE THE MOLES

If I had a quarter for every time I was around drugs or was offered drugs and turned them down, I would never have had to worry about making money with music. I was straight before 'straight edge' was a thing. I didn't just do it to extend the precious years I have left on this earth; I wanted to avoid anything that might be a distraction from the music that meant everything to me. I wanted a lifestyle that was opposite to the one my father had. I went to the gym, ate healthily, drank lots of water, and took vitamins.

Ray and Phil also stayed away from cigarettes, alcohol, and drugs, though neither of them was as paranoid as I was about dying young. We never wanted to waste a moment of our life, so after we had a tremendous hit with 'Kites,' we all seriously considered dropping everything and moving on with far more challenging, experimental music. It was more than a consideration, it was fate, but before I dropped my pop star persona, I accidentally dropped something else.

'Kites' was still a big hit and we were in London hanging out with the guys in Status Quo. We went to a nightclub where all the local musicians and scenesters hung out, and I was feeling pretty good so I ordered a vodka tonic, figuring I'd only have the one and remain in control. While everyone waited for the waiter to return with our drinks, I went to use the men's room. When I came back, my vodka tonic was on the table. Usually, I would gingerly sip drinks, but I wanted to celebrate our success and figured, 'What the hell,' so I took a big gulp from my drink, and it was refreshing. There was just enough vodka that I could taste it, but it didn't burn my throat, and the tonic water was pleasantly bubbly and bitter.

Some girls from a group we toured with, The Paper Dolls, were with us, with a few of their friends in tow. After my big sip, one of them smiled and looked directly into my eyes.

'I thought you might want to know,' she said. 'Our guy just slipped some acid in your drink. I hope you're okay with it and have a good time.'

I had never done acid because I'm terrified of losing control.

'When the hell?' I replied. 'Who would do that? I don't want that.'

'No, you'll love it,' she said and laughed. 'Just go with it.'

I've never been the kind of person who just goes with anything, but what choice did I have? Within fifteen minutes, I started feeling really bizarre. I was keenly aware this wasn't what I wanted, and I started to panic, which made everything much worse. I said I needed to get some air and went outside the club. I was practically panting, yet I couldn't get enough air in my lungs, and every time I breathed it sounded like a wind squall through a tunnel. My heart pounded, and with each beat, the earth shook so hard—so hard the sidewalk started to crack, I felt like the ground was going to collapse beneath my feet, so I stumbled over to a lamppost for support. I clung to it like I was in a deep ocean, and it was a flotation device. For the next six hours, I hugged the post for dear life.

It must have been around midnight when some people asked me what I was doing. Maybe they were checking if I was all right, but their voices were warped and distorted, and they echoed so much I couldn't understand what they were saying.

'I need to stay right here' was all I could summon. They were the only words I still knew, so I kept repeating them. I was sure that if I let go of the post, I would get swept away somewhere and die. In the lamp-lit streets, my mind was causing horrendous hallucinations. The road flooded with blood, and it pooled around my ankles and started rising toward my knees. People around me were gradually decaying, and skeletons were floating in the ocean of blood. Screaming drowned out any other noises around me. I don't know if it was my own screaming or if it was in my head, but it wouldn't stop. And when I closed my eyes, my skin started burning, so I kept them open and stared at the flesh on my arms, which was bubbling like boiling water. I knew if I closed my eyes again, my arms would disintegrate and I wouldn't be able to hold onto the pole anymore.

I hung onto it until morning, when it started to get light. As the acid started to wear off, I remembered that I was supposed to drive home that night, but I didn't feel up to it. I stayed a bit longer, and when I was again able to speak full sentences, I called a taxi, had the driver take me to a hotel, and slept until it was afternoon. Then I took another cab back to my car and drove home, shivering all the way. More than ten years later, I wrote 'Inside Out' about my bad trip, and we eventually did a video for the track that includes images of lampposts that still make me shudder.

Simon Dupree & The Big Sound were very much a Portsmouth band. The only time we felt at home in London was when we were recording or performing, and the city dwellers never embraced us the way they did with trendier British bands. Maybe in reaction, we sheltered ourselves from all the influences of London and everything that was going on in the 'cool' scene. We were never cool, which greatly benefited us. I have never been cool, and I hope I remain that way because I just want to be whatever I am. I don't want to have to fit a mold. And I never want to gear anything for mainstream acceptance, as we did in Simon Dupree. I hated that.

Living in Portsmouth, you didn't have to act cool, so we always had great shows there and the whole of the south coast, including the Isle Of Wight. Several of those shows were booked by the notorious gangster Wilf Pine, who was part of the English mafia. That may seem scary, but we were the darlings of the English mob, including the notorious Kray twins, Ronald and Reginald Kray—racketeers, robbers, and, yes, murderers—who loved our music almost as much as they loved the money they made from our sold-out concerts. Really, though, it was more than just a financial relationship. They liked us as people and took us under their wing, making sure promoters paid up, watching our backs to make sure nothing went down at our shows, and catching us onstage whenever they could.

This relationship lasted well into the Gentle Giant era. After one of our sold-out shows on the Isle Of Wight, Pine and his cohorts, Mick and 'The Canadian,' came backstage after the gig.

'Fantastic show, guys,' said Wilf in a raspy working-class accent. 'So, are you boys hungry?'

As a matter of fact, we were. We hadn't eaten before the show, there was no food spread or catering backstage, and all the pubs in the area had stopped serving food. With all the local restaurants closed as well, we'd be lucky if we could find a fast-food joint that served greasy fish and chips.

'So, what kind of food do you like?' Wilf continued.

'Uh, Indian,' I said. 'But everything's closed.'

'Don't you worry about that,' Wilf said. 'Come with me.' We got into his car and his driver took us to a great nearby Indian restaurant. As I feared, it was closed. Wilf got out of the car, walked up to the front door of the restaurant, and pounded on it.

'Hey! Open up!' he shouted. 'It's me.'

After a few moments, the door opened. Wilf talked to the restaurant owner and explained that he would consider it a personal favor if they opened up the kitchen and cooked some food for everyone in the band. The owner nodded, turned to one of his employees, and told him to fire up the ovens and cook some appetizers and curries. A few minutes later, we were sitting at the table with Wilf, Mick, and The Canadian, and the wonderful smell of cooked meat and spices wafting from the kitchen. Thanks to the sway Wilf and his thugs had over the community, we enjoyed an amazing meal that night, secure in the knowledge that all of our equipment would be safely under supervision at the venue until we came back for it.

Being loved by the Isle Of Wight Mob was sometimes a double-edged sword. There were times when the police would get too close to whatever Wilf, Mick, and The Canadian were involved in, and they had to bolt out of town until the heat died down. On more than one occasion, they stopped off at Phil's house in Portsmouth and had him stash jewelry until they came back for it. It was an odd relationship, but one that certainly benefited us—and Phil.

Once, Wilf showed up at Phil's in a Rolls-Royce. 'I gotta go out of town on business,' he told Phil. 'Would you mind watching my car until I get back? It's all right if you drive it around. Have a good time,' he said, and he left before Phil could respond.

A minor historic moment in the career of Simon Dupree & The Big Sound happened in July 1967. Right before we toured Scotland, keyboardist Eric Hine came down with glandular fever, so his doctor grounded him from touring. We needed a replacement right away. Elton John was just starting out—only at the time, he was still going by his birth name, Reg Dwight. He was managed by a guy named Dick James, who had him working under a retainer of £10 per week.

Ray and I went to London to meet Reg, and he was incredibly nice and very humble. Of course, it's hard not to be humble when you're making less than £2 a day—something we had no way of knowing at the time.

We asked him if he would play something for us, and, without a pause, he launched into a litany of piano music: blues, American standards, British pop. It was like someone had tossed a nickel into a player piano.

'Can you play organ and Mellotron?' I asked.

'Sure, if it's got keys, I can play it.'

'How about weird, psychedelic stuff?'

'Yeah, mate,' he said. 'No problem.'

It was clear he'd be able to play anything we threw at him, so we asked him to fill in for Eric on tour. 'Hey Reg, what we can offer you is £25–30 a week,' I said, hoping he wouldn't ask for more.

'Holy shit!' he shouted. 'Really? I've never seen that kind of money.'

We would never have guessed that this was almost three times what he was making, but we were happy to pay it. He was a fine keyboardist, and he was saving our asses. After we met Reg, we went home, then he came down to Portsmouth to rehearse with us for a few days before the tour.

Reg was chatty and open with us, and we grew close in no time. He wasn't out of the closet yet, and it wasn't long before he unloaded some personal shit on us. He had a girlfriend who wanted to marry him, and he didn't know if he loved her as a friend or as more.

'I dunno what to do,' he confided in us. 'I don't really want to get married. Should I get married, should I not get married?'

We liked Reg but we barely knew him. How could we possibly give him advice on something so serious?

'You know, Reg, I'm sure you'll do what you have to do,' I said. I knew it was hardly constructive advice, but it was the best I had.

'Yeah, fuck it,' he said. That was the last we heard about the subject.

Reg knew a lot about pop music and loved talking about his favorite groups. He wasn't just knowledgeable about English music. He knew just as much about what was happening in the States, though neither of us had been there yet. We bonded on the black blues we all listened to on the American Air Force Radio.

Some of the shows on the Scottish tour were in nearby towns. Others were a hundred miles or more apart, which required long drives in the van. Every few hours, we'd stop at a café to take a short break, have a coffee, and maybe take a piss. And then we get back into the van and head back out. That's when we learned another quirk about Reg.

'Hey guys, look what I've got,' he said one day, shaking a snow globe that probably cost about £5.

'Reg, why do you want that? Isn't it a little pricey?' I said.

'Maybe. I dunno. I just wanted it.'

So it went every time we stopped. Reg always picked up something odd: commemorative spoons, a yo-yo, a candlestick. And he never worried about the price. Once, he picked up a watch that looked expensive. I figured maybe I should talk with him before he spent his entire per-diem for the week.

'Do you think you should think about whether you really need something before you buy it?' I asked. 'I mean, especially if something costs a lot and you don't need it on tour.'

'I like to collect stuff,' he replied, nonplussed. 'It'll remind me of being on tour when I get back home and look at the stuff. Why, do you want any of it?'

'No,' I said, and I laughed.

I kind of felt sorry for Reg. He seemed unable to stop himself from buying useless things. Pretty soon it wouldn't matter, and he'd be able to buy anything he wanted.

We stayed friends with Reg after Eric returned to the group, and we frequently talked about working together in the future. Meanwhile, we swam forward with Simon Dupree, but at times it was more like treading water. We started to talk more to John and everyone at EMI about heading in a different musical direction. Understandably, they weren't too keen on the idea.

In an effort to appease us, my brother-in-law booked us a session at Abbey Road in mid-'68 to record something more experimental than anything we had done and release it under another name. Ray, Phil, and I wrote a weird song called 'We Are The Moles,' which we structured in the style of The Beatles at their trippiest. We played droning, spacy riffs and phased the instruments in and out of the mix. We layered chiming keyboards on top and added freaky studio sound effects to the vocals, which included lines like '*We are the moles and we stay in our holes / Hiding our faces, revealing our souls.*' We didn't take it seriously at all. We just had fun, and there was a fast vocal part that was a little like 'I Am The Walrus,' which we all thought was great.

It was easy to do, and we did it quickly so we would sound spontaneous. We had a good time tapping into this strange, surreal side of ourselves. When we'd finished it, we recorded a B-Side, 'We Are The Moles Part II,' which started with marching sound effects and then turned into this ethereal, nonsensical ditty with the three of us harmonizing the only line in the song, '*We are the moles,*' in various ways. It ended with madcap clapping and calls for '*More!*' which Ray and I found hysterical. We wrote the whole thing in the studio in five minutes and recorded it in ten.

Parlophone released 'We Are The Moles' in 1968, and, to our surprise, it started getting airplay. The press was chattering. Everyone was trying to figure out who was in this mysterious band with no credited members. The song hit the Top 100, and when people started wondering if The Moles were The Beatles in disguise, it reached #75 and started going up the charts. We thought this might be the beginning of an anonymous side project that would be fun to do and imagined going back into the studio to record a whole album of silly, psychedelic songs.

That was before Syd Barrett burst the bubble. In an interview with the weekly *Melody Maker* music paper, he said, 'The Moles are just that shitty group Simon Dupree & The Big Sound.' Once he'd intercepted our galactic flight, the engine stalled, and 'We Are The Moles' dropped right off the charts. It was such a dick move. Rather than allow the mystery around us to build—at no expense to him—he ratted us out.

Having the mysterious shroud of The Moles yanked off instantly halting our forward momentum was aggravating and made us want to escape the back-stabbing English pop scene and do something more obscure that catered to our musical interests instead of the fickle tastes of the mainstream. We needed new blood. I needed a change, and I got it. I just didn't realize how much change I would experience over the next few months.

In late 1968, we went into Abbey Road to record the single 'For Whom The Bell Tolls,' which had chirping birds, a ringing bell, horns, and marching drums, but was otherwise a baroque pop song with yearning, mellifluous vocals. Eric Hine and I wrote the B-side, 'Sleep,' which had soulful vocals and prominently featured both Ray on violin and Phil on trumpet. I was credited on that one as Dupree—as in Simon Dupree—which I thought was funny. The song got some radio play, and we played many shows that year.

In 1969, we returned to the studio and recorded 'Broken Hearted Pirates,' a silly, up-tempo song that starts with a seafaring pop melody and features seagull sounds, piano, whimsical flutes, horns, and lyrics about, well, sad pirates. It was a disaster and a bad career move.

We had already been convinced to change course and record a psychedelic song that was outside of our milieu, and 'Kites' was huge. So, John King thought we should try another quirky song written by an outside songwriting team. At the time, The Foundations had a hit called 'Baby Now That I've Found You,' which featured an orchestra and big arrangements, and suddenly, every label wanted their bands to do a song like that. So, we did 'Broken Hearted Pirates' by Michael & Anthony, which was practically a parody of what we were doing before 'Kites.' It wasn't just redundant; it seemed like we had lost our footing. When we performed the song on the popular German music program *Beat-Club*,

Left My father, Sergeant Major Lewis Shulman, Army Air Corps, No. 1 Parachute Regiment, during World War II.

Below The Shulman family, 1952. *Left to right*: Eve, Ray, Rebecca, me, Phil, Lewis, and Terry.

Right Me and my brother Ray in the living room of our house on Eastney Road, Portsmouth, 1958. **Below** With my brothers Ray (*center*) and Terry (*right*) in our back garden, 1961.

Opposite page, top The four Shulman brothers: Terry, me, and Ray, with Phil standing at the back, Eastney Road, 1957. **Below** My father playing trumpet at the South Parade Pier ballroom in Southsea, Portsmouth, 1962.

Right Me playing the famous Fender Stratocaster, 1965. **Below** Our first promotional shoot for Parlophone Records, for 'I See The Light,' 1966.

Opposite page, top Simon Dupree & The Big Sound playing live at the Indigo Vat Club, Portsmouth, 1966. **Below** Simon Dupree & The Big Sound promo shoot for 'Kites,' 1967.

Jimmy James
VAGABONDS

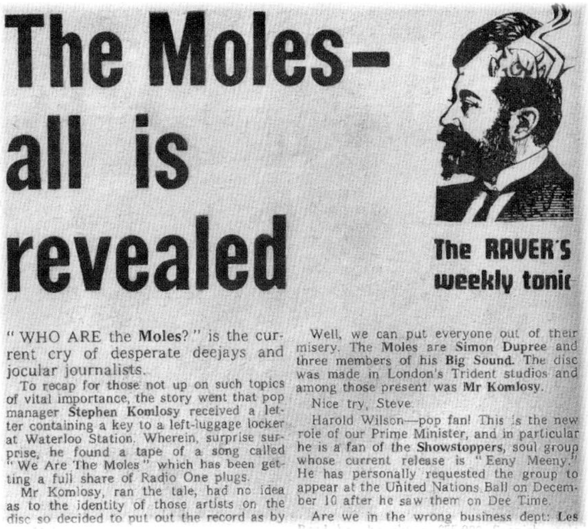

The Moles–all is revealed

The RAVER'S weekly tonic

"WHO ARE the **Moles?**" is the current cry of desperate deejays and jocular journalists.

To recap for those not up on such topics of vital importance, the story went that pop manager **Stephen Komlosy** received a letter containing a key to a left-luggage locker at Waterloo Station. Wherein, surprise surprise, he found a tape of a song called "We Are The Moles" which has been getting a full share of Radio One plugs.

Mr Komlosy, ran the tale, had no idea as to the identity of those artists on the disc so decided to put out the record as by

Well, we can put everyone out of their misery. The **Moles** are **Simon Dupree** and three members of his **Big Sound**. The disc was made in London's Trident studios and among those present was **Mr Komlosy**.

Nice try, Steve.

Harold Wilson—pop fan! This is the new role of our Prime Minister, and in particular he is a fan of the **Showstoppers**, soul group whose current release is "Eeny Meeny." He has personally requested the group to appear at the United Nations Ball on December 10 after he saw them on Dee Time.

Are we in the wrong business dept: Les

Left Syd Barrett of Pink Floyd reveals that The Moles are actually Simon Dupree & The Big Sound, 1968. **Below** Me with Eve (*center*), Ray (*left*), and Phil (*right*) in Bristol, 1968. One of the few moments we were all together in front of a camera.

Opposite page On the set of *Beat-Club* in Hamburg, 1967. We were supporting none other than The Jimi Hendrix Experience.

Above Reginald Dwight, who later became Elton John, on tour with us in Simon Dupree & The Big Sound in Scotland, 1968.

we embarrassed ourselves horribly by further fueling the parody by dressing up like pirates and hopping around the stage like idiots.

The only consolation of recording 'Broken Hearted Pirates' was hanging out with the actor and comedian Dudley Moore, who came into Abbey Road to play piano on the track (though for some reason he wasn't credited). Long before he was nominated for an Oscar for his lead role in *Arthur*, Moore was best known for performing with Peter Cook in the hysterical comedy revue *Beyond The Fringe*. He told us he liked our music, and we enjoyed chatting with him. All three Shulman brothers wrote the B-side of 'Broken Hearted Pirates,' 'She Gave Me The Sun.' The music was buoyant and sparky, and Phil nailed the horn parts, which sounded great. Maybe that one should have been the single.

After 'Broken Hearted Pirates,' it was clear we had slid off the rails and needed to get back on the track or board a new train. We were annoyed with John, who had pushed us in musical directions we didn't want to pursue. Ray and I were reluctant to confront him since he was our sister's husband, so Phil did the honors. He had often argued with John about business decisions, anyway, so, in no uncertain terms, he told John how unhappy we were with his recent decisions. That ended our relationship with him.

For the sake of accuracy, we didn't fire John King, and he had no plans to leave. But one day in the middle of one of several arguments with Phil about the unsatisfying creative path we were on, John slammed his fist on the table.

'I don't need this shit,' he shouted. 'Fuck it, Phil. You've pissed me off one time too many.' Phil was the bad cop. For the sake of Eve, Ray and I played the good cops and asked John not to leave. If we had known they would eventually get divorced, we would have shown him the door ourselves. As it was, we were just paying him lip service. We were ready to move up to a more professional level of management. Sometimes everything works out for the best.

CHAPTER SIX
COLD FEET

Our search for a new manager brought us to the esteemed English record producer Gerry Bron, who had worked with tons of big acts including Gene Pitney, Uriah Heep, Bonzo Dog Doo-Dah Band, and Manfred Mann. We knew Gerry through the Abbey Road scene, and he was the one who'd connected us with Elton John's first manager, Dick James, about having Reg (Elton) fill in for Eric Hine on our Scotland tour. Gerry liked Simon Dupree, and he believed in us as pop stars and musicians. But he also had a greater vision for more forward-thinking music, and he was starting a new label and looking for groups to invest in as well as manage. It seemed like a great match—and, for a while, it was.

The last single we put out in Simon Dupree, 'The Eagle Flies Tonight,' was another song by Michael & Anthony. It was a pretty, earnest pop song with bursts of horns, splashes of strings, and a syrupy melody made for the radio. Except radio had moved on. Still, we could have kept going for a lot longer than we did. Our concerts were still packed, and the press couldn't get enough of us. I was on the cover of *Rave*, *Melody Maker*, and other publications, and wherever we went, crowds of kids were there waiting.

It's important to realize that the record business in the 60s wasn't like today. We put all our singles together along with some other songs we tracked at the studio during our three-hour sessions, and Parlophone released it as our only album, *Without Reservations*, in August 1967. That was before we'd recorded 'Kites,' though the song was added to later pressings. Our fans loved it and were delighted to have all of our songs, including some that had never been released, on one album. Playing shows throughout the UK and some of Europe and releasing nine singles (not including the Moles seven-inch) between 1967 and 1969, we were constantly in the spotlight. So, even though some of our singles weren't hits, our biggest songs—'Kites,' 'I See The Light,' 'Reservations,' and 'Day Time, Night Time'—were real crowd-pleasers and kept the kids screaming like we were the second coming of The Beatles. So, it's easy to understand why EMI balked at the idea of the Shulman brothers changing course musically after only one album with Simon Dupree & The Big Sound. We had a good thing going, and they didn't want us to fuck it up. In some ways, we were getting to the point where we were beyond caring. We wanted to move forward as musicians, and the pop community was holding us back.

Maybe I would have been more aggressive about breaking up Simon Dupree before we recorded our last two singles if something else wasn't weighing heavily on my mind. In 1968, after returning from a major tour, I proposed to Jennie. It seemed like the right thing to do. I needed more stability. I wanted a family, Jennie was Jewish, and I hadn't met anyone else who seemed like marriage material. Was I crazy about her? I don't know. I loved her, but I'm not sure I was *in* love with her. Nevertheless, she accepted my proposal. We were engaged.

A part of me was reassured that there would be a financial cushion while we continued our musical pursuits with another band, and, if all else failed, Ray, Phil, and I would have 'casinos' to fall back on. Thinking like that would have been pragmatic. But fuck, man, I was twenty years old, and I wanted to sprint across the tightrope without a safety net. To anyone else, it looked like I had a charmed life. I was on the cover of teen magazines, and Simon Dupree were playing loads of gigs for adoring fans. I was becoming a big international star, and my beautiful fiancée was planning this big Jewish wedding that was like something out of a fairy tale—and her parents were paying for it. Everyone was happy for me... except me.

During the last tour before the wedding, we were in Stockport in Northern England and I was warming up in the dressing room when, out of the blue, I started sweating profusely and my heart pounded like a jackhammer. I flashed right back to my dad coughing, struggling to breathe, and then dying right in front of me. I was terrified, and the fear made me feel sicker. The room was spinning around me as I collapsed in a chair and plopped my head into my hands. Ray ran and got me a glass of water, which I managed to gulp down. Someone else found a paper bag for me to breathe into, which didn't help at all.

'Derek, are you okay?' asked Phil. 'We have to do a show.'

I focused on being onstage and went through the set in my head, and that helped. I took deep breaths, in and out, in and out. After about an hour, my heartbeat slowed, and I felt okay again. *What the hell was that about?* I thought, right before we went onstage.

I played the concert and I was fine onstage, but when we finished I felt strange. I was wondering if I should see a doctor when I had a second attack. I gasped for breath, and my vision was clouded with dots like static on a TV screen. I was dizzy, so I lay down in bed and feared for my life. It was complete dread, and I didn't know what I was afraid of, other than dying on tour. I prayed to whatever God might be out there to get me through. By the time I finally felt better, I had sweated clean through my sheets.

'Is anything going on with you?' asked the doctor I visited the next day. 'Has anything changed in your life?'

'Not that I know of,' I said. 'Why am I feeling like this?'

He asked me if I could think of anything coming up that I was worried about. And then it struck me. I was getting married in less than a week. I asked myself if I was getting cold feet and decided my feet were fine. I just couldn't marry Jennie. But I had to. It was too late to cancel. Jennie's family had already spent thousands of pounds on the venue, staff, catering, and flowers for the wedding of the century. Between 250 and 300 people were coming, including press from most major outlets. Everyone was finalizing their plans, and many people had already sent me gifts.

I called my sister, who I always went to when I needed life advice.

'Are you okay, Derek?' she asked.

'No, not really,' I replied. 'Everyone is forcing me to get married. I don't want to. I can't go through with it. This is not going to work.'

'You don't have to do this,' she calmly said. 'If you think it's a mistake, cancel the wedding. If you really don't want to get married, it's better to accept that now than regret it later.'

The next person I spoke to was my mother, and she was just as supportive as my sister. 'If this is actually making you ill, Derek, then you've got to know in your heart that this is not the right thing to do,' she said.

Everyone said they would support my decision, whatever it was. Phil made it clear that if I didn't get married, we would all lose the financial stability Jennie's parents could provide for us. But ultimately he said he didn't want me to be stuck in an unhappy marriage.

The next day, I called Jennie's father. I hadn't even talked to Jennie, but my decision was made.

'I'm sorry. I'm not going through with marrying your daughter,' I told him. That's when the bomb exploded. Harry screamed at me and told me I was horrible and ungrateful, and how dare I do this to his daughter. He said I didn't deserve her and not to bother coming to him for help. He called me a failure and said I'd never make it in music. He shouted whatever he could that he thought would hurt me, and when he was out of insults he hung up.

I felt rotten and depressed. I wasn't panicked anymore. I was empty.

A day or two later, I got together with Jennie to apologize and explained that I had gotten sick and I wasn't ready to get married. She cried and told me she loved me. When she regained her composure, she asked me if I didn't love her anymore.

'It's not that,' I said. 'I mean, I do love you. I'm just ... I'm not ready. I don't know why.'

While I took some time away from Jennie to figure out what was going on in my head, I was sluggish and depressed. I didn't want to do anything with anybody, and I wasn't thinking straight. The only time I was happy was when I was onstage. Our manager, Gerry, suggested I get out of Portsmouth and away from my routine.

'Why don't you stay with us in London for a couple of days?'

I thought about it for a minute and decided a new location might help me find a better headspace. Gerry lived in North Hampstead, London, with his wife, Lilian, who was a cellist and a very vocal presence. She was twenty years older than me, and to say she was not the most attractive person in the world was an understatement. On top of that, she was loud and had an opinion about everything. But I was grateful to her and her husband for putting me up while I figured things out.

That night, I woke up at about 2:30 in the morning to the sound of the door opening.

'Who's there?' I whispered as a shadowy figure inched toward me. It was Lilian. She said she was checking in on me to see how I was doing, which is an odd thing to do after 2am. I assured her I was fine.

'Okay, Derek. Well, if you need anything... anything at all, I'm here for you.'

The way she said 'anything at all' sounded like an invitation. Weird, but no big deal. 'Uh, okay. I'm going back to sleep.'

'Are you cold?' she whispered. 'It's a big bed. I can slip in there with you if you like.'

My stomach leaped into my throat. That was definitely an invitation. Even if she'd been as beautiful as Brigitte Bardot, I wouldn't have invited my manager's wife into bed.

'No, no. I'm okay,' I said, trying to push down the waves of panic that were starting to rise. 'I'm just tired. I'll roll over and go back to sleep now. By myself. Good night.'

'If you change your mind, I'm here for you.' She walked to the side of the bed, leaned over, and put her palm on the edge of the mattress. 'I know it can get lonely when you're away from home.'

She stroked my cheek. I didn't say a thing and prayed she wouldn't move her hand anywhere else. I had to summon all my willpower not to scream. The next ten seconds seemed like ten minutes. I was sure she could hear my heart pounding, and I hoped she didn't think I was getting excited. At last, she stood back up and left the room.

I packed that night to leave the next morning.

'You know, Gerry,' I said when he woke up and came downstairs, where I was waiting. 'I'm feeling much better now. I just needed a good night's rest. I have some things I need to do in Portsmouth, so I think I'll head back. Thanks so much for the invitation. And be sure to thank Lilian for me as well.'

Before he had the chance to say anything, I bolted out of the house and caught the next train home. Fucking hell.

I talked to Jennie soon after, and we agreed to postpone our wedding indefinitely but not cancel it completely. We clung to the hope that I would get over my jitters and we could try again when I felt better and had more clarity. Though I didn't know it at the time, it was a gentle way to say goodbye.

Leaving Jennie was a milestone in my life. It shook me up psychologically and made me question what kind of a person I was, what I wanted, and why I couldn't marry a perfectly great Jewish girl when I knew I wanted to start my own family. A few months later, I was no closer to epiphany, but at least I was over the hump of emotional turmoil. Jennie and I tried rekindling our relationship. We went out on dates. We even slept together, but there was no spark. Our time together was over.

I had come to a major crossroads, and I knew my life moving forward would change dramatically. There would be no marriage, and Simon Dupree & The Big Sound were over. It was time to stop taking the safe path forward. I needed to take chances, whether they worked out or not. It was time to listen to the voice in my head that was telling me, *You don't want a backup plan. That's not who you are. You need to do what you want to do right now because life is short.*

Of all the pop stars we knew, Elton John might have played the biggest role in the Shulman brothers' transition from Simon Dupree & The Big Sound to Gentle Giant. Reg was an incredible music scholar and collector. He listened to everything that was going on in Europe and America. When I told him we wanted to play a different kind of music, he suggested we listen to some bands for inspiration. One of them was Spirit. We checked out their first two albums, *Spirit* and *The Family That Plays Together*, which combine a bunch of musical styles including psychedelic rock, jazz, blues, and folk. It was intriguing, inspiring, and not that dissimilar to the kind of music we were already considering. Elton also suggested we listen to

Frank Zappa and Miles Davis, two other artists we grew to love.

At one point when we were still doing Simon Dupree, Reg told us he was a songwriter as well as a pianist and he'd love to write a song for us. We had enjoyed touring with him, so we said we'd love to hear anything he came up with. The next time we saw him, he played us a really good song on the piano called 'I'm Coming Home,' and we went right into Abbey Road studio and recorded it for a future single. Then we got caught up in a whirlwind of angst and drama. I was ending my engagement, we were becoming disenchanted with the band, and we were talking about breaking up. So, 'I'm Coming Home' never got released, and it fell through the cracks for decades. Then, in 2021, I saw that Elton was playing in New York, so I called his agent Barry Marshall, who, funnily enough, used to book Simon Dupree & The Big Sound. Barry got me two tickets, and before my wife and I went to the show, I tracked down the recording of 'I'm Coming Home,' which I had on a cassette tape. I gave it to Elton backstage after the show. He hadn't remembered doing it with us and said he couldn't wait to hear it. The next time I talked to him, he told me he loved the song and that it brought back some great memories of being on tour and hanging out with us.

Rewind back to 1969. I'm talking to Reg about finding musicians for our new band, and he says he has written a bunch of new stuff and might be interested in joining us. 'That could be really great,' I tell him, and we agree to get together to listen to his new songs.

Ray and I met Reg in London, and we were excited to hear what he had put together. As much as we wanted to work with him again, as soon as he started playing the tape, we knew the music wouldn't fit our new direction. His new songs were good, but they were rooted in R&B and pop, and that was exactly what we wanted to get away from. We knew that he still wanted to play commercial music, and if he joined our new band, he wouldn't be happy. We told him we didn't think it would work, and he was gracious about being gently rejected.

We changed the subject and kept chatting, and Reg told us he wanted to change his stage name, too.

'Oh yeah?' I said. 'What are you thinking?'

He told us he'd chosen the name Elton John because he was a big fan of Soft Machine, whose sax player was Elton Dean. And he got the surname John from the vocalist Long John Baldry, with whom Reg had played in the band Bluesology.

'Reg, that will never work!' I spouted. 'What a stupid name that is.'

'Maybe you should come up with something else,' said Ray, who was trying harder than I was not to laugh.

Not long after that, the music Reg wrote with lyricist Bernie Taupin started to take off. By 1970, 'Your Song' was a major hit and ELTON JOHN was playing to packed houses at the Troubadour while we were scrambling around Guilford trying to get gigs. Clearly, Reg had the last laugh.

Ray and I and even Phil knew we couldn't keep Simon Dupree & The Big Sound going. It had gotten to the point where we would play shows and could feel the audience waiting for us to play the hits. As much as we had enjoyed seeing guys singing along and young girls screaming in ecstasy when we played those songs, it wasn't artistically rewarding anymore. It felt cheap. We wanted crowds to listen intently to *everything* we played and to have to focus on multiple rhythm and tempo changes to understand our music. We didn't want to write predictable songs anymore. Verses and choruses were okay, but we didn't want the hooks to be so obvious that fans didn't even have to pay attention to dance along with the music.

We were all in regarding the new musical direction we wanted to take, and we knew we couldn't do that with our bassist, Geary Kenworthy, nor sadly my old school friend, keyboardist Eric Hine. They were good pop musicians, and they played well for a mainstream crowd. We needed guys who were capable of playing complex, multifaceted music and changing direction on the fly. We wanted to make the kind of music Spirit made without sounding like Spirit, and we needed to play with musicians who could do anything and contribute ideas and parts that were as forward-thinking as ours. Securing the right lineup was going to be hard enough. Before that, we had to convince our label and our team that we didn't want to make pop music anymore; our priority was no longer to get played on the radio.

When John King stepped down, we had talked to various managers, including Don Arden, who worked with Jerry Lee Lewis, Little Richard, Gene Vincent, and other guys we admired and listened to on American Air Force radio. But these guys didn't want to take risks.

'You've got a great name and an established fanbase. Why would you throw that away?' Arden had said.

'We need to do something different,' I said. 'If we can't put a new band together, we don't want to do any more music. That's how strongly we feel.'

Arden laughed. He may have thought we were making a bad move, but he respected our integrity. 'Well, good luck then,' he said. 'Just not with my money.'

In retrospect, we were fortunate that Don wasn't interested in us back then. We'd cross paths with him again soon enough.

Some of the other people who found out we were breaking up Simon Dupree & The Big Sound and starting a new, more adventurous band were similarly surprised. They shouldn't have been. When The Beatles became more adventurous and started prioritizing meticulous, well-crafted studio productions over peppy live performances, they had an influence on a range of like-minded musicians that was almost as influential as the wave of excitement and enthusiasm they generated with 'Love Me Do' and 'I Wanna Hold Your Hand.' Suddenly, lots of pop groups were trying new, left-of-center types of music. When they were teenagers, Robert Fripp and his school friend Gordon Haskell played together in the pop/soul band The League Of Gentlemen before Fripp formed the more progressive King Crimson in 1968 (Haskell joined the band for a short time in 1970). Jimmy Page from The Yardbirds joined forces with Band Of Joy vocalist Robert Plant, the singer's childhood friend John Bonham, bassist John Paul Jones (who had played with Page in various session gigs, including some for the Yardbirds), and, in one brief tour, transformed from The New Yardbirds into Led Zeppelin. Two members of the failed London rock band Episode Six, vocalist Ian Gillan and bassist Roger Glover, helped carve a new face for Deep Purple in 1969. Mid-60s jazz and rhythm & blues outfit The Graham Bond Organisation featured future Cream bassist Jack Bruce and drummer Ginger Baker, as well as guitarist John McLaughlin. Rhythm & blues band The Soul Agents brought the world a young Rod Stewart. Anon, a band featuring Mike Rutherford and Anthony Phillips had just broken up, as had Garden Wall, which featured Peter Gabriel, Tony Banks, and Chris Stewart. All five musicians were students at Charterhouse School in Surrey, and they joined forces as Genesis in 1967. Bassist Chris Squire, vocalist Jon Anderson, and drummer Bill Bruford were in Mabel Greer's Toyshop until the group broke up in 1967 and they formed the more progressive Yes. And Steve Howe played in the English beat band The Syndicats, the psychedelic pop group Tomorrow, and the rock band Bodast before joining Yes in 1970. Maybe most of the guys in those bands didn't get to play *Top Of The Pops* until they were reborn with their more intricate, progressive groups, but, over the years, we had a lot of good times with many of these guys.

I'd like to be able to say Simon Dupree & The Big Sound ended on a euphoric high note. It did and it didn't. In the final days of the band, we were booked to play a week of dates at the Stockton Fiesta, a cabaret club. We were still very popular, and I was trying to make a graceful exit, despite hating every second of it. We never wanted to be a house band, so when we played a venue like that, we'd book three days at the most. The week before our first gig, Joe Cocker was playing the first of five nights. He was so drunk he couldn't stand up without hugging the mic stand. Crowd members were booing and pelting him with objects. After being hit with one too many beverage cups, he staggered off the stage and the show was over. The club's management canceled the rest of his shows and told him to get the fuck out and not to come back.

They contacted us and asked if we would play Cocker's remaining shows in addition to the three for which we were already booked. None of us wanted to play the gigs, but the money was good, so we accepted. We played everything the crowd wanted to hear, but we were just coloring by numbers. But at least we wouldn't be competing with any hot-shit opening bands, since the venue had booked a hypnotist named Chick Mick.

It wasn't unusual for cabaret clubs to book a variety of acts—magicians, ventriloquists, comedians, and, yes, hypnotists—and, during his show,

Mick joked with the crowd and hypnotized various volunteers. We figured they were plants and paid little attention to his act. Then, on the last night we were booked to play with Chick Mick, our drummer Martin Smith and bassist Gary Kenworthy asked him how it worked.

'Well, you want me to show you?' the hypnotist asked.

'Yeah,' we told him.

'Go ahead, give it a try. Hypnotize us,' Phil said.

Chick Mick started his routine. 'Okay, watch my hand and listen to my voice. You're getting sleepy.' Us bigshot Shulman brothers looked at one another with leering skepticism.

'What the fuck?' said Phil. 'We're not getting sleepy.' For sure, the three of us were not, but I'll be damned if that hypnotist didn't put Gary and Martin right to sleep. Within minutes, he had them waddling around, quacking like ducks and squawking like chickens. Then he snapped his fingers and they went back to normal but had no idea what had happened to them.

'So, when are you gonna hypnotize us?' Martin said. Maybe hypnotism only works on weak minds—and rhythm sections. It was the funniest thing, and as a final memorable backstage experience for Simon Dupree, it helped end the band on more of an up note than I had expected.

CHAPTER SEVEN

MIND IF I TUNE UP?

With Gerry Bron's financial backing, we were able to disband Simon Dupree & The Big Sound and take the next nine months off to write a batch of experimental songs for our new band and recruit and hire new members who were skilled enough to co-write and play the material.

'Derek, I believe in you and your brothers,' Gerry said. 'I'll support you because I know you can do this.'

Phil and his wife, who had bought a large house in Portsmouth, were renting rooms to students studying at nearby schools. One of them was a music fan who knew Phil, Ray, and I were starting a new band. One morning, he knocked on Phil's door before heading to class.

'A good friend of mine is a musician in Germany, and he wants to get back to England,' he began. 'His name is Kerry Minnear, and he was in a band called Rust when they broke up. Now he's stuck there, but he's a great musician. He went to the Royal Academy Of Music and studied composition and theory. I just thought you might want to talk to him, since you're doing this new thing.'

Phil thanked the student and then told us about Kerry. By the time we tracked him down, he had returned to England and was living with his parents in the West Country. Fortunately, there weren't too many Minnears in the phone book, so we gave him a call.

'Your friend says you're really good,' Phil began. 'If we pay for your train fare to Portsmouth, would you want to try out for us? We're not doing stuff like Simon Dupree anymore. We want to do something really different. So, are you interested?'

'Yeah, I'd love to,' he said. 'I need a gig, and I think I can get in with what you want to do.'

Kerry was a classically trained musician who had a gift for playing angular, off-kilter passages on keyboards, but he also enjoyed and was more than capable of playing a good melody. He was a fantastic person—upbeat and friendly—and consumed with creating chords, patterns, and licks that served the songs instead of his ego. He had only been semi-professional with Rust and had never done any major tour, but he was eager to learn and contribute to something new.

Kerry stayed at Phil's house in Portsmouth, and we met him soon after he had settled in. He played some songs for us that he had composed, and we were amazed. The melodies and progressions he played had only existed in our heads until that moment. It was clear we were on the same page. From that point, Gentle Giant was not just a fetus. With the arrival of Kerry, it was born. Between Kerry's composing knowledge and Ray's classical background, there was an immediate bond, and once they started writing, they couldn't stop. Once again, the stars had aligned. Not only was Kerry the catalyst for what we became, but he was kind, patient, and even-keeled, and he had the right disposition to cope with the pressure of being in a touring band. He could also be charmingly naïve, which was sort of sweet.

About five years after Kerry joined Gentle Giant, we were playing a big headline show in London to support our album *The Power And The Glory*. Backstage after the show, a pretty, petite young woman the rest of us instantly recognized walked over to Kerry. They started speaking, and though Kerry couldn't identify her, he recognized she wasn't from the UK.

'Oh, you sound American. Where are you from?' he asked.

'I'm living in California now, but I'm originally from Connecticut,' the woman said, then changed the subject. 'I really like your music. I think it's great.'

After about thirty minutes of chit-chat, Kerry asked the most amazing thing: 'Do you do anything in the music business?'

'Yes. Yes, I do,' she said.

'So, are you a singer, or do you work for a label or something?'

'Well, I'm in a group called The Carpenters,' she said humbly, after a brief pause.

Kerry was chatting up Karen Carpenter and he didn't have any idea who she was! He had never seen her picture. He didn't know her music. It was unbelievable. She was sweet and not at all insulted. Maybe she enjoyed not being instantly recognized, but hearing him ask her if she does anything in the music business was hilarious. And her answer—'Well, I'm in a group called The Carpenters'—was priceless. Ray and I were nudging one another, snickering. Kery didn't say, 'Oh, I'm sorry. I didn't recognize you.' He was completely nonplussed, and they dated for a couple of weeks.

With a gifted keyboardist and songwriter who could match musical wits with Ray, we needed a versatile guitarist who could captivate a crowd with unusual riffs, chords, and time signatures. We put an ad in the *Melody Maker*, which drew hundreds of responses. In the weeks that followed, about 120 guitarists came to rehearsal space we rented for these auditions in Tottenham Court Road, London. One of them was a big Jamaican Rastafarian guy. We told him to come over for an audition, and he walked in smoking a huge pipe. We started talking to him about the adventurous, anything goes spirit we wanted to inject into our music, and he suggested we consider playing reggae instead. Ray showed him the unconventional chord structures for 'Peel The Paint.' As soon as we began the song, he ignored Ray's direction and played an upbeat reggae passing that clashed horribly with what the rest of us were playing. It was excruciating. NEXT!

We were feeling pretty pessimistic when Gary Green showed up with his older brother, Jeff, who was a roadie for Soft Machine. Gary was three years younger than me, and he played mandolin and recorder as well as guitar. As soon as he stepped onstage with us, he wowed us by doing something none of the other prospects had even considered.

'Hey guys, do you mind if I tune up?' Gary asked.

After dealing with 100 or so hopeless guitarists who thought they were the next Jeff Beck, it was great to hear someone who cared enough about being in tune before trying to impress us with his playing. Gary had great timing and could play unusual tempos and nail abrupt rhythm shifts, but he was more of a blues-based player than Kerry or Ray, so he was as good at locking into a groove as he was at playing straight melodic or textural parts. We were feeling pretty good about him. Then, in the middle of a song, his brother grabbed him by the arm and whispered in his ear, and Gary blanched.

We later learned that Jeff had seen the words 'Simon Dupree & Big Sound' in big letters on Martin Smith's bass drum, and after mentioning it to Gary, he almost packed up and fled to the train station. A while after we hired him, he told us what went through his mind when he saw our logo: 'Oh, no. Not *that* band?' Let's just say he wasn't a fan. He didn't want to play pop music any more than we did.

Thankfully, instead of following his instincts to leave, Gary stuck around and continued to wow us with his skills. We launched into something Kerry had written, and Gary followed the rhythmic shifts and improvised licks that complemented the song. As far as we were concerned, he was in the band.

Drummer Martin Smith was the only leftover from Simon Dupree & The Big Sound, and we had hired him toward the end of the band to replace Tony Ransley, who lacked flair and chops. Martin played with us in our new band for two albums, but, ultimately, he was the wrong guy for us. Finding the right man for the job is always a Herculean task. There are lots of good drummers but very few great ones.

We have Gerry Bron to thank for more than just our Gentle Giant label deal. Indirectly, he also led us to our band name. Every month or two, Gerry sent one of his staffers to our practice space to check in on us and listen to what we were doing. One of these people was Colin Richardson, who came to see us while we were working on a pile of incomplete but solid music that Kerry and Ray had come up with. We started practicing 'Alucard,' a six-minute-long track that would later become a staple of our set and the name of our future reissue label. As we played, Colin smiled and bobbed his head along with the complex rhythm as best he could.

'What do you think?' I asked him after rehearsal.

'Boy, you know, it's heavy and it's quiet,' he said. 'It's gentle and then there's just this giant sound. It's like a gentle giant.'

BINGO! It had been a productive day. Colin went back to Gerry with a glowing progress report, and we had our new band name. Plus, we had worked 'Alucard' to the point where it was almost ready to record—the back and forth between the spacy keyboards and the horns sounded especially good.

We sat in band meetings and came up with all these crazy ideas. One time, we were working on combining some of the different parts of 'Alucard.' Suddenly, Kerry jumped up. 'Let me score this and I'll see if I can make it work.' he said. He started scribbling notes on music sheets before we disbanded, and by the next time we got together he had composed several versions that allowed us to merge different parts in clever ways without sounding forced or pretentious.

Back in Simon Dupree, I had helped compose and shape the simple, straightforward songs. In Gentle Giant, I willingly took a back seat to Kerry and Ray and allowed them to handle eighty to ninety percent of the songwriting. Gary contributed to the guitar parts, but he had great respect for Ray and Kerry as well, and he worked closely with them to write passages that contrasted with what they were playing yet complemented the music. For me, the challenge was finding vocal melodies and arrangements that shined alongside all this wild stuff. It was a major challenge. This was unorthodox, unusual music that could easily have remained instrumental, so it would only benefit from the right kinds of vocals. This was anxiety-provoking for me, but at the same time, finding ways to fit my voice to this strange music was interesting and enlightening, and I enjoyed pushing myself to make it work—to rise to the challenge. I had to. Maybe it was because of my competitive nature, but I felt that I had to step up to the plate and keep in musical stride with everyone else, because if I couldn't, I was an idiot, and I didn't deserve to be the singer.

Phil and I both worked on the lyrics, which were more literate and analytical than anything we had done in Simon Dupree. He loved to read and was influenced by existentialists like Albert Camus and Jean-Paul Sartre, and I was more interested in making observations about what was going on in the world around us. We were both so excited about the new band that, in the beginning at least, we were a good songwriting team.

Sometimes we argued about which lyrics to use, but we knew we were a part of something bigger than ourselves.

We wrote and finessed around twenty songs, then scheduled some shows to see how audiences reacted to the new music, figuring a trial by fire was the best way to test our skills and up our game. I can't remember anything about the first Gentle Giant gig, but a bit of research revealed that we performed for hometown fans at the Fairfield Parlour, Portsmouth Polytechnic's student union, on May 9, 1970. The promo text on the flyer mentioned the band would be 'featuring ace singer Simon Dupree.' This must have excited fans of the Big Sound—but maybe not enough. A local paper reported a 'disappointing turnout,' though it added, 'Despite the [attendance] letdown, the band impressed with what many described as a brilliant debut performance.' I'll take that.

I think the reason I can't remember the show is because nothing earth-shattering happened, so in that respect, I'll chalk it up as a good Gentle Giant show, and there were so many of them. For those in the know, there was a buzz about Gentle Giant from the start. Gerry Bron got us a deal with Vertigo Records, which was a new label founded by Olav Wyper, who had been the marketing manager at Philips/Phonogram. He and his team were interested in signing experimental bands, and they liked what we were doing. So did the critics.

Since we had road-tested most of our new songs in and around London before we entered the studio, we knew which ones the crowds liked most and which one we played best. We whittled our set down to eight songs before we entered the studio, and since we were so well rehearsed, we were confident that we'd be able to record an album that would earn us a brand new fanbase while expanding those who appreciated the more eccentric side of Simon Dupree.

Fans who were ready to progress with the Shulman brothers were thankfully blown away. Predictably, those who wanted us to play run-of-the-mill psychedelic pop and simple R&B were a bit confused. As I saw the looks of bewilderment and awe on their faces, I thought, *Just wait 'til you hear the album!*

CHAPTER EIGHT

A TALL TALE

Gerry Bron introduced us to Tony Visconti, a transplanted American producer who was developing a solid reputation. He heard the first Gentle Giant demos we made and said, 'Yes, please!'

Tony was the ideal producer for us. It was 1970, and he had worked with T. Rex, Badfinger, Strawbs, and David Bowie. We were lucky he made the time to fit us into his schedule. Right after he finished a T. Rex album, we met him at Trident Studios in London and then recorded a series of three-hour sessions. He slid us in between other sessions with David Bowie and T. Rex. We had to be productive in the hours we had, but we never felt like he was rushing us or was thinking about other projects while we were with him.

Being with Tony was incredible. There was electricity in the air. We were making history. We had worked with great producers like George Martin and Dave Paramor, but Tony was far better for us at this stage in our career. As a gifted musician as well as producer, he was a great mentor. He was knowledgeable about classical, jazz, folk, rock, classical, and pop—all the elements we applied to our songs—and he understood our objectives, even when we weren't entirely sure what we were doing. That led us on our path to sonic freedom. We weren't at the end of the road, by any means, but Tony helped us realize that our only limitations were self-imposed and that we had the talent and creativity to break barriers.

We did a bit of preproduction with Tony first, but we were so excited about the songs and had spent so much time rehearsing them that they were mostly good to go. We put everything we had into that album—all of our technical skills, off-the-wall arrangements, and vocal techniques. In that respect, it was the opposite of Simon Dupree & The Big Sound. More specifically, it was nothing anyone had heard before. It was strange, but deliberately so. There was no lack of compositional skill in those songs, and if we occasionally missed the mark, it wasn't because we were shooting in the dark. Kerry and Ray wrote their parts on sheet music. Nothing was jammed out or thrown together. At the same time, in the beginning, we were stumbling around and finding our footing. We were still in our gestation period, compared to what we would do together over the decade. But it was a great start.

We worked hard with Tony, and we loved it. We also enjoyed the downtime, during which we became good friends with the guys in Bowie's band, including guitarist Mick Ronson and drummer Mick Woodmansey, who were working on Bowie's album *The Man Who Sold The World*. Tony joined us in the pub after their sessions and made sure we all felt comfortable with one another. He was all about creating camaraderie between his friends, so he initiated conversations that helped break the ice.

Bowie dropped in several times to say hi, but he'd disappear soon after like a spaceman beaming back to his ship. He didn't have a big ego and wasn't aloof or standoffish; he was shy back then and seemed uncomfortable in social situations. When he was around us, we exchanged niceties, but he didn't say much. I think he put all of his personal expression into his music, for now lacking a lot of the communication skills that he'd so capably master down the road.

When we were in the final stages of recording *Gentle Giant*, Tony took some time off to work with T. Rex. All we had left to do was overdubs, so Tony suggested we drop in and watch T. Rex record in the studio. In a way, it was more like a freak show than a learning experience—or maybe we learned what we didn't want to do when we went back into the studio. Marc Bolan was finishing his guitar overdubs, and we hung behind the studio glass and watched. As the tape rolled and the gritty, glammy music blared from the speakers, Marc made agonized faces as he played double stops on his Les Paul. One second he was on his feet, the next he'd dropped to his back, kicking the air like he was trying to ward off wild animals, all the while continuing to manhandle a barbed blues lead from his guitar. There was no audience there, but Marc was determined to go wherever the music took him.

After Marc left and we headed back into the studio, I spoke to Tony.

'What the hell was that about?' I asked. 'What was going on with Marc?'

'That's just what he does,' Tony replied. 'It works for him. If something works, remember what you did, and don't be afraid to do it again.'

It was good advice, but what Marc was doing looked a bit iffy to me, like he was trying to impress whoever was watching. 'That guy's full of shit,' Phil said. But, of course, he wasn't. We toured with T. Rex later, and Marc was as uninhibited onstage as he had been in the studio, kicking up dirt and rolling around, and though his playing was a bit primitive for my tastes, there was no question he was rocking up a cyclone.

Tony had the musical knowledge and engineering skills to enhance the songs of any of the artists he worked with, whether they were basic bar bands or sonic extremists. He enjoyed putting his touch on a recording without altering the core essence of the music, and that's what made him such a great producer. In our case, he enjoyed helping us fine-tune our songs. With our blessings, he turned a knob here and tweaked a fader there to bring out the best in our performances. His passion for the project was contagious, and as a kicker, he wrote the liner notes for the album. As it turned out, he was also a damn good creative writer:

A TALL TALE

BY TONY VISCONTI

Giant took notice of the long shadows and decided to quit for the day in the apple orchard. He stretched, took forty steps and covered the quarter mile to the mouth of his cave. He sat down and pulled a sweet smelling cork out of a two hundred gallon jug. Scrumpy is what he poured into a mug having the same capacity as a bathtub.

As he quaffed he perceived that something strange was in the air, stirring the serenity of the Somerset countryside. He slowly rose to his full height and whispered, 'Ar, there be a good sound floatin' in the east wind. I think I'll investigate.'

You must understand that the giant doesn't go out much, except when he sees his girlfriend in France now and then (she's the daughter of Gargantua)—and twice a century at that! Now he had another good excuse to break the routine of his work at the orchard.

He travelled swiftly through the night, carefully avoiding populated areas. When he came to the Salisbury Plain he decided to see if his stone ring was still standing. He made it as a boy, just for fun. As he approached, two long-haired youths sitting against a slab looked up. One said, 'Man, this stuff is pretty good gear. I've just hallucinated a great big far-out lookin' giant over there.'

The other said, 'Far out man, I see him too.'

They sat motionless for a few moments, then the giant turned and continued his quest towards the south. When he was out of their sight the first one whispered wide-eyed, 'Too much man, us having the same hallucination.' The other youth had fainted.

Sure enough, the sound was coming from Portsmouth way. To the giant's delight it came from a cottage out in the countryside, far from the centre of town. Inside, six dedicated musicians were tearing off a rendition of 'Why Not?' at a thousand watts; that's enough to rip the top of anybody's head. All except the giant's. He just laid on his stomach, rested his head on his folded arms and listened with an ear to each open window for good stereo.

The band stopped after three hours and Ray said to Kerry, 'Let's go out and dig the stars.' They opened the front door and nearly walked up the giant's nostrils. They jumped back inside shakin' all over and both said at once, 'There's abigfaceoutthereit'sbigit'sbig—oh!'

The others noticed immediately that something was wrong so they all went out to have a look. They saw the head of a great big giant, sleeping peacefully. Phil was at the head of the group. He turned and said, 'Gary, did you spike our tea again?'

Just then the giant opened his eyes. 'Be 'ee the boys as were makin' that good sound?'

Martin, at once put at ease by the friendly accent answered,

'Yes, it was us. I'm sorry if we made too much noise. You see, we moved out here so we wouldn't bother anybody and—'

'Bother anybody? But that's the gentlest music I've ever 'eard apart from thunderstorms.'

Needless to say they all got on very well after the giant had said that. Frank the roadie moved the instruments outside and they played the rest of the night for him. Somewhere in Portsmouth a seismograph reported a mild earthquake when the giant was dancing.

In the morning I drove down from London with the group's manager Gerry and my friend George the artist. We drove around to the back of the cottage and gaped at the group laying in the grass listening to stories of the giant's distant past. Derek ran to us as the car lurched into reverse and bade us to halt. He explained everything and soon we were listening to the amazing things the giant had to say.

Before the giant left, it was suggested that he pose for a picture with the group. No matter how I angled my Polaroid I just couldn't get everyone in the picture. I have some photos of six guys and a big boot, six guys, a big eye and part of a big nose: but I couldn't get a decent picture of the giant and the band together. George was more successful. The giant placed him at the top of a tall tree and in fifteen minutes George had done the rough sketch.

Well, there you have it. The story of the Gentle Giant. You may think it's fantastic, but then, so is the music.

We loved Tony's liner notes and were astonished that, as busy as he was, he'd taken the time to write them just to help us out. I still love thinking about all the people who bought the album and read Tony's fantastic tale while listening to our eclectic blend of rock, jazz, classical, and folk and then examining the gatefold covert art depicting the head of the smiling giant on the front, and the back, which showed the giant holding the six of us in his outstretched palms. That came from Tony as well:

'I want to introduce you to a guy named George Underwood,' Tony said to us one day. 'He's David Bowie's best friend from school, and he's a brilliant artist. I think you guys will hit it off.'

Tony had been right about everything so far, so we thought, *Okay, great, let's meet the guy*. We found out that George and Bowie used to play in the band George & The Dragons but broke up after an argument over a girl. George punched Bowie in the left eye, and since he was wearing a ring, the resulting injury caused Bowie's left pupil to become permanently dilated, accounting for the difference in color between his eyes. The damaged eye couldn't be repaired, but the friendship quickly mended.

George lived in Putney, so when we came in from Portsmouth to meet him, Tony put us up on the floor of his spare room. We didn't know what we were going to do for the album cover, so we hoped George would have some ideas. He suggested we base the artwork on the band's name since we were a new group with an unusual moniker. He drew a picture of the gentle giant, and we loved it. He suggested that the giant gently cradle the band members in order to create a connection between us and get our images on the album without a huge, tacky band photo. It was iconic. It was beautiful. It was Gentle Giant.

Gentle Giant has been called one of the first great prog-rock albums to follow King Crimson's *In The Court Of The Crimson King*, which came out in November 1969. It's a flattering comment, but not one with which I'm altogether comfortable. The problem with many so-called 'prog' bands is that instead of making complex passages that fit their multifaceted songs, peaking and dipping in intensity at the right times to provide memorable conflict and resolution, and weaving their compositions together with strong melodies, they want to be musical mathematicians. They make their songs complex because they can, not because they should, and embark on circuitous journeys that never take the listener anywhere, and, therefore, amount to nothing more than treading water. Some of the greats—and I refuse to name them—have fallen into this trap from time to time. And even we came close at moments before we established a firm foundation.

Everyone in Gentle Giant had a low threshold for boredom, and whenever we did something that sounded like something else or was too repetitious, we got sick of it and either created something else to evolve the part or threw it away and started over. We hated bands that put an abrupt three-minute Mellotron part in a song or five minutes of a classical music passage in an effort to emulate the London Symphony Orchestra. Kerry and Ray could compose symphonies if they wanted to, and we could easily smell bullshit when other bands tried and failed. We could have done it well, but that was never going to be our signature.

It might seem strange, but we wanted to be the opposite of grandiose. Other bands made double-album concept records, but the closest we came to that was on our loosely thematic fourth album, *Three Friends*, which wasn't about alien civilizations, mythology, topographic oceans, or ancient military conflicts. To us, all that stuff defined pretension, and while naysayers have accused us of being pretentious over the years, I don't think we ever were. I just think they didn't try or care to understand our musical goals, which included writing inspiring, forward-thinking music for people who were tired of having everything spelled out for them, but who enjoyed great sing-along vocals as much as accomplished playing. To that end, I was the vocalist, but Ray, Phil, Gary, and Kerry handled complex harmonies with ease, giving us the baroque choir element that separated us from many of the bands to whom we were compared.

If our unwavering desire to be different from everything else made us pretentious to some, so be it, but it was never a result of being arrogant or feeling superior. We just knew what we could do with music, and we weren't about to sell ourselves short to be more easily digestible. We didn't want to write or play three-chord rhythms with a vocal on top, then a middle-eight and a guitar solo (we had already done that). We preferred to think of our pieces of music as being like cinematic passages that evolved over the course of the song, creating different images for the listener to latch onto. The instrumental passages and vocal sections were parts of the composition and were structured to make the songs coherent. Each of the parts was essential for the songs to develop and evolve.

'Quiet And Cold' would have been a shuffling blues song without Ray's passionate street-corner violin parts, which set the stage for my yearning vocals and Kerry's jaunty xylophone solo. The twittering bird and meowing cat sound effects were borrowed straight from the Beatles school of audio overload and contributed to the narrative approach to the song.

'Alucard'—one of our trademark tracks—included one main hook based around a Pentatonic scale that we intercut with skittering organ lines, abrupt horn blasts, meter fluctuations, and effect-treated vocal harmonies.

The longest song on the album was the nine-minute 'Nothing At All.' Kerry wrote the beginning of that and brought it to us at our first rehearsal together. He sang the beginning, and we all liked it. We quickly realized how well it showcased Gary's Renaissance-style arpeggios and our featherlight vocal harmonies. But we felt like it was a little too fragile, and it went on for too long. So, we combined it with another song we were working on that had a fatter, heavier groove. Suddenly, we had this dense riff, stealthy bass line, and aggressive vocals. Then, Gary let fly with a flailing multitracked guitar solo we panned from left to right channels and then back again.

The midsection of the song is an extended drum solo from Martin that's eventually accompanied by jazzy piano, and then the song returns to the pensive vocal harmony of the opening verse. If we had really thought about it, we would have asked, *Who in their right mind would put a long, phased drum solo on a studio album?* It's a dumb thing to do on an album, but we weren't thinking. We were just acting and reacting. And we must have realized subconsciously that it would come across really well in concert—that we could extend it to showcase Martin's chops. Crowds loved endless drum solos.

The songs on *Gentle Giant* are not perfect, but they were a joy to work on. It was a tremendous learning experience for all of us and a heavenly departure from what we had done in Simon Dupree & The Big Sound. We paid careful attention to what everyone else was doing, and since we each brought different skills to the studio, we all came out of the experience as more eclectic musicians. We were all reborn as a better band to grow and improve with each other. We were all part of this Giant thing, and while Ray, Phil, and I actually shared DNA, we were all brothers with the shared goal of making music that would change the world. We were all good, but Kerry and Ray proved how naturally gifted they were and how well they played off one another. I felt lucky to be a part of the explosive creativity.

We started promoting the album a while before it was available in the shops. If we didn't tour, we would just have been sitting around, so we booked any gigs we could and played some great shows. We were on the bill of a memorable concert in Hamburg, Germany, at the Open Air Festival. It was the first of many concerts we played with Black Sabbath. They were incredibly nice to us. We talked about The Beatles (Ozzy's favorite group) and the wave of great music coming out of England, and, over the years, we grew to be good friends. It had been just a few months since Sabbath released their groundbreaking self-titled album, so they were still fairly straight and sober. At later shows, we were in the eye of the hurricane as the band discovered decadence, debauchery, and especially cocaine. But that stuff came in America after they released their second album, *Paranoid.*

The festival in Hamburg included Uriah Heep, who Bron also managed, as well as Humble Pie, Manfred Mann, Renaissance, East Of Eden, and Keith Emerson. We were always treated well in Germany, and the fans there loved us. Considering the strength of the lineup, we were surprised that only about ten thousand people attended the two-day event; the grounds seated twice that many. I don't remember being upset by the crowd size, though. We thought it was funny to look out from the stage and see a half-empty festival.

We saw Reg Dwight and spent some time with him on July 4 in Portsmouth at a daylong stadium show that featured Hookfoot, the band he played in right before he went solo as Elton John. He seemed happy for us and reiterated how talented he thought we were. He also pointed out that it was a good thing he hadn't joined us because he had much bigger commercial aspirations than we had. It seemed like an odd comment, and we figured he was trying to save face. Little did we know how right he was.

Another fun show was at the Marquee Club in London, one of the city's most historic rock venues. On July 15, we opened for Slade, which might seem like an incompatible pairing, but at the time, there was no friction between glam rockers and prog bands, and the gig itself was hilarious. Slade were really fun to be with and constantly joked around backstage. We went down really well with the crowd, yet it was only one of a few shows we ever played at the venue. Since we were a big up-and-coming rock band, it seemed strange to us that the Marquee didn't reach out more often, but it was symptomatic of the reaction we received throughout England at the beginning of our career. We never felt as welcome at home as we did in Italy, Germany, Canada, or, when we finally got there, America. I believe our problems in the UK were triggered by the British press, some parts of which were indignant that Simon Dupree & The Big Sound had the *nerve* to become a 'new, progressive' band. It was almost as if we wore badges in the UK that read 'UNCLEAN.'

Our *Gentle Giant* record release show was in Glasgow, at a club called Morpheus. It was a meaningful show, especially for Phil but also for me, since we'd both been born in Glasgow, and playing there symbolized how much we had accomplished since we lived there in poverty. That was a great show, as were gigs across Europe. But the final three shows in London emphasized how we were not destined to be darlings of the city's art scene. *Melody Maker*, which had frequently praised Simon Dupree, called our performance at the Lyceum 'twee' and declared that the way Gary, Ray, and Kerry traded instruments during the show was 'pretentious for the sake of it.' As much as we hated being called pretentious—because we despised pretension—we appropriated the phrase and used it as a symbol of irony, even naming our 1977 compilation album *Pretentious For The Sake Of It.*

While the scenesters didn't climb into the open arms of Gentle Giant, the mainstream press praised us, including the BBC, which was important to generate record sales. *Gentle Giant* didn't land us back on *Top Of The Pops* or anything, but it was recognized and admired by a wide variety of tastemakers, including Frank Zappa, Jimi Hendrix, Jethro Tull, Black Sabbath, and comedic actor Sherman Helmsley (who played George Jefferson in *All In The Family* and *The Jeffersons*). He declared Gentle Giant his favorite band, and, later in our career, he would come into our lives in a wild and unexpected way.

GIANT STEPS

CHAPTER NINE

SENSORY PLEASURE

We spent more than a year writing and recording our first album, then we focused on touring. We were enjoying the shows, getting a good feel for our new fanbase, and tinkering with new material backstage and during whatever downtime we had back home.

All of a sudden, Gerry told us we needed to hurry up and release the follow-up to *Gentle Giant* to keep the momentum going. He wanted us back in the studio with Tony right away. There were a couple of songs that hadn't made the first album, so we had those to work with, as well as bits and pieces of music we had put together, but nothing was fully realized.

I appealed to Gerry's supportive side: 'We just need a little more time, to get the songs right.'

'We don't have more time,' he shot back. So, into the studio we went.

We tracked the mostly finished songs we didn't use on the first album, then used a click track to record all the other leftover bits we liked. Finally, we spontaneously built the rest of the parts onto the click. Kerry and Ray wrote everything, and we'd record the passages as soon as they came up with them and figure out where to put it all later.

Between these hectic sessions, we toured around England from the beginning of January 1970 until the end of March. Our lives were a fragmented collage of gigs, van trips, writing sessions, and studio stints. There's a saying that art imitates life, and our second album, the highly experimental *Acquiring The Taste*, reflects that axiom. It's the only Gentle Giant album that wasn't completely written before we started recording it.

A lot of people have told me it's their favorite, the best we ever did. To me, it's a very odd record, and I've never liked it very much.

That's not because the songs aren't good. Even with the band in accelerated motion, Kerry and Ray wrote some excellent, creative, and forward-thinking material, and the performances were good as well. But I found the chaos of spontaneous creation unsettling. I prefer order to disorder. We weren't fully prepared to be thrown into the shark pool. We frantically thrashed around to stay afloat, and we did so quite successfully, but for me, it wasn't an enjoyable experience. Critics loved the album, which was not like *Gentle Giant* yet just as adventurous and free-spirited and inspired many of the same reactions.

We recorded *Acquiring The Taste* back with Tony Visconti at AIR and Advision Studios in London. Recognizing that we were experienced musicians with a working knowledge of the studio, Tony allowed me and Ray to sit at the boards and work the machinery. It seemed like he was training us to produce, and he encouraged us to choose the sound design and effects that best complemented the compositions.

'These songs have your mark all over them, so I don't want to be heavy-handed with the production,' Tony said. 'If you have an idea, go for it, and I'll help you to make it work.'

I'm so grateful to Tony for handing us the reins. He didn't allow us to make mistakes that would damage the album, but he was open to any new ideas that would enhance our vision and felt the project benefitted from the different perspectives we put into it. So many producers are territorial and want the musicians to steer clear of the board. Tony was more like a guide and a guru. He showed us how to work together as a band under extreme pressure. He had the insight to know that we were the best people to judge how we should be recorded and what we should sound like, and he opened the doors for us to be self-sufficient.

Maybe I didn't like writing and recording the songs with the frenetic energy of a manic painter who has a gallery show in a couple of days and is starting from a roomful of empty canvasses, but I loved learning how to control the session. Phil, by contrast, was frustrated by the whole process. Maybe he resented Tony for making me his wingman. Maybe he was frustrated that we were being forced to produce on a corporate deadline and didn't have the time we usually took to fine-tune our music. Phil and I were like oil and vinegar when we weren't recording, but put us in a bottle, shake us up, and everything comes out well-blended and flavorful.

Even when he was unhappy, Phil was devoted to the band and always played his parts well. He was a Shulman, after all. He, Ray, and I always rose to the occasion, as did Kerry and Gary. The broken link in the chain was our drummer, Martin. He was a jazzer, not a freeform, adventurous player, and he missed a lot of the changes. He managed to get by on the first album because we'd practiced so damn much, but during the sessions for *Acquiring The Taste*, he wasn't cutting it. He hit the drums with the wrong feel. We needed a solid rhythm section behind our experimental music, but Martin played like he was still stuck in a pop group from 1969. He couldn't keep up. We needed someone sharp and forward-thinking, yet he was more like an apprentice, which held us back. We'd already done our apprenticeship in Simon Dupree. We were no longer in the here and now, learning every step of the way. We were consistently aiming for the future, and we didn't have the patience to lock ourselves in place to tutor and teach.

We knew we would have to put up with Martin's shortcomings until we could find a replacement. That was partially on us, since we'd hired him, but it was a major source of frustration. What happened next was far more frustrating. We finished *Acquiring The Taste* in time to make our 1971 release deadline and proudly handed the tape to Gerry, who hadn't heard anything we had done in the studio with Tony. At first, it seemed like he was in a good mood. He was upbeat and looking forward to his first exposure to our latest sound. Soon after he hit play, his smile turned sour. With every song, he grimaced and clenched his teeth. His eyes started to bulge.

'What the fuck is this?!' he blurted out.

'What do you mean?' I said. 'It's the album.'

'Okay, but it's a demo, right?'

'No, this is what Tony gave me. It's done.'

To our shock, Gerry hated *Acquiring The Taste*. He said it was the worst piece of shit he'd heard in his life. 'I can't work with this!' he exclaimed. 'Experimental music is one thing. I don't know what the fuck this is.'

This was a huge problem. Gerry hated the album, yet he had funded the band, and he was still our manager. He set up tour dates for us, but his heart wasn't into it. Whatever he saw in us when we put out *Gentle Giant* was no longer exciting to him, which I couldn't understand. Our debut album was more labored over than *Acquiring The Taste*, but we had improved as performers and songwriters by the time we wrote and recorded the new songs, and we were clearly the same band. We hadn't reached the peak of our powers, but we were getting there. Yet Gerry saw the album as a huge step backward and said he could no longer tell where Gentle Giant was going.

We were dumbfounded, frustrated, depressed, angry. We were a progressive rock band. No two Gentle Giant albums sounded the same, and we didn't want them to. For us, that's what being progressive meant. Our greatest fear was to parody ourselves the way we thought Simon Dupree & The Big Sound had done with 'Broken Hearted Pirates.' When we signed with Gerry, he had been on board with our desire to constantly evolve, expand, and progress.

As a symbolic 'fuck you' to anyone who called us pretentious and thought our demanding music was an exercise in self-indulgence, or worse, shitty songwriting, Phil and I designed the controversial cover art, depicting a saliva-dripping tongue protruding from an open mouth and toward what appears to be a bare butt. When the gatefold sleeve is opened, the drawing extends to reveal the buttocks as a juicy peach. We thought it was clever, if not entirely subtle. We were tired of being compared to Simon Dupree & The Big Sound, we felt betrayed by label people who wanted us to be more mainstream, and we wanted to be judged on our own merits, not on the success of other so-called progressive bands. So, we put out album art that said we weren't going to lick anyone's ass to be successful, and we weren't going to listen to anyone who told us what to do. The only ones we answered to were ourselves.

Along with the controversial cover art, the packaging for *Acquiring The Taste* included an essay by Phil:

> *Acquiring The Taste* is the second phase of sensory pleasure. If you've gorged yourself on our first album, then relish the finer flavours (we hope) of this, our second offering. It is our goal to expand the frontiers of contemporary popular music at the risk of being very unpopular. We have recorded each composition with the one thought—that it should be unique, adventurous and fascinating. It has taken every shred of our combined musical and technical knowledge to achieve this. From the outset we have abandoned all preconceived thoughts of blatant commercialism. Instead we hope to give you something far more substantial and fulfilling. All you need to do is sit back, and acquire the taste.'

Ultimately, Gerry Bron quit managing the band. He still liked us as people, but he felt so betrayed by the album we had submitted to him that he could no longer support us or our music. That's where Simon Dupree & The Big Sound's gangster connections came back in. Wilf Pine and the Kray brothers' compadres in London were Don Arden (father of the future Sharon Osbourne) and Patrick Meehan, who conducted business together and founded Worldwide Artists Management in 1970. So, when we severed ties with Gerry, Pine's people suggested we contact Meehan, their colleague in the mob. Worldwide's biggest clients at the time were Black Sabbath, who by 1971 had transformed from a straight, serious psychedelic blues band to a dark, drug-and-alcohol-fueled 'metal' band (before the term was coined) with demonic iconography and some Satanic lyrics. The team also managed The Groundhogs and The Edgar Broughton Band and co-managed Yes with Brian Lane. They had a far greater profile than Bron, so we were happy to make the leap.

Right away, Worldwide booked us to play a two-day festival in Heidelberg, Germany. The British Rock Meeting Heidelberg Open Air Celebration, as it was called, foreshadowed our turbulent future with the company. The event featured Black Sabbath, Deep Purple, Fleetwood Mac, Rory Gallagher, Fairport Convention, and others. We arrived at the airport in plenty of time to catch the flight and file onto the charter plane. The sky was clear and the conditions seemed to be optimal. The pilot announced we were ready for takeoff. I closed my eyes and leaned against the side of the headrest, hoping to catch a nap before we landed.

The plane began its ascent and then abruptly lurched ... hard. At the same time, there was a mechanical scraping noise. Mick Fleetwood, who wasn't wearing a seatbelt, screamed, fainted, and slumped to the floor of the plane. Three nearby overhead compartments opened, spilling their contents. The pilot wrestled with the controls and the plane began a steep bank to the left. A voice crackled over the loudspeaker.

'Ladies and gentlemen, this is your captain speaking. We're experiencing some minor technical problems with the aircraft which explains the turbulence you might have felt. We'll be returning to the airport out of an abundance of caution. Please remain seated with your seatbelts fastened. We should be on the ground shortly.'

The plane landed safely, and we returned to the boarding area with no idea what had happened or when we would be able to reboard the plane. I was starting to wonder if we were going to make it to Germany in time for our set when a flight attendant announced that it was safe for us to return to the plane. Our tour manager talked to the flight crew and learned that three of the four engines on the plane had failed, and had we not had such a skilled pilot, we might not have made it back to the airport. We were assured that the mechanics had repaired the plane, the engines were now fine, and we should promptly reboard. A few minutes later, the flight took off, and Gentle Giant and blues-rock master Rory Gallagher were the only bands left on the plane. Everyone else found an alternate source of transportation.

Friction in the air dovetailed with friction on the ground. Gary and Martin had been snapping at each other for days. The two had been at loggerheads ever since Gary stole Martin's girlfriend. Gary wasn't smitten with her or anything, but he craved companionship, and since he had left his old girlfriend behind in London when he came to Portsmouth to work with us, he figured Martin's girlfriend would do. She was friendly to him, so he moved in and outcharmed Martin to win her over. When we were on tour in Europe, there was such bad blood between them that there was no way we were going to go on much longer without a blowout. That incident came backstage in the middle of the European tour.

'Bandmates are supposed to be like brothers,' Martin shouted, after a six-pack too many. 'How could you do this?'

'Hey, she didn't want you,' Gary said. 'She likes me better.'

'I really care about her! You're an arsehole,' said Martin, practically in tears.

That just egged Gary on. 'Maybe you should spend more time working on your playing and less time trying to win back some bird.'

Those were fighting words. The two came to blows backstage, which marked the only time a member of Gentle Giant threw punches. Neither of them was physically injured, but Martin's pride was crushed. Between us riding him about his inferior playing and Gary stealing his girl and popping him in the nose, the runway was cleared for Martin's imminent departure. Gary certainly had been underhanded with Martin, but we needed him as a guitarist and songwriter, so there was no question as to who would stay in the band and who would go. Martin was already on the outs with us, and really, Gary only sped up Martin's inevitable and necessary break with the band. Gary stayed with Martin's ex for about a year before he hooked up with someone he liked better. There's a reason lots of women won't date musicians.

I think Martin was relieved when we fired him in late September 1971, in the middle of a tour. That left us in the unenviable position of immediately finding a new drummer and continuing like nothing had happened. We interviewed dozens of new drummers over two days in London. No one was right, and everything seemed hopeless as the final candidate stepped up to audition. We were expecting yet another drummer who thought he was the only one onstage and overplayed like Keith Moon on amphetamines, or a player who wanted to play traditional 4/4 beats without flair. Instead, we got an eighteen-year-old kid named Malcolm Mortimore who surprised us by keeping up with us and injecting some colorful fills into the songs.

We asked Malcolm and a few other players to come to our rehearsal studio in Portsmouth for a more intensive second audition, where he was confident and played with an abundance of energy and style. His meter wasn't always perfect, but we figured he was nervous and not entirely familiar with all the changes in the music, so we invited him to join the band. Malcolm moved to Portsmouth and, in between unpacking his belongings, had a week to learn our entire set before our next show in early October. He did pretty well with us on his first run of shows. I don't know if he was running on adrenaline, touched by his muse, or if we were so happy to have someone with confidence behind the kit that we overlooked any mistakes he made (which wasn't likely, since we rarely overlooked anything). Malcolm had a great touch and good technique, and he evolved into a great drummer who would go on to play with Tina Turner, Tom Jones, Van Morrison, Mick Jagger, Coliseum, and others. But when he joined Gentle Giant, he was far less musically experienced than we were, and all the style in the world couldn't cover that up.

CHAPTER TEN

COLLISION COURSE

We never copped to being simply a prog-rock band, but if fans and critics were going to call us prog, we decided it would behoove us to follow some of the tropes. Hence the concept album *Three Friends*. Phil and I came up with the idea and loosely based the storyline on our experiences growing up in Portsmouth in a working-class environment while striving to be a world-class band. When we were back in school, we were on the same level as the other students, and we were treated equally—at least in theory. Our mates were the kids we saw every day, and we had a shared set of experiences that bonded us such as joking around in class, hanging out at lunch, and playing sports together. Then we left school, and everyone branched out into our own different worlds. Our friends weren't together all the time, and we could no longer connect with them the way we used to. It's a fairly universal experience that we all go through on some level.

In *Three Friends*, three former classmates all go in separate directions after school, and when that happens, they can no longer be real friends anymore. I wanted to illustrate how social class is connected to the kinds of barriers that are built over time. When someone ascends the ladder of success, they develop different values and morals, and, even if they continue to wave the flag for the working class, they're doing so from gilded towers; they can't personally relate to the struggles of the common man, and they may accidentally act in a condescending manner, which makes their former friends resentful. Similarly, the person who maybe isn't as bright or lucky as his former friends slides further down the totem pole and becomes less accomplished than the more middle-class people with whom he formerly associated. Everyone branches further into their own worlds and none of them connect. Class and vocation drive them apart, and those three school friends end up in completely different places and can no longer relate to one another. When you've got one person in a position of upward mobility, another who's in homeostasis, and a third who's on a downward trajectory, society dictates that they can't be true friends.

We didn't base the characters on any particular people we knew, but we tried to draw a parallel between the three friends in the album lyrics and our experiences in the music business. There were bands we used to play with in Portsmouth that were still performing in clubs, while we were touring the world and making some money. Many people in their position tended to look at us not as hometown heroes but as ingrates. They used to hang out with us, but then, when we became successful and hardly even played our hometown anymore, they became bitter and tried to delegitimize us: 'Oh, they only made it because they sold out,' or 'Yeah, I hear they've turned into total cunts, and they're all hooked on drugs.'

We didn't have time for that kind of negativity. We were following our dream—going, going, going, playing bigger and bigger venues, getting reviewed by more popular magazines and newspapers, being interviewed on television. While we weren't driving Rolls-Royces or living in mansions with our own chefs and security guards, we were making some money and holding our own—and, in that sense, we were breaking out of our former class and into a different level of society.

We had the concept nailed down, and as 1972 dawned, we looked forward to returning to the studio to write an album that was just as good, musically, as *Acquiring The Taste*, but less polarizing. We wanted to keep our fans happy and reach a new audience that liked prog rock but didn't want to listen to music that was too challenging to grasp on a first or second listen. Ray and Kerry were more prepared this time, having written new songs during their downtime on tour, and I was excited about recording my vocals. I was sure our fans would love the direction we were going in.

It was a typically dreary English winter's day when we piled into our trusty old Zephyr Zodiac to head from Portsmouth to London to meet up with Malcolm and the engineers at Advision Studios to start recording the album. I never used to mind driving long distances. When we weren't running behind on our way to a concert, a recording session, or a promotional gig, being behind the wheel or even in the backseat of a car driving down the motorway was generally relaxing. Then, everything changed forever.

Ray was driving and Phil was in front with him. Kerry and I were in the back. The Zephyr wasn't a sleek sports car—thank God. It was a sturdy, metallic tank of a vehicle. That's probably what saved our lives. We were in Guildford, halfway to London, when Ray lost control of the car. I was looking out of the windshield as the wheels lost traction and we started to slide sideways to the right. Ray tried to compensate by spinning the wheel, but instead of turning the wheel clockwise in the direction we were skidding, which is what the experts tell you to do, he spun it counterclockwise and lost control.

I hoped the Zephyr would make a terrifying spiral and stop, then we would continue on our way. Instead, the car flipped over and skidded toward the other side of the highway. The force exerted on my body made me feel like I was on a rollercoaster headed toward a steep drop. We burst through the guardrail, and the car righted itself as it began to plummet. As soon as the wheels left the pavement, I was sure this was the end. I knew that when we hit the ground, the exploding glass would slash us like flying knives, the impact would snap our necks and pulverize our spines. Our organs would be crushed. I wasn't being hysterical. I was completely rational. It would be a horrid mess, but at least it would quickly be over.

I should have been horrified. Ever since my dad died, I had been haunted by my own mortality. But now, strangely, I was completely calm. I don't think I've ever felt as serene as when I realized I was about to die. I simply registered what was happening and accepted the situation.

Okay, this is it, I thought. I didn't have images from my life flashing before my eyes. There was total Zen ... and then a huge bang. I was sure I was in the last moments of my life and the world would soon fade to black. Well, we'd had a great run. I had lived the dream. I was ready to go.

I closed my eyes and waited. And waited. When I opened them again, I could see everything around me, and I wasn't in any pain. I wasn't dead. Somehow, after the car toppled from the road, it had landed upright on a narrow pathway. The tires had burst and the wheels were jettisoned to the valley below. They were history, as was the car. But we were okay. The spot where we'd landed was almost exactly the width of the vehicle. If we hadn't landed wheels down, or if we had slipped six inches one way or the other, we would have plunged a hundred feet onto the railway tracks below.

I had a small scratch on my head that wasn't even bleeding. I brushed bits of broken glass from my lap and felt my arms, legs, and feet to make sure I wasn't injured. Then I called out to everyone.

'Are you guys okay?' I asked, not knowing what to expect.

One by one, voices:

'Yeah, I'm fine,' said Kerry.

'I'm okay,' Phil said.

Ray seemed stunned, but a few seconds later he confirmed that he, too, had emerged unscathed. We might have been in shock. We spoke conversationally, as if we had endured a flat tire, not a near-death experience.

'Can everyone still play?' I asked. 'Are you okay enough to record?'

No pauses there. Everyone answered in the affirmative. We were all excited to get to the studio and make the record.

Then Phil raised a practical point: 'Okay, we're sitting on the edge of a cliff. How the hell are we going to get to London?'

I looked down at the railroad tracks. 'Do you guys think we can make it to the train?' The cliff we'd landed on was high but not terribly steep.

'Let's climb down,' I said. 'We can't be too far from Guilford. And we can catch a train from there to London.'

The only problem was getting safely down the hill without twisting an ankle or falling and taking a tumble. There was no other option. We climbed out of the wrecked car and carefully zigzagged down the hill. There was a path at the bottom that led directly to the train to Guilford. We bought tickets and boarded the train none the worse for wear, and then we got off at Guilford and transferred to a train to London. From there, we got a taxi to Advision Studios and walked in right on time, ready to work with the engineer Martin Rushent on our first self-produced album.

Given what we had just experienced, we could have panicked or fallen apart, but we were so focused on making a great record that we didn't even think about the accident, and we didn't mention it to anyone. It was unique to the four of us, and therefore it didn't need to be addressed. We had stared down death and walked away, so the horror and bad luck of having crashed was dwarfed by the good fortune of emerging unscathed. We were so determined not to fuck up and lose precious studio time that we were pragmatic to a fault. The Sturm Und Drang of post-crash trauma would have to wait until after the record. The worst was behind us. What could really go wrong now?

I don't believe we had something or someone watching over us, and I'm not big on fate or destiny, but the chances of undergoing a drop from the motorway onto a tiny hilltop and emerging practically unscathed are infinitesimal. It was almost like we'd made some rock'n'roll deal with the devil. Gentle Giant would be allowed to continue its crusade in exchange for delayed but significant emotional trauma, interpersonal conflict, and intangible frustrations down the road.

Ray didn't drive for a long time after the accident. I still dislike long car rides, and I get nervous when I'm merging onto the highway, especially when it's raining. And we all suffered from recurring nightmares of the crash, sometimes with different, horrible endings. Compared to what could have happened, however, we got off lightly. We were extremely lucky, and our good fortune fueled our willpower, so we were able to compartmentalize. We put what happened behind us and summoned the motivation to carry on with what we had planned. In a way, Ray and I did the same thing we'd done after our dad died. We compartmentalized, strapped on our instruments, and returned to the practice room. On various levels, that's probably what kept us together as bandmates for more than twenty-five years.

When we finally arrived at Advision, Malcolm and Gary were waiting for us. We didn't talk about the near-death experience at first. We just got on with the business at hand and started working on preproduction for the new songs. We had decided to self-produce *Three Friends*, having learned so much sitting in with Tony on *Acquiring The Taste*. No one knew what we wanted as well as we did, and now that we had the skills to set up mics and man the board, it made sense to cut out the middleman. A great producer can help make a good album sound amazing (some have even made bad albums sonically pristine), but we knew we had the material for a great album, and we didn't need help fine-tuning our creative ideas. When you're that focused, a producer can actually be a third wheel.

As we had feared, however, Malcolm's inexperience slowed our progress. He would sometimes speed up and slow down while he was playing, and maybe we should have been more understanding, but I was determined to get the record done right, with as few hiccups as possible. And Malcolm was hiccupping like a kid who drinks too much soda. He was nervous, and it messed with his timing. The more we criticized him, the more mistakes he made. He wasn't used to dealing with hotheaded musicians, and we weren't willing to put up with anything less than perfection. It was a bad combination.

Time and again, Malcolm kept missing the 'one'—the first beat of a musical measure, which is supposed to solidify the rhythm. I tried to help him out by standing in front of his kit with my headphones on, listening to the playback, loudly counting for him while he drummed. Kerry did the same from the control booth. It took some work, but we got the tracks down, and he sounded good. Maybe we should have used a click track, but for some reason no one thought of that. In the end, his drum breaks and technical skills would shine throughout the album.

The way Malcolm mixed jazz drumming with rock—I'd never heard anything like it. But he was so focused on his playing, he was unable to sync with the chemistry of the rest of the band. In retrospect, he was so far behind us as a professional musician that there was no way he could catch up. We were perfectionists and he was young and still learning his craft. I suppose we could have handled it better, but the only solution was to find another drummer, which we would soon do. But first, we had to get through a monumental tour opening for Jethro Tull, at what was probably the peak of their career.

That was revelatory in two ways: we played big arenas night after night, and we got to watch Tull putting on a fantastic show full of creative stage design and lighting that gave us direction for what we could do with our own productions. Tull were supporting the monumental *Aqualung* and premiering songs from their soon-to-be-released masterpiece *Thick As A Brick*. There was a strong mutual respect between us and them. They gave us full use of their lights and plenty of stage room, and they made it clear to promoters and staff that it was fine with them if our set went longer than our allotted time. When we were on fire, they wanted to see us play an extra song as much as our biggest fans did, and we were grateful for that.

We all quickly became friends, hanging out on one another's buses before and after the shows and nerding out about our favorite music, books, and movies. None of us were after-show party people, so we never got fucked up and threw televisions out hotel windows. Ours was a real friendship, not one spearheaded by drugs and alcohol. I was closest to the guitarist, Martin Barre, partially because he was a friendly, stand-up guy, but also because vocalist Ian Anderson's first impression of us made him gun-shy.

Ian was heading into our dressing room at the beginning of the tour to say hello and wish us well when he heard Phil and me having a heated argument. The door was closed, but we were loud enough that Ian turned the other way and went somewhere else. The distancing didn't last, though, and within days Ray, Phil, and I were having esoteric conversations with Ian as well.

The audiences at the Tull shows were eighty-five percent male. There were loads of guys who were there with their friends. Very few of them had girlfriends at the shows, which made them quite different from the times we had opened for Slade or T. Rex, or even back when we headlined large venues with Simon Dupree & The Big Sound. That probably had a lot to do with the kind of music we were all playing, but at the same time, Ian Anderson was not exactly a sexy frontman. He's no Paul Rogers or Ian Gillan. So, not only was the music largely unappealing to females, but the musicians weren't the kinds of guys girls wanted to gaze at onstage. It wasn't until prog bands with decent-looking singers and catchy songs started getting airplay that a greater number of girls started coming to prog shows.

The one good thing about that was that if we had our girlfriends with us on the road, we never had to worry about them having any interest in the types of guys who were sneaking backstage after the shows. It was funny because instead of girls coming backstage and wanting us to sign their breasts, like we'd experienced with Simon Dupree, there were boys coming up to us wanting us to sign their tour programs and copies of our sheet music. That's the nature of the beast when you're a band like Jethro Tull or Gentle Giant and not Led Zeppelin or The Rolling Stones.

We learned another important lesson playing with Jethro Tull. Until we hired a highly skilled drummer with immaculate timing, we were never going to blow the headliners off the stage, and we'd be lucky to come across as the highlight of the night when we were the showcase band. Malcolm's internal clock was even more off-kilter live than it was in the studio, and there was no one to stand next to him and count off the beats. Sometimes he'd play so fast we'd finish the set in seventy-five minutes instead of ninety. It was like punk rock before punk.

Malcolm wasn't just a sloppy player; he also took foolish risks. He loved to speed around on his motorcycle, and I'm not sure he was a much better daredevil than he was a drummer. Before a gig in Vienna, Austria, he had a nasty spill on his bike and seriously bruised his left arm, which the doctors put in a cast. Since we didn't have time to find a replacement, Phil attached a drumstick to Malcolm's cast and wrapped it with a mountain of duct tape. It didn't work very well, but at least we played the show.

Then, fate really cracked Malcolm across the head. In late March 1972, he crashed his motorcycle and was thrown from the bike, breaking his left arm, left leg, and pelvis. He needed intensive physical therapy and months to recover. We had wanted to replace him anyway, but we didn't think we'd have to do so before we could audition a new batch of drummers. After Martin's accident, we offered the gig to ex-King Crimson drummer Mike Giles, but that didn't work out. We were in a bind. We had to either cancel shows or hire someone else right away and return to the road.

PART TWO

UP AND RUNNING

GIANT STEPS

CHAPTER ELEVEN

FAIRY DUST

We knew John Weathers from his work in Joe Cocker's backing group, The Grease Band. He was working in a carpet factory when we tracked him down and asked if he would fill in for us on a tour of the UK while we looked for a full-time replacement for Malcolm. We hoped he would work out, but after our previous misfortune, we didn't want to make John an offer he couldn't refuse but that we might later regret. Nonetheless, John was excited by the opportunity to play with us, and within days we dove into rehearsals. He was a talented player who instantly adapted his style to fit our approach. So far, so good.

John's first tour with us was both a trial by fire and an accidental test of humility. We were so caught up with walking him through all the hairpin turns of our music that we weren't paying attention to the tour schedule that our management was putting together. Then I saw some calendar notes that mentioned something about Jimi Hendrix.

At first, I was confused. Jimi had died in 1970, and I'll never forget the pit I felt in my stomach when I found out he was no longer with us. He was on top of the world, and then he was gone. Simon Dupree had shared the stage with him at festivals in Europe and watching him play was mesmerizing. He was a trailblazer as a songwriter, player, and showman. When we were on the same bill, we went out and did a couple of songs and then Jimi went on and blew us away. I was never happier to be destroyed like that. He was a phenomenon and a thrill to watch. He was so ahead of everyone else, he made us look like a tiny ripple in a pond—and we were damn good. How could anyone who claimed to be untrained be that good? I had seen Clapton, Jimmy Page, Jeff Beck, and Rory Gallagher, and this was another level of talent. As far as the greatest moments in rock go, it was right up there with seeing The Beatles.

When you're that good, you've got a right to be arrogant. But Jimi was such a nice person—soft-spoken but sweet, and always positive—and one of the coolest people we had ever met. We were younger and didn't have anywhere near that kind of star power, yet at the couple of shows we played with him, he complimented us, took the time to sit with us and talk about music and life, and treated us like equals. Then, he and his band were off doing their thing, winning over the world, and we were building our career. The next time we met him, he was a much bigger star, yet he was just as pleasant and friendly as he was the first time we met him. And then he died.

When we found out, we all cried. We were crushed when we realized he would make no more music. It was unimaginably tragic that so much talent could be snuffed out like that. We had followed his career like his other excited fans, eager to get our hands on everything he released, and at night I sometimes dreamed of playing with him again.

Now, though, I wondered why our name was on this flyer with a picture of Jimi Hendrix after he was gone. I figured it must be a cover band, but why would we be opening the show? Soon enough I learned that it wasn't a cover band. It was actually Jimi. The venues that booked us wanted us to play before a screening of the concert film *Jimi Plays Berkeley*. It wasn't just a tribute show or two, either: there were twenty-four dates opening for this movie. Years later, I saw the film *This Is Spinal Tap*, and the scene where the band plays a venue with a marquee that reads 'Puppet Show and Spinal Tap' brought me right back to our shows opening for *Jimi Plays Berkeley*.

I figured that these shows might be a good way to break in John Weathers, since none of the venues were huge. But having headlined as part of Cocker's band, it didn't fill him with confidence to find out that Gentle Giant would be the support band to a movie. The tour started on a dubious note on April 1, in Blackburn. We played for about 250 people, left the stage, and then the Hendrix movie was set up, but no one could get the soundtrack to play. Instead of screening a silent Jimi concert film, the promoter canceled the rest of the show and gave back half of the 60p (about 75 cents) admission fee.

Here are some debacles from other shows: the film never arriving; horrible acoustics; concertgoers spending most of our set at the bar; the night where there were so few attendees that the promoters urged fans to move up and sit at wooden tables and chairs in front of the stage; our equipment truck failing to arrive in time for a show; John nearly getting into a fight with a fan who came backstage and announced that he'd rather see us with Martin or Malcolm; Phil tearing his trousers when they got caught on a microphone stand; us canceling out of sheer frustration. Comically, *Three Friends* was released in the US, England, and the rest of Europe in the middle of our 'Hendrix' tour.

In a weird way, the humbling tour with the Hendrix movie lit a fire under us to get back in the studio and write an album that would cement our status as a headline-worthy band that transcended labels like 'prog,' 'psychedelic,' and most of all 'pretentious.' We were motivated, charged, and working non-stop to become better songwriters and performers, to present a better range of dynamics, and to be a more commercially accessible band without sacrificing artistry. Some of the frustrations we had experienced during the *Three Friends* cycle injected us with piss and vinegar, which made us a better band. Maybe more than anything, the immediate chemistry between us and John eliminated the need for babysitting and handholding. He was a pro, and he presented us with ideas for great rock beats and held down the rhythms like an experienced sailor holding down the helm in high winds. Any struggles we'd had getting drummers to nail tempos, rhythms, and fills were over. We had found our man. John was a giant among Giants.

He was also as dedicated and motivated as we were, so when we proposed going right back into the studio after we finished touring, he was all in. That was the Gentle Giant way. We would never take an extended break to fuck around on the beach or take a pilgrimage to Mecca to find ourselves. We weren't in the financial position to go on a long holiday, and besides, we didn't want a break. We enjoyed writing and recording and performing together, making creative strides, and becoming more accomplished—not for fans or our career, but for our own musical growth. We wanted to play the music we wanted to listen to. Downtime wasn't conducive to that.

We had enjoyed making *Three Friends*, and we figured that having a central theme again was a good place to start with the new record. The original idea was to write a fleshed-out song about each member of the band. I'm not sure that came through in the end, which is just as well, since writing a musical epic and internalizing it as something like 'The Ballad Of Derek' (though we would never have called it that) would be silly and, yes, pretentious. In the end, Phil and I agreed to base some of the lyrics on literature and philosophy and loosely intertwine them with stories drawn from our personal lives. 'The Advent Of Panurge' was inspired by *Gargantua And Pantagruel* by François Rabelais, 'A Cry For Everyone' was rooted in the existentialism of Albert Camus, and 'Knots' dipped into ideas from a book of the same name by Scottish psychiatrist R.D. Laing. These grand themes encouraged us to explore a wide variety of sounds and styles, from the elegiac medieval melodies of 'Raconteur Troubadour' to the beat-heavy rock outs of 'A Cry For Everyone' and the instrumental 'The Boys In The Band.'

At first, Phil was as excited about the new music as the rest of us and wanted to devote all his time and attention to the band. Gradually, though, that changed. Phil had a family, and his wife wanted him to spend more time with her and their kids. At that point, I was so far from that type of thinking that I couldn't imagine how he could think of anything but the band. Eventually, the conflict would prove to be too great for him, but when we recorded *Octopus* at Advision Studios between July 24 and August 5, he was able to tune out any outside distractions and completely focus on the music. It was an amazing collaboration, and we were all deeply involved in the process, generating ideas that enhanced and complemented the songs that Kerry and Ray wrote, creating a more developed version of Gentle Giant with which we were all pleased. When we finished writing, we had our most rounded and fully formed statement date.

I've often thought of the band evolving in life stages. Our self-titled debut was us as toddlers learning to walk, excited about everything whizzing around us. *Acquiring The Taste* was us as kids, establishing our values as creatives and trying all kinds of ideas to discover what worked. *Three Friends* was our awkward adolescence and the realization of personal flaws that held us back despite the unwavering drive to move forward. In that context, *Octopus* was Gentle Giant discovering our sea legs and finally living up to our potential. With it, we turned from spotty teens to young adults.

The studio sessions for *Octopus* were occasionally fraught, as was almost everything we did. A little discord is useful for generating passion, emotion, and energy from band members. But there's a balance. Too much disenchantment is never good. Each of us wanted to place our musical mark on the new songs, which at times led to arguments. More often than not, though, we had a great time. John injected a more rock-oriented vibe into the songs, resulting in some of our heaviest and most enjoyable songs.

Whenever we became frustrated, our engineer, Martin Rushent, had a way of calming us down and bringing us back to earth. We were producing the album ourselves, as we had *Three Friends*. Martin made it sound great and kept us reigned in. Not only was he an excellent engineer, but he could always tell when we could use some levity, and he'd always have an anecdote ready or a joke on hand to lighten the mood, sidetrack us, and get us to focus on what we enjoyed about making music.

When we encountered a creative obstacle and started to get fidgety, Martin came to the rescue. 'Hold on, guys,' he'd say. 'Let me play something back for you to see what you think. Be quiet for a sec?'

Martin had set up six twelve-inch reels around the studio and had a loop of one-quarter-inch tape perpetually running throughout the sessions. He cued up a two-track Studer playback machine. 'I have an idea,' he said, and pressed play.

We watched the wheels of the machine turn, and instead of hearing Gentle Giant, out came this crazy recording of The Troggs—the band most famous for 'Wild Thing'—arguing with one another after listening back to a hopeless take of a song they should have left on the cutting-room floor. Their engineer, Clive Franks, had become so sick of the bickering that he hit the talk-back mic, pressed 'record,' and captured the absurd conversation:

> **RONNIE BOND (DRUMS)** Whether you think so or not, that is a number-fucking-one, and if that bastard don't go, then I'll fucking retire! I fucking do!
> **DENNIS BERGER (PRODUCER)** I think it is a good song. I agree, it is a good song.
> **RONNIE** But it fucking well won't be unless we spend a little bit of fucking thought and imagination to fucking make it a fucking number one. You gotta put a little bit of fucking fairy dust over the bastard, you know?
> **DENNIS** Oh, we'll put some fairy dust over it. I'll piss over the tape.
> **REG PRESLEY (VOCALS)** I'm a fairy!
> **RONNIE** Do you know what I mean? I don't know what it needs then.
> **DENNIS** Aah!
> **RONNIE** But I know that it needs...
> **DENNIS** I know that it needs strings. That, I do know...

The Troggs argument goes on and on for another fifteen minutes, following a tight audio edit, and was one of the most hilarious interactions caught on tape I'd ever heard. It took us out of a dark period of uncertainty and had us pissing ourselves laughing. For the rest of the session, whenever we disagreed about anything or started getting frustrated, Martin would interrupt—'I have an idea...'—and turn up the sound on the track with the Troggs recording. His little producer trick brought us back to earth and made us realize we weren't negotiating to save hostages. We were supposed to be having fun doing what we loved, and that epiphany erased the cloud of tension from the room more effectively than a dehumidifier removing excess water from the air. For months or maybe years afterward, we quoted bits from the Troggs argument recording back to one another and smiled. It became a great inside joke.

With Martin at the controls, we recorded *Octopus* in about two weeks at Advision Studios and finished just in time to prepare for our first US tour, promoting *Three Friends* in North America, which saw us opening for Black Sabbath. We'd known them since the early days and cheered them on as their self-titled first album revolutionized heavy music. Now, they were heading to the States to promote their second album, *Paranoid*, which was a game-changer in both the US and the UK. It was their first tour of America as well, and we were excited to be chosen as the opening band, though that had much to do with our shared management company. We weren't as heavy as them, but they were loved by loads of fans seeking a new sound, and we figured that anyone who connected with good songs would be able to appreciate Gentle Giant. Besides, Black Sabbath generated headlines everywhere they went, and we hoped some of that attention would rub off on us and maybe open a door for us in the US.

From the moment The Beatles played *Ed Sullivan*, every English band has fantasized about conquering the States. The opening date of the tour was in Savannah, Georgia, but we flew to Toronto, Ontario, first to get our work visas straightened out. Then we headed to Buffalo, which was our first contact with American soil.

'What kind of a place is this?' I asked Ray. 'This doesn't look like the America in the movies.'

Almost before he had time to answer my rhetorical question, we were on a plane from Buffalo to Charleston, South Carolina. As we disembarked, a wave of wet heat washed over us. It was sticky and a little hard to breathe, and there were palm trees everywhere. It was a culture shock beyond our expectations. We had been in hot climates before, but never anywhere so humid. It was sixty-five degrees or so back home in England, and here we were in South Carolina, sweating as if we had just finished a game of tennis.

We got to the venue, County Hall, and hooked up with Black Sabbath. We loved those guys, and they were happy to see us. Connecting with other musicians from working-class backgrounds was always comforting. County Hall was a dilapidated building that resembled a big underground bunker. We played for about thirty minutes and received the kind of lukewarm reaction opening acts often get from big crowds. We didn't think much of it and looked forward to watching Sabbath.

They began with ominous, introductory music, and then the band took the stage dressed like high priests of the Satanic temple. Now, this was new! The volume was ear-splitting, and as they launched into the soporific drone of 'Black Sabbath' the crowd stood transfixed. Then Ozzy started to sing. He sounded nasal, as usual, and his voice was scratchy coming out of the PA, which, I guess, pissed him off. Partway through the third song, he hoisted the mic stand above his head, flung it over the amplifiers, and stormed offstage. Show over. More than five hundred angry fans started throwing shit, and when they saw us at the side of the stage, they began aiming at us, as if we had somehow wrecked Ozzy's voice and made him cancel the gig. The cops stormed in and dispersed the crowd, which flooded into the street, where they continued to voice their displeasure by shouting and smashing things. It was a grand introduction to the American policing system—and a sign of things to come.

Black Sabbath had gotten heavily into partying and were especially fond of Peruvian marching powder (aka cocaine), which caused them to fidget and talk, nonstop, sometimes making sense. Touring with them looked good in a press release, but Gentle Giant's musical adventures were a stretch for the ears of most Sabbath fans, and even when we turned up the amps and played our loudest songs, the kids screaming 'Iron Man' and 'Paranoid!' weren't interested in watching a technically complex, sonically dynamic band try to win them over with subtlety or musical variation. They wanted to be stung by the buzz of steel wasps again and again. We joked around and did our best to gain the crowd's favor, as we had done when we played with Sabbath as Simon Dupree & The Big Sound, but back then Sabbath hadn't cemented their fanbase. Now, they had, and Gentle Giant wasn't on most of these kids' radars.

Once, Ozzy and I were sitting next to one another on a plane heading for a gig. He was drowning himself in alcohol, spilling almost as much as he was consuming, when he stopped and turned to me.

'Derek, are you a millionaire?'

'What?' I replied.

'Are you a millionaire?' he repeated. 'I think I am, but I'm not sure.' He returned to drinking. A minute later, he said, 'Can you believe I'm a millionaire? It's nice, but it's strange. It's good.'

Neither of us knew it at the time, but we were both being ripped off by our manager—him far worse than me—and neither of us was anywhere close to being a millionaire. In fact, he and his bandmates were practically broke.

Touring with Black Sabbath was bittersweet, filled with euphoric highs and depressing lows. And there was plenty of time to relax—not because Sabbath only booked gigs every few days (as they did in their later years), but because they canceled multiple dates on the tour. The day after the Charleston debacle, we played Nashville's Municipal Auditorium. As soon as we got offstage, the promoter announced that Sabbath couldn't make the show, leaving the middle band, Black Oak Arkansas, with the misfortune of playing a double set that pissed off the Sabbath fans.

The next three concerts were postponed, so we had a three-day vacation in Nashville. It was a good place to be. They had good restaurants and some cool music stores and pawn shops, where we bought a couple of nice guitars.

Then there were other days when we wished we were on the road with a more serious band like Jethro Tull. After another Sabbath cancellation, we got stuck at the Holiday Inn in Warren, Ohio, for four days. The town was so bereft of culture that it was like being in prison. As aggravated as I was, I felt bad for Black Sabbath, and I worried that one or more of the guys would overdose and die on tour. Once you've grown up with nothing, it's hard to know when (or how) to say no to a diet of free booze, drugs, and sex. It was sad for us as we'd known all of them before they were famous, but while it was always great to see them, they were never the same.

It wasn't enough that our first tour of America was plagued with cancellations. There was also a full-scale, arson-fueled riot—and it wasn't even Black Sabbath's fault.

We were booked to play the three-day Erie Canal Soda Pop Festival, held between September 2 and 4 in Chandler, Indiana. The event took place on Bull Island, a nine-hundred-acre facility on the border between Illinois, Indiana, and Kentucky, and went down in music festival history as one of the most poorly organized and badly run events of the era. We took a bumpy ninety-minute ride to the site on September 3. We thought we were hours ahead of schedule, but when we got there, so many of the bands on the bill hadn't shown up that we immediately had to take the stage. The audience had been standing for hours in the heavy rain.

We stepped onstage and prepared to deliver a great show, only for an electrical generator to short-circuit, causing Kerry's organ to malfunction. We had to end the set early, but that was a scratch on the surface of the snafus that plagued the event. Many of the big bands on the bill canceled or refused to play due to poor communication, mismanagement, and an absence of security. To their credit, Black Oak Arkansas, Foghat, Eagles, Cheech & Chong, Albert King, Canned Heat, Rory Gallagher, Ravi Shankar, and The Amboy Dukes showed up and performed, but fans who'd braved the storm to see Black Sabbath, Fleetwood Mac, Bob Seger, Slade, The Doors, Nazareth, The Faces, and The Allman Brothers Band were shit out of luck. The venue ran out of food and water after more than two hundred thousand fans stormed the grounds, which were equipped for a mere sixty thousand, and looting, rioting, and mass destruction ensued. We got out of there soon after we played, and we later found out that unruly rioters burned the main stage to the ground. In addition, someone died of a heroin overdose, someone else drowned in the Wabash River, and some unruly crowd members killed a local resident's cow.

The last show we played with Black Sabbath was on September 15 in Los Angeles, at the Hollywood Bowl. Captain Beyond opened, and we played next. It looked like it would be a triumphant end to a chaotic tour. The streets felt like a movie set. There were towering palm trees, music culture everywhere, and the Hollywood sign glinting in the sunlight on Sunset Boulevard. The smiling Giant from our first album was staring out from a city billboard placed by our label to advertise the release of *Three Friends*. Then, everything turned to shit.

Before the show, the singer from Captain Beyond accused me of hitting on his girlfriend (which I had not done), and a fistfight almost broke out between us before their set. From the moment we took the stage, the audience made it clear how unwelcome we were in their city. While we played, they flung beer bottles, quarters, and other projectiles. Normally, we could keep our cool in uncomfortable situations, and for a few songs we dodged the thrown objects, but when a cherry bomb landed onstage and exploded a few feet from my mic stand during the intro for 'Funny Ways,' we felt like we were in danger, and I felt like I had to say something. So, we did something no performing band should ever do. We stopped playing.

'Hey, guys,' I said into the mic. 'Can you please calm down and cool off? We'll be finished playing soon enough.' I thought being polite might encourage them to stop throwing stuff. Then Phil stepped up to the mic.

'You're all a bunch of cunts!'

It was an accurate assessment, but not one that calmed the crowd. The boo that followed was louder than a drum solo, and the sky immediately filled with too many objects to duck. We finished our set and walked off without anyone getting hurt, though we had to change and shower to get the beer, soda, and spit out of our clothes and hair.

If our performance confused the crowd, Black Sabbath were even more confounding. Everyone in the band was wasted. It was Los Angeles, for fuck's sake—who would expect anything different? But we all counted on a powerful show. Sure, Sabbath were heavy partiers, but when they showed up, their heavy music overshadowed their inebriation, and they usually destroyed, playing songs that shuddered with pure power.

I wondered how much of that intensity came from the cocaine. During the LA show, the salad bowls of blow the band were snorting backstage took its toll. Toward the end of the show, Tony Iommi dove into an extended guitar solo. One second he was bending hellish noises from his overdriven guitar, the next the instrument was feeding back tonelessly and Tony had face-planted on the ground. He didn't trip or collapse, and at first we thought it was part of the show and he would jump up and melt more faces. We looked forward to it, and we all looked at each other and laughed about how entertaining Tony was.

The crowd were on the same wavelength, and they cheered for five minutes while Iommi remained on the ground. He opened his eyes but didn't get up. Some of the band's techs held him upright while he finished his solo, which was a dissonant mess. Then his handlers walked with him offstage, where he collapsed. Thank you, goodnight. The next night in Sacramento was canceled, and that was the end of that tour.

A few days later, we continued the *Three Friends* tour on dates with Yes and the Eagles. The former had already hit the mainstream with 'Roundabout' from 1971's *Fragile* and were polite and friendly—if spiritually eccentric—Englishmen. The Eagles had just released their debut album, and 'Take It Easy' and 'Witchy Woman' were all over the radio. By contrast with Yes, they were arrogant and obnoxious, and they treated us like hired help. We hadn't been treated that badly on tour since we opened for The Beach Boys.

I didn't get it. How could they look down on us? They claimed to love good music, and we were a challenging, melodic rock band who were fun to watch. They were a simple soft-rock group with a few catchy songs. We'd passed that level years ago in Simon Dupree. And, despite their popularity, they were hardly arena-ready. Their harmonies were off-key, their tempos inconsistent. Maybe they felt threatened by us since, musically, we were far superior to them. Still, they were so full of themselves, I can't imagine how we could have made them feel small. They were selling shitloads of records while we were struggling to stay on the road.

Even though there were six of us, they gave us only a small portion of the stage and minimal lighting. When we started doing well, they loaded more of their gear onto the stage before we played. Every night, the backdrop was moved forward, and we had one foot less room to work in. By the last show, I could barely stand on the edge of the stage, let alone move around while we performed.

At first, we tried to be friendly.

'Nice show,' I said, after one of their sets early on the tour.

'Yeah, Don Henley replied. 'That's how it's done. You guys fuckin' blow.'

Yeah, we fuckin' blow you off the stage every night! That would have been the ideal response, but I said nothing.

We played some shows with Frampton's Camel and Steve Miller in Texas, and, to our surprise, discovered we had a strong following there. *Three Friends* was beating sales expectations in America. We also did well in Quebec and Montreal, which wasn't so surprising, since the Canadians seemed to like challenging, experimental music. We had planned to continue the *Three Friends* tour in Italy, but then Jethro Tull invited us to join them for another month of their US *Thick As A Brick* tour. As much as we loved Italy, it was a better career move to delay the tour and return to America with Tull. They were huge, they were good friends, and the people who liked their music also enjoyed Gentle Giant. The only drawback was the tour schedule. Tull were playing for two nights at numerous venues, and since we didn't have hotels booked or planes to shuttle us between faraway cities, we could only play one show in each city. Captain Beefheart & The Magic Band or Wild Turkey played the second dates.

Being in the States with nothing scheduled between shows was too stressful for Phil, who missed his wife and son. When we were out with Black Sabbath, most of us were annoyed by all the cancellations. Phil was crushed. Being onstage was the only thing distracting him from not being home. He spent most of his time in our room at the Holiday Inn, his ear connected to the receiver of the phone by his bed. He spent hours talking to Roberta, who was having a hard time being a single parent and consistently urged him to come back home.

Back then, international calls were timed to the second at exorbitant rates. It was a total racket of unconscionable price-gouging fueled by loneliness. At a time when there were no competitors to lower prices, phone companies and hotels charged a fortune for overseas calls. During the Black Sabbath tour, Phil spent over eight hundred dollars on phone calls, which was a lot back then. When we returned to the States with Tull, he spent even more time on the phone with his wife, and it rarely made him happy. So, he booked flights back and forth between whatever American city we were in for a day and Portsmouth, sometimes returning just minutes before we were scheduled to go onstage two days later. It was disruptive to the rest of the band, who drove between gigs, and switching from homebody to touring rocker was tearing Phil apart like a newspaper.

In stressful times, the unpredictability of rock'n'roll sometimes delivers a welcome relief, or at least interesting stories. One night in May 1973, we were sulking in our dressing room somewhere in Texas when our publicist, Jessica, entered with a short black fellow holding a Chinese take-out bag.

'Gentlemen, this is Sherman Hemsley,' she said. 'He's a big fan, and he would love to say hi.'

We had no idea that Sherman was a famous TV actor, having played George Jefferson on *All In The Family* and *The Jeffersons*. Those shows weren't broadcast in England. But though the timing wasn't ideal, we were always fine with meeting fans.

'Hey, you guys are unbelievable,' he gushed. 'You know, you have one of the best bands I've ever heard in my life.'

'Well, thanks, man,' I said. 'That's very nice of you.'

'I brought you a special gift that I think you'll like,' he replied, reaching into the plastic bag and pulling out two foil takeout trays.

Oh, he's bringing us Chinese food, we thought. It seemed like an odd gift.

Sherman opened one of the containers, and it was filled with dried mushrooms. I didn't see any sauce or noodles, and since he was a stranger, I wasn't about to try the food. Still, I wanted to be polite.

'Is it chop suey or something?' I asked. 'I'm sure it's great. Let's save it for later.'

'No,' Sherman laughed. 'They're magic mushrooms. You'll really enjoy them.' I flashed back to my nightmare LSD trip.

'Oh, thank you very much,' I said, stumbling on my words. 'I'm sure they're wonderful, but I'm going to pass.' Kerry, Ray, and Phil also turned down the 'shrooms, but I think Gary and John tried a little, and some of the people who were backstage with us happily accepted the rest.

CHAPTER TWELVE
COMPLETE CONTROL

When we were in Simon Dupree & The Big Sound, we felt lucky that the local gangsters had befriended us and seemed to be looking out for our best interests. And we were happy that our connection to the Kray brothers in Portsmouth led to a relationship with Worldwide Artists Management after Gerry Bron quit. But maybe we should have realized there are substantial drawbacks to doing business with gangsters.

Back then, managers were notorious for striking crooked deals with artists and holding these horribly one-sided contracts over their heads like a razor-sharp guillotine blade. Patrick Meehan and Don Arden were business partners and two of the most intimidating managers in the business, and both had ties to the British mafia. Arden had signed numerous bands from the Birmingham area, including The Move and The Small Faces, who we played with several times before they became The Faces. At a time when they were releasing hit records and playing big shows, they were on a salary of ten pounds per week. Arden and Meehan's team bought them fancy cars and the musicians drove them around like they owned them. In fact, they owned nothing. When they realized they were being bilked and tried to renegotiate their deal, Arden called them into his office—but not to offer them more money.

'Look,' he shouted with bulging eyes, his face reddening. 'You have a contract. You signed it, and that's it! If you try to hire a lawyer to get out of it, you might just find yourselves unable to walk.'

The Faces knew Arden didn't make empty threats. He was a thug; he had guns and Billy clubs. He worked with a network of criminals, and there were stories of members of his team holding disgruntled musicians upside-down from open windows, the vice grip of the mob being the only thing preventing gravity from sending them into a death plunge.

But Patrick and Don like us, we thought. *They wouldn't mess with us*. We soon learned how wrong we were.

When we signed with Columbia in the US, we were promised a $150,000 advance for *Three Friends*. When we finished recording *Octopus* and still hadn't received the money, we wondered if we had missed something. Columbia was a good company, and they did a good job supporting us. In fact, the label's president, Clive Davis, introduced us at one of his huge, weekly meetings. Everyone from the company was sitting at a huge table, and Clive called us 'the big new UK thing.' We felt like a goldfish that had jumped out of the bowl. We cowered in the corner of the room as thirty-six industry guys in suits mentally gauged our worth to the company. We couldn't wait to get out of there.

Clearly, Columbia expected big things. When *Three Friends* reached only #197 on the US album charts, our product manager told Phil that we needed to up our game on the next album. If he had stopped there, we might have been none the wiser, but then he added, 'We paid you a lot of money, and it would be great to see that it was worth spending that on you.'

'What are you talking about?' Phil said.

'The $150,000 we paid you when you signed,' said the label guy.

'No fucking way! We never saw the money!'

Phil told me about the conversation, and I knew right away that something smelled sour. If we had been paid a hundred and fifty grand, we wouldn't have been operating under such a tight budget. Phil had house payments. There were crew guys on salary, and any spare money we made went back into the band. After we returned from the States, Phil and I confronted the management, and we were told that the entire advance had gone on tour expenses. That didn't make sense. We had guarantees for all the Sabbath shows that were canceled, and all the other tours were great for us. Venues were packed, we sold lots of merch, and our earnings were far outweighed our expenses.

Phil hunted down the paper trail and gathered evidence that showed that not only were we owed the full $150,000 from the signing advance, but other payments we got weren't as much as we were owed—and some never arrived. The more we dug into the paperwork, the more we realized that Worldwide was stealing from us.

That was disturbing for obvious reasons, but we knew we had to handle the situation with kid gloves. Worldwide had made it clear that they liked us and our music, and we didn't want that to change in any way. At the same time, we weren't going to roll over while we were getting screwed. As problematic as our contract was, we soon found it was far more equitable than the legal papers that had been drawn up for our friends in The Groundhogs and especially Black Sabbath. Our tour manager, David Hemmings, who worked for WWA and managed the emerging Judas Priest, spilled the beans about how badly every band was being treated. Several weeks later, we heard he had 'committed suicide.'

We scheduled a closed-door meeting with Patrick Meehan Sr. and his son, Patrick Meehan Jr., Sabbath's product manager, and some other people from the company. We wanted to make sure Black Sabbath were there. Our contract was one-sided, but Sabbath's deal was so bad it reverted ownership of anything Black Sabbath had to Worldwide Artists, much as Arden had done with The Small Faces. Only, Sabbath were earning far more money for Worldwide Artists than practically all of their other bands combined, and WWA needed to hold onto their prized livestock. Black Sabbath thought their managers were encouraging them to act like rock stars to help them live out their fantasies while everyone got rich. In reality, the management were distracting Sabbath so they could steal everything from them. Sabbath were snow-blind. The showers of cocaine and groupies were tantalizing, but they were merely distractions. With groupies reaching into the front of their pants, the band members would never feel the hands of management removing their wallets from their back pockets.

I was the one who told the guys in Sabbath that their contracts were worthless and that they needed to attend this urgent meeting if they wanted any chance of renegotiating their deal. At first, they were skeptical, especially Ozzy, but I was able to convince them that they were not rich rock stars and that they owned nothing. The management contracts they had signed made Worldwide Artists the custodians and owners of Black Sabbath's houses, cars, boats, bank accounts—everything they were *permitted* to use. They were devastated. All they had left was a meeting to attend to try to hold onto a fraction of their earnings.

Gentle Giant met with WWA to discuss our issues first, and as we opened the doors to the office, we were terrified. It felt like entering the lion's den at feeding time. We hoped that speaking out would get them to pay us what we were owed or agree to invalidate our contract. We were their first band to realize we were being fucked and say, 'We want out.' But even though we were livid, we walked into the meeting calmly and rationally, determined not to lose our tempers.

'Thanks for meeting with us,' I said to Patrick. 'Now, what's that deal you got us at Columbia? Because we're not seeing any money from it.'

'Well, yeah, it's in an account for you. Don't worry about it.'

'What account?' I shot back.

'It's fine. It'll be there.'

He smiled through gritted teeth, and we could tell he was lying. There wasn't a whole lot we could do, but because the Krays liked us, they had convinced Arden and Meehan not to completely fleece us. As outrageous as it seems today, in the 60s and 70s, so many bands went through this kind of thing at the beginning of their career that it was almost accepted in the industry as a rite of passage. You paid your dues by getting fucked over.

I had always naively thought that we were smarter than everyone else, and maybe that's why Patrick Meehan didn't treat us as badly as his other acts. I thought he respected our intelligence and our intelligent music, and I swore I never would have signed a horrible record contract. Then, much later in my life, I looked back at our old contract and saw how dismal it was. We owned a mere four percent of our album sales, which is minuscule even for a new band. And there was my signature on the page. We were suckered into the swindle, just like everyone else.

We figured there might be strength in numbers, and that if the other WWA bands were aligned with us, maybe we'd all get out of the situation with unbroken kneecaps and a few quid. The second meeting was the one that tore the band-aid off our relationship with Worldwide Artists. This was the game-changer attended by us, Black Sabbath, and The Groundhogs. Phil and I were able to show them that our receipts didn't add up to what we were owed. Patrick glanced them over, begrudgingly copped to an accounting error, and promised to pay us back some of the money—but not the $150,000, which he still insisted had already been spent on us.

Next, Meehan Sr. and his son met with Sabbath. In no uncertain terms, he told them that if it wasn't for WWA, Sabbath would never have made it out of Birmingham. He added that he and his peers were overseeing Black Sabbath's career so that they could continue to enjoy a self-indulgent life free of paperwork or commitments. Then he explained the details of their management deal, point by ugly point. Each phrase and clause he read made it abundantly clear that Worldwide Artists had legal ownership of all things Black Sabbath. Tony and Ozzy grew pale, and it looked like their faces would slide off their skulls.

'You mean, I don't own *anything*?' Iommi asked in disbelief. 'I don't own my house? I don't own my cars?'

Ozzy, who had brought a bottle of whisky into the meeting and was self-medicating as he learned he was practically homeless, was furious. Suddenly, he gripped the neck of the bottle and drew back his arm like a football quarterback, spilling booze down his arm, shoulder, and onto the floor. He whipped the bottle at Meehan; it whirred past his head and shattered against the wall. Meehan's face turned red. At that moment, we were all wishing Ozzy's aim was slightly better, but had that been the case, he would likely have wound up far deeper in debt.

Our friends in The Groundhogs were even more fucked than Sabbath. They had signed an equally horrible contract, and they didn't have the fame or resources to bounce back the way Ozzy and Sabbath did. Disillusioned and depressed, they broke up for a year before frontman Tony McPhee restarted the band with a completely new lineup (twice).

We were shaken but far from bankrupt. In the end, we paid £90,000 to buy out our contract, which wasn't finalized until the end of 1974. Even so, we made enough from touring and selling merch to remain in the black. At the same time, we became more cynical. We lost trust in

Above Our first promotional shoot as Gentle Giant for Vertigo Records, for the release of our debut album, *Gentle Giant*, in 1970.

Above Columbia Records promotional photo shoot for *Three Friends*, 1972.

Left A Columbia Records billboard promoting *Three Friends* near Sunset Boulevard during our first US tour in 1972. **Below** Gentle Giant playing live at PalaLido, Milan, Italy, January 4, 1973.

Above Gentle Giant onstage during our US tour in 1975. **Left** Our road managers setting up the stage at the Autostade, Montreal, August 30, 1975.

Opposite page, top Gentle Giant live at the Musikhalle in Hamburg, Germany, April 10, 1974. **Below** A backstage promo shoot from 1976.

Right Advision Studios, 1976, during the *Interview* album sessions. *Left to right*: Paul Northfield, Phil Freeman (*in background*), Ray Shulman, and me. **Below** Ray, me, Phil Freeman (*kneeling*), and Paul Northfield (*right*) setting up microphones at Advision.

Above Chrysalis Records UK promotional photo shoot for *Playing The Fool*, 1976.

Above Playing the 'Shulberry'—a custom-built electric ukulele/mandolin hybrid, made specifically for 'Playing The Game'—on our 1976 US tour.

managers, labels, booking agents, and others who profited from the artists they signed, and we realized that if we were going to thrive as Gentle Giant, we had to take complete control of our business and our music.

I already had experience keeping the lights on for my family in Portsmouth, and I had been producing our music for a couple of years. Little did I know, the experience I gained when we severed ties with WWA and I became the manager of Gentle Giant would set me up a decade later for a career as a record label executive.

When we finished touring the US with Tull, we went right back on the road to make up the Italy dates we had postponed. It was certainly a tour to remember and a huge turning point in the band's life. In addition to playing all the major cities, we played three concerts in Sicily, and, somewhat strangely, Patrick Meehan wanted to join us at the shows. We weren't asked if it was okay with us. He just told us he was coming, so we quietly acquiesced and hoped for the best.

When our plane arrived from Rome, our Italian promoter greeted us at the gate. 'Ciao, Paisan,' he said to Patrick. The promoter told us we would be boarding a smaller plane that would take us to Catania, where a 'Mr. Christaldi' would meet us. We were specifically instructed to tell the man that it was a great honor to play in Palermo and Catania and to thank him for the opportunity.

When the plane landed in Catania, three black limousines were waiting for us on the tarmac. As we exited the plane with the other passengers, several men in designer black suits got out of their cars, greeted us, and took us back to their vehicles. One of the men opened the door of the middle car that we didn't enter, and out stepped a short, bald older Italian gentleman who looked like Marlon Brando in *The Godfather*. We figured out right away that this was Mr. Christaldi. We already knew that Patrick had ties to organized crime in England, but when you saw the way Mr. Christaldi greeted Patrick in Sicily, it was clear that his mafia connections ran far deeper—all the way down to the Cosa Nostra.

We immediately thanked Mr. Christaldi for having us in his town and allowing us to play in Sicily. I think we were driven as much by fear as genuine gratitude, but our sincerity touched him, and he insisted we all have dinner with him and the promoters after the show. By the time we finished the concert, it was 1am, and we figured Mr. Christaldi had probably gone home. But when we got offstage, there he was. We joined him for a multi-course Italian dinner with all the trimmings and didn't finish eating until 4am.

The next day we traveled to Palermo. We figured we had survived the trial by pasta and thought and that Mr. Christaldi had other 'business' to worry about. But when we finished our encore in Palermo, there was Mr. Christaldi and his entourage. Once again, it was dinner time, and we were showered with ebullient praise and fine cuisine. At least we had a day off for our nerves and stomachs to recover before we played Bari. When that show was over, nobody was waiting for us, which filled us with a strange combination of relief and disappointment.

While we were in Italy, we were supposed to play the PalaLido Arena in Milan. The morning of the show, we arrived from Treviso to discover that the municipality of Milan had canceled the gig and banned future rock concerts because of rioting hours before our show. We spent our day off in Milan visiting restaurants and enjoying the local food and wine.

Ray and I had a glass of wine each. Gary imbibed much more. When we got to the hotel and retired to our rooms, there was an enormous crash from next door where Gary was staying. It was so loud that everyone in the hotel must have heard it. The manager rushed to Gary's room and opened the door. There was Gary in the bathtub. The sink was in pieces on the tile floor, with shards of broken glass surrounding it. Gary sat there uninjured with a sheepish grin on his face.

We couldn't imagine what had happened. Then Gary told us he had slipped while getting into the bath. It was like a game of Mousetrap. As he tripped, his foot somehow smashed into the window, and the glass and wooden frame fell into the sink, which broke on the impact and shattered on the floor. It looked like The Who had rolled through town and taken revenge on the bathroom, which, aside from the tub, was destroyed. There went our gig money from the night before.

GIANT STEPS

CHAPTER THIRTEEN

AND THEN THERE WERE FIVE

We had figured being back in Italy would be good for us—especially Phil, who had grown more distant and aloof. He'd be closer to his family and could talk to them more easily since they'd be in practically the same time zone (one hour difference). Looking back, I think it was obvious that Phil's days with the band were numbered. There's no question that he enjoyed the shows in Italy and the mafia-provided meals, but he was moodier than ever and clearly torn between staying in the band or leaving us and becoming a full-time family man. He wrestled with every possibility that would allow him to tend to both worlds, which must have been soul-ripping. And it drove the rest of us crazy. We weren't about to kick him out, but if Phil wanted to leave, we couldn't stop him.

Finally, Phil broke. His wife gave him an ultimatum: the family or the band. At the core, he was a family man more than a touring vagabond, so he left. In retrospect, I can confidently say that choosing family over the band was the right thing for Phil to do. At the time, though, I didn't see it that way. I was still single, so I couldn't understand how he could abandon his brothers (not just his blood brothers but all of us) and bail on us. He barely explained himself when he left because he didn't know what to say. But that didn't help mend burned bridges.

Phil was frustrated and confused. He was angry and we were pissed. Worse, we had been given little warning, no time to vent our anger or try to talk him out of leaving. He simply went to the airport and flew home after one of our shows in Italy, leaving us in a lurch. I understand now why he did it, but I'll never figure out why he did it that way.

We had planned to return to the studio immediately after we got off tour to start work on the follow-up to *Octopus*, but without a co-lyricist and key musician, that wasn't going to happen. Ray and I even questioned whether we wanted to continue without Phil. We were never the Three Musketeers, but from the moment Simon Dupree & The Big Sound took off, we had been the three Shulmans. Now, the dynamic was different, and it seemed like our game was thrown off.

One day, Ray and I were walking the streets of London in the drizzling rain. I sniffed and gazed dazedly at the slick, shiny road. 'You know we can replace Phil,' I said after a long silence. 'Things are different, but, I mean, you and I are still the Shulman brothers. We started all of this, and I'll be damned if I'm gonna throw it away.'

'I don't know, Derek. Everything feels weird and not exactly right.'

'Do you want to quit?'

Ray paused and I felt a gnawing sensation in my stomach. 'No, he finally said. 'I want to keep going. If Phil wants out, I guess that's his deal.'

We didn't know how Phil's absence would change the band, but the most important thing was we were both still in. Kerry, Gary, and John didn't want the band to break up either. Neither did our fans. The separation with Phil was acrimonious, which was a shame, and in the fallout, Ray and I completely cut off contact with him for the next ten years—long after Gentle Giant called it a day. As a bittersweet consolation, any power struggles in the band were over. I was now the frontman and major decision-maker, and everyone was comfortable following my lead.

Like our father, Ray was a masterful musician who could play any instrument placed in front of him. I was no slouch either, and I was already handling some of the bass, saxophone, and recorder parts. So, when Phil left it, wasn't too hard to carry on as a live band without him. Our first show as a five-piece was on February 23, 1973, at the Corn Exchange in Devizes, England, opening for Thin Lizzy. We were due to return to the US in March and wanted to play a couple of warm-up gigs beforehand.

To a large extent, you can choose your venues and tour bands, but you can't pick your audience. We expected to have to work on some of the new musical cues for our touring show, maybe toss in some jokes to win over members of the crowd who were there for Lizzy (I often introduced myself as a celebrity rock star like Mick Jagger or Eric Clapton, which was usually good for a laugh). We didn't expect to face a wild, aggressive crowd, let alone members of the Hell's Angels motorcycle gang, who came to bust heads. Violence erupted without provocation, and all I could think about was the stabbing at Altamont in 1969. I urged everyone to stop fighting, but to no avail. So, we finished playing and got the hell out of here. Good thing security arrived before anyone was severely injured.

Our next show was on March 4 at King Alfred College, a teacher-training institution in Winchester, where we confirmed to any of the scholarly folks in the crowd that their counting skills weren't off and there were just five of us up there. 'For anyone who was wondering where Phil is, he's no longer in the band. He's gone back to teaching,' I said, which elicited laughs from some members of the crowd, who thought I was joking.

Octopus came out in Italy in October 1972 and in England in early December. We were worried that it wouldn't be released in America in time for our tour, and that our fans wouldn't know the new songs. It eventually hit American record stores in late February, with a different cover. For some reason, Columbia Records decided not to use Roger Dean's fantastic artwork of an angry-eyed octopus surfacing from the depths (maybe because they thought it might be confused with all the work he did for Yes). Instead, they went with an image by artist Charles White of a dead octopus inside a jar. The lid was screwed closed and marked with the band's name. It looked okay, though, and it arrived in time for fans to familiarize themselves with the new, heavier material on the album—and John's fierce drumming.

Trying to break America was always a challenge for us and our team. We didn't always see eye to eye with our label reps, and some promoters seemed to be on a different planet altogether. Shows with Wishbone Ash, Humble Pie, and even J. Geils made some sort of sense, and we had a good time opening for King Crimson. Why someone booked us a handful of shows with Sha Na Na, on the other hand, is anyone's guess. Our fans showed up and gave us a standing ovation. Conversely, some of *their* crowd didn't think much of our challenging music and took to chanting 'Sha Na

Na' between our songs. Playing tunes from *Octopus* was a nice break from our prior set, but the songs, and especially the lyrics, reminded me of Phil, which was depressing.

By mid-1973, we were keen to return to the studio to record our next album. Ray and Kerry had a batch of songs, and I worked on some musical stuff, but we were a little gun-shy about recording the first Gentle Giant without Phil. Everything we worked on reminded us that he wasn't there. The lack of fervent discussions about different ways to present the songs was unsettling, and without Phil's literary references, I was unsure how to start writing my lyrics. After extensive brainstorming, we solved the problem. Instead of allowing Phil's absence to be the elephant in the room, we made it the focus of our music. Driven by John's four-to-the-floor beats, we wrote passages that were more concise and direct than any we had done before, but which were also shaded by our frustration and anger at having been abruptly abandoned, and our determination that we would persevere and succeed despite the abrupt change.

The new songs took shape quickly and triggered a rebirth of Gentle Giant. Entering Advision Studios in July, we worked efficiently and effectively, though not always joyfully. I wouldn't say it was stressful. We were at the top of our game musically and determined to make a great album, which we did, but for me and Ray, love for music was the only thing that masked our depression. For the first time ever, I wasn't happy to be in the studio. Singing didn't lift me up. I didn't enjoy producing. It wasn't a labor of love but was closer to an obligatory chore. And I felt fucking awful—sad, anxious, annoyed.

Ray, who was usually well-adjusted and even-keeled, was also down, and since our moods always marked the music we wrote, *In A Glass House* was dark, aggressive, and much less progressive. It wasn't purposeful, it was entirely subconscious, and it wouldn't be too much of an exaggeration to say it was Gentle Giant's post-traumatic stress album.

As much as Phil and I had fought, he was our older brother. We respected his intelligence, wit, musical skill, and business acumen. Now, he was gone, and we were in grief. Phil hadn't reached out to us, we were stubborn, and we intuitively knew he was going to be out of our lives for a long time, maybe forever. The emotional turmoil was evident in my lyrics and the melancholy tone of some of the music. Even so, we rose to the occasion and finished the album in time for its scheduled release two months later.

In A Glass House was an entirely different beast for Gentle Giant, and it created a daunting dualism in me. I knew the music was good—maybe even great—but I felt so bad. It was an album marked by ambivalence. After we wrote the songs, we listened back with a certain amount of trepidation and said, 'Okay, what did we do here? Is this good? Is this us? Are we Gentle Giant without Phil?' It was a very strange cycle. At the same time, I don't think Gentle Giant couldn't have grown into the band we became if Phil hadn't split. Left to our own vision, we were able to focus on groove and feel and become a much more rock-oriented band.

Though he was relatively new to the band, John Weathers took control and threw us a lifeline when we were foundering. The way he drummed on *Octopus* gave us extra dimensions to explore. He could play intricate, tricky meters and soft, subdued beats as well as anyone. Yet, it was his ability to shift effortlessly into overdrive and propel us in a more straightforward rock direction that took Gentle Giant to our next musical plateau. I can't overstate how important John was in providing an accidental, unwritten, unspoken form of therapy when we needed it most. Subconsciously, *In A Glass House* was like putting the old Giant in his coffin, saying goodbye, and continuing as a new Giant with our reputation and integrity intact.

The album title is a direct reference to the adage about people who 'live in glass houses.' To us, the stone-throwers included management, fickle labels, and fair-weather fans—and, yes, our acrimonious split with Phil, which colored many of my lyrics. I didn't want to make an album full of literary references and existential commentary. I wanted the songs to be fresh and to express how I felt about what was going on with the band, in our lives, and how the social and political climate of the time was impacting everything around us. And a lot of that was colored by my mental turmoil. As a five-piece touring band, we knew we couldn't have as much instrumentation onstage, so we didn't write as many parts into the arrangements. There was plenty of violin and some horns, but guitar took a more prominent role, and while we still strayed from convention and included many tempo and rhythm changes, the songs were more accessible and conventionally melodic—for Gentle Giant.

When we started working on *In A Glass House*, I was conflicted, but I still felt like that turmoil was generating the purest, most honest musical expression of which we were capable. From a pure physical and emotional level, it was my favorite Gentle Giant album. Later, however, as I began to reevaluate what we had done, I came to regard it as one of my least favorite records. More recently, I've looked at it for what it is—a good, authentic snapshot of where we were at that point in our career. With decades of hindsight, and having reconciled with Phil in our silver years, I can say that moving on as a five-piece was a blessing in disguise, and his decision to devote himself to his family was one he needed to make. We were getting more popular, and there was a greater demand for us to tour internationally, which would have been horrible for Phil. And, considering how many major career decisions came our way over the second half of the band, it benefitted us to have one bandleader taking care of business, instead of two jockeying for position. I just wish we all had had more time to prepare for what transpired, and that everyone had parted ways on good terms. As our lives progressed, we discovered that while history tends to repeat itself, you can't rewrite the past, which sadly would cause many years of acrimony.

It would have been great if *In A Glass House* had been the commercial resurrection we needed and immediately supercharged our career in America, the UK, and beyond. That didn't happen. The executives at Columbia took one listen to it and had a knee-jerk reaction—it was too dark, and it wasn't *Octopus*. To our shock, they refused to release it.

As some small consolation, Vertigo liked the album just fine and released it in Europe on September 21, 1973. Our fans loved the record too, and no one complained that it was bleaker or more introspective than *Octopus*. It sold well in Europe and set us up for some big headline tours there.

Columbia's lack of interest didn't poison us in the US, either. The album was one of the most popular import albums of the year, and it resonated strongly with our American fans, which would later lead to our decision to reissue it in 1992 on our own Alucard label. This was a brand-new era for

Gentle Giant. We were no longer on Columbia, we were almost through with WWA, and we'd signed a new management deal with Terry Ellis, who we knew because he also managed Jethro Tull.

Ellis had co-founded Chrysalis Records with Chris Wright in 1968. He knew our music well and was excited to work with us. It was a win/win, and everything changed for the better. We didn't have to look over our shoulders anymore to see if anyone was screwing us, because the only one we saw when we glanced behind us was the friendly smiley Giant. We had tour managers to make sure we received our guarantees, and everything happened as planned, which is never a sure thing when you're on the road in a foreign country. We hired Eric Brooks, who had mastered the nuts and bolts of tour managing while on the road with Jethro Tull. He worked with us for around two years and did a fantastic job, cleaning up spills and making sure the Giant machine was well-oiled. He was all business too and avoided the lurid elements of the job that attract too many tour managers (wrangling groupies, procuring drugs, making sure the party is raging). That was fine with us—the more effort he put into communicating with venues and hotels, getting us where we needed to go, and ensuring we were paid, the happier we were.

With Terry's guidance, we signed to Capitol in North America and Chrysalis for the rest of the world. At first, we focused our efforts on touring Europe, since *In A Glass House* wasn't being released in the US. We had a bit more money and were headlining more shows, so we took a cue from the stage productions of Jethro Tull and Yes and put more resources into our visual presentation. We started with a projection screen, and that rapidly became multiple screens splashing surreal, Giant-themed images across the back of the stage. We barely played any of the songs from our first two albums anymore, focusing instead on the evolved material from *Three Friends*, *Octopus*, and *In A Glass House*, the latter of which had entire crowds on their feet. As a five-piece, we were at the peak of our playing powers, and our performances were close to flawless. Usually, our production enhancements made for a better show, although there was one time when that wasn't the case—at least for Gary.

Gary started out by doing a pretty piece on acoustic guitar, and I was preparing to come out from backstage and start singing 'So Sincere.' Ray entered first. In the fog and darkness, I didn't notice the electrical wires crossing the stage. I stumbled over one of them but didn't fall over. Something went *CLANGG!* and Gary and Ray looked behind them giggling. They thought I had tripped and was on the ground, but the noise was actually caused by the wire snapping into the guitar stand, which went flying, as did the guitar it was holding. Gary's roadie picked the Les Paul off the ground to hand it to him in time for him to finish the song. He should have figured it was out of tune and grabbed another guitar. But it wasn't just out of tune. It was in two pieces. When it fell on the stage, the headstock snapped right off. Gary had to finish the set with a Telecaster, and when he got offstage, he was bereft that his prize guitar was broken.

Gary's guitar was in desperate need of repair. Not long after the show, I found out I needed some fixing as well. During the tour, I had started experiencing severe stomach pains. I figured I was suffering from physical exhaustion. If I had been having a great time on the road, and if the shows had been standing room only, I would have gutted it out and finished the tour. But the *only* time I felt good was onstage. Before and after the shows, I was anxious, doubled over in pain, and I had to be in a quiet room with soothing music, breathing deeply and practically meditating for the pain to pass. The cue to stop touring came after I started vomiting blood. We canceled a twelve-date tour of France and I went straight to the doctor, who diagnosed me with bleeding ulcers.

I had wrestled with gastric issues in my late teens and early twenties, and throughout my life, I've experienced semi-regular stomach discomfort to varying degrees whenever I've gotten anxious or upset. Stress causes some people headaches or anger issues. For me, it goes right to my gut. Instead of flying to France and playing shows, I went back to Portsmouth, rested in bed, watched my diet, and took medicine until the ulcers healed.

When I felt pretty good again, we got back to work on our next record. We had already written most of the songs for *The Power And The Glory* on the road, so we were ahead of the game. After a bit of tweaking, we returned to Advision Studios in December 1973 and worked for a solid month to perfect the songs. I played a bit of tenor sax on 'So Sincere,' but there weren't a lot of horns on the record. Instead, we emphasized Gary's guitars and Ray's violin (acoustic and electric). Kerry played an assortment of keyboards, including piano, Hammond organ, RMI Electra Piano, Fender Rhodes, Minimoog, Clavinet, and Wurlitzer, as well as marimba, vibraphone, and cello.

Despite the abundance of time we spent in the studio recording all of the different tracks, the process was smooth, almost effortless. Music doesn't often come out of thin air. Even great songs usually require at least some pushing and pulling, sweating and screaming before they're born. That wasn't the case for *The Power And The Glory*. Every morning, we couldn't wait to get back into the studio to try out new ideas. We arranged the songs without much exertion, and even with all the instrumentation, producing the album was a breeze. After the angst and turmoil that went into *In A Glass House*, *The Power And The Glory* was like a gift—affirmation that we still loved being together and making our original style of music. And we had gotten damned good at it.

If every album we did represented the evolution of this metaphoric Giant, *The Power And The Glory* was our reinvention after a bad divorce. Having survived the bitterness of *In A Glass House*, it was like getting remarried to a band I loved being with. The record came so easily and without drama, we felt powerful and glorious. That would have been reason enough for the album title, but really it came from the lyrics I wrote about the corruption that stems from having too much power. The songs weren't exactly political, in that they didn't address specific people and events, but they were inspired by feelings of uncertainty and distrust that had developed in First World nations between the people and their governments. England is no stranger to governmental scandals, and having toured the US numerous times, we were aware of how much the Watergate fiasco—which dominated news headlines—and the arms race had shaken people's confidence in their leaders. Without being preachy, I wanted to address the adversarial relationship between leaders and those who vote for them. More specifically, I had been thinking about how the people at the top of society wield the most power, and how the majority of society, who are at the bottom of the hierarchy, have practically no power at all, aside from their votes at the ballot. It was the closest we came to making a protest album.

We submitted the album as our final contractual obligation to WWA and signed to Capitol Records in the US. Everyone was relieved to discover that *The Power And The Glory* was Gentle Giant at our best. It was challenging and multifaceted yet melodic and upbeat enough for mainstream audiences, and it was well-received wherever we went on tour. At the same time, we were eager to get back to the studio again, to start work on the first album for which we'd have complete creative control. We would make all decisions regarding musical content, marketing, promotions, and management decisions—since I was now officially managing the band.

To our delight, *The Power And The Glory* charted at #78 in the US—a wonderful surprise, given that our last official release there was *Octopus*. We headed back to the States to open for Traffic on October 8 in Denver, Colorado, then played a five-night headline run in West Hollywood at the Whisky A Go-Go. The five-hundred-seat club was packed every night, with hundreds more fans lined up hours in advance of the shows but unable to get tickets.

In a very tangible way, the Whisky shows marked a turning point for Gentle Giant. We no longer felt like we needed to prove something to win over American crowds. We had already won them over, and they were jumping around, singing along, and smiling with sheer joy as we played. It beat the hell out of the days of playing to hostile audiences and dodging debris. After our Hollywood triumph, Capitol immediately pressed thirty thousand more copies of *The Power And The Glory*. To celebrate, we went to San Francisco for a few days, but aside from some good Chinese food and a pleasant stroll through the artsy Haight-Ashbury district, we were too consumed with thoughts of making new music to be tourists. We spent the bulk of our time in the hotel, putting together ideas for new songs. One of the reasons we never took long breaks was because we didn't like to sit around. Why risk sightseeing and losing momentum when you could be building the path, brick by brick, to your next victory?

Our catalogue was so eclectic at that point that we could play with just about anyone. On the *Power And The Glory* tour, we performed shows with Aerosmith, Golden Earring, Quicksilver, J. Geils Band, Chick Corea's Return To Forever, Dr. John, and Frank Zappa &The Mothers Of Invention. To our delight, we found out Frank was a big fan, and when he was asked in an interview if any new bands were inspiring him, he said he couldn't think of anyone except Gentle Giant. Loftier praise we couldn't have asked for.

Then, right when we were risking getting a tiny bit too big for our britches, we did a poorly attended Friday afternoon in-store appearance in Cleveland at Record Revolution, which was near the venue where we were playing. Every time someone walked through the door, a representative from Capitol asked them if they were ready to meet Gentle Giant, only to be greeted with blank expressions. The customers didn't know who we were! The signing was scheduled while schools were still in session, so the bulk of our teenage fans were in class.

To go from the absurd to the ridiculous, as we took our seats for the signing, one of the store's employees picked up a mic and a written note to introduce us: 'Ladies and gentlemen, let's give a big Cleveland welcome to ... General Grant!'

Whoever scribbled the intro must have had atrocious handwriting. In response, we wrote on the wall signed by bands visiting the store, 'Gentle Giant, not General Grant.'

Not long after that, we were scheduled to open for J. Geils in Philadelphia, but when the headliners canceled, the label got us another gig opening for Dave Mason at a college outside Trenton, New Jersey. I guess I should have taken a closer look at the itinerary. When we stepped onstage, I went up to the mic and said, 'Hello, we are Gentle Giant. It's great to be here in Pennsylvania with all of you!'

Aaaargh! I might have been better off introducing us as General Grant.

CHAPTER FOURTEEN

IN THE MIDNIGHT HOUR

I hadn't realized I was pushing myself too hard until we got back to Portsmouth. I woke in the middle of the night, stood up, and felt an inferno raging in my stomach. I doubled over, flopped back into bed, and curled into a fetal position. I called out to Ray, who urged me to try to relax, get some rest, and pay more attention to my health. I didn't exactly listen until a few days later when I collapsed on the floor. It was time to return to the gastroenterologist.

He conducted a series of tests and then performed an endoscopy to remove a couple of bleeding duodenal ulcers. I was advised not to overexert myself for two months and to rest my voice, which meant no singing, no interviews, and minimal talking. To my dismay, we had to cancel a string of UK shows. But in retrospect, I'm lucky I didn't do more damage to my body than I did. During our five weeks in the States, I had been in denial about developing another ulcer—or suffering again from an earlier one. I had endured chronic stomach pain and acid reflux on tour, but I'd convinced myself it was anxiety and tried to fight my way through it. I guess I lost.

There was no way I was going to stay inactive for two months. When I started feeling better, I started working with Kerry and Ray on songs for our next album. A month in, I told them I was fine and insisted we go back on tour. We spent the first part of 1975 in North America, and we started off with a wallop, performing a headline show on January 14 at the twenty-thousand-seat Montreal Forum. To poke a bit of fun at ourselves, we had the rear projector flash the word 'pretentious' over our heads at the start of the show. Good thing we could spell. Not everyone can. A few days later, a New York marquee at a major venue read 'Presenting Genlte Giant.'

When we headed back into rehearsals in the spring of 1975, we were confident and fired up. Fueled by the waves of positive energy on tour, we vowed to turn the new songs we had written into the most uncompromising statement anyone had ever heard from us. It had to be adventurous, it had to rock, it had to be ebulliently melodic—and more than ever, we had to be able to explain the intent behind every note. We had watched from afar as the Giant played in the sandbox, found meaning and direction, questioned the world around him, and set out on a path that earned him recognition and longevity. Now, we were six albums in, and it was time for him to make his mark as a fully formed, sentient, and empathetic entity.

We worked through the spring and summer and then went into Advision seeking a new form of validation. We had survived crippling interpersonal turmoil, fought our way out of inequitable contracts, circumvented undesirable situations, and endured agonizing illness and injury. Now, we were self-produced, self-managed, and driven by an intangible force to succeed on our own terms. We had never been part of a scene, and we didn't need industry powerbrokers to break us. We were still living on the South Coast of England, and we were still quite popular. Other bands moved to London because, hey man, it was the thing to do. We wanted no part of that. I'm sure most people at the record company thought we were a pain in the ass, and maybe, in their minds, we offered them less than we delivered, but this was our lives, our careers. We had come too far to compromise and learned too much to be willfully obscure. We knew exactly what we were, and it was time to show everyone our hand.

Having focused on nothing but Gentle Giant for five years, and having played with John for almost three, we were at top form musically, personally, professionally, and lyrically. We were clear-headed and focused like night owls. That's the spirit from which *Free Hand* was born. And, as much as we loved *The Power And The Glory*, *Free Hand* came out when we were at the top of our game.

Free Hand was our first record with Chrysalis in the UK and our second with Capitol in the US. We knew there was some great stuff on it, but we had no idea how solidly the public would connect with it. The album hit #40 on the UK chart and reached #48 on the *Billboard* 200 in America and #49 in Canada. We couldn't have been happier, but we couldn't figure out whether listeners recognized and appreciated the undiluted artistic expression involved, or if they liked that the songs were hooky, melodic, and rocked like an earthquake in hell. Either way, we never expected *Free Hand* to take off in the way it did—and maybe that's one of the reasons it did. Throughout our time in Gentle Giant, we never thought about legacy or where we'd be in ten years. It was all about the here and now. We did what we wanted because we liked playing what we wrote and listening to what we played, and no one was doing anything like it at the time.

So, why did we combine so many styles and sounds into our diverse, multifaceted music? Maybe it has something to do with feeling confined in Simon Dupree, but I think it has as much to do with willful isolation. We were cocooned on the South Coast and operating solely within the microcosm we created. We were a close-knit family, not outcasts who escaped their upbringing and never looked back. As such, we wanted to share our good fortune with friends and family, and we even took Uncle Chaim and Gary's father, Jim, on the road with us on occasions, which they loved. As I would learn in my later career as a music executive, we naively made the right moves—at least for ourselves.

Being authentic and proactive is the only way you can achieve anything worthwhile, as opposed to trying to be like someone else or to follow their path to success. Knowing that the formula worked and had yielded our best-selling album confirmed to us that we were doing something right. And it gave us a bit of leverage heading into our next tour, which, as was so often the case, was back in North America, where we commanded the largest crowds.

During the tour, we played some shows opening for Steppenwolf, Jefferson Starship, J. Geils Band, Strawbs, and Rick Wakeman, but we headlined most of the time and performed with an elaborate full-scale stage production that included a slide show synchronized to the music. We already had a reputation for switching instruments onstage, and on the *Free Hand* tour we continued the tradition. I played bass on several songs while Ray played violin. Ray played bass and horns. It was fun for us, and it was interesting for the crowd to see us present some of our songs in a different fashion. We also created medleys of songs from different albums and sometimes added new instrumentation and visual effects to keep audiences paying attention. I've always been impressed by bands that recreate their album songs note for note, but I find it more enjoyable to see groups improvising, switching up arrangements, and revising their music on the spot.

We could never have done it without John's exceptional drumming, so it's a good thing we didn't lose him for good in Quebec City. After we'd finished playing, he was still feeling energized, so he stayed at an after-party long after the rest of us returned to the hotel. It was January and way below freezing when a young couple offered him a ride back to his hotel, which he gladly accepted. During the drive, the couple started snapping at each other. As the bickering turned into shouting, John tried to tune out the dissonance, hoping the driver would remain in control of the wheel. Then the driver slammed his foot on the brake pedal, and the speeding car swerved and slid to a stop.

'Get the fuck out!' the man screamed. Assuming the driver was kicking his girlfriend out of a warm car and into the freezing winter, John opened his mouth to suggest he reconsider. But the driver had no intention of booting out his girlfriend. Irrationally, he was kicking John out in the middle of nowhere at three in the morning, and his girlfriend wasn't protesting.

There was nothing John could do. He stepped out onto streets glittering with snow and ice. The car sped off, and John had no idea where he was, so he stumbled toward what looked like a distant stoplight, unaware whether he was headed toward his hotel or away from it. Either way, he was miles from his destination, and his fingers and toes were growing numb. He saw a few cars and tried to flag them down, but the drivers either didn't see him or didn't want to pick up a potential serial killer in the middle of the night. Fearing he would freeze to death, John rambled toward the light, and in one of those incidents that's so unlikely it seems like an act of fate, a cab pulled to the curb at the traffic light and let out a passenger.

John waved his arms and screamed louder than a heavy metal vocalist. The cabbie honked back at John, then waited as our drummer stumbled to the car and back to the hotel.

I'm not sure it was our best show ever, but one of my favorite Gentle Giant concerts was in 1974 at Shrine Auditorium in Los Angeles. Everything clicked, and when I sang, I wasn't thinking about the lyrics, the melody, or even what song we were on. Everything just came out of me—perfectly timed, delivered with passion and heart, and I had nothing to do with it. I was the vessel. I practically left my body, and I could see myself performing, watching in awe like a fan in the front row. The mix was perfect, and Gary, Kerry, Ray, and John were a precision orchestra, feeding one another's impulses and playing every note with clarity and conviction. It was beautiful. At that moment, we were the best band on the planet. After two encores, the seven thousand people in the audience refused to leave. They continued to roar, and we felt obliged to go out again. We told the audience that we didn't know any more songs, but still they refused to leave. We looked at each other and John suggested we play 'In The Midnight Hour,' which we always jammed in soundcheck. It was a magical moment for the band.

It was what all musicians strive for—all the elements coalescing in harmony—to be cherished all the more since it isn't all that common. When you're a touring band, there are so many moving parts, many of which you have nothing to do with, and any of them can malfunction at any time. Sometimes they involve support staff, who can wind up being far more consequential than anyone could have guessed. After working for us for almost two years, our friend and tour manager Eric left the music business to go to law school. We were happy for him, but at the same time, we had no idea who could fill his shoes. Terry suggested we hire a woman named Rita, a buxom blonde who had been Jethro Tull's first violinist.

'That's all well and good,' I told Terry. 'But what does she know about being a tour manager?'

'Oh, don't underestimate her,' Terry replied. 'She's sharp as a knife, and she's a no-nonsense businesswoman. She'll be a great replacement for Eric. And why not give a woman a chance?'

'Sure,' I replied. 'We'll absolutely give a woman a chance.'

We brought Rita onto the team, and she proved right away that she was smart. She was well-read, a great conversationalist, and able to de-escalate stressful situations. Then we learned her flaws. She liked to party, and when she was wasted, she became less professional and more unpredictable. One night after the show, she was hanging out with a few of the crew guys in one of their rooms, drinking and smoking weed. High as fuck, she went outside to get some air, and while she was out there laughing loudly to herself, Gary walked by.

'What's going on?' he asked—a reasonable question to ask someone who's standing by herself cackling. 'What are you doing?'

Rita's face turned as red as her lipstick. 'What do you mean?' she snapped. 'What are you implying?'

'Nothing,' he said. 'I Just wondered why you're out here alone.'

'I don't like your attitude!' she said, then began a profanity-filled tirade that went from obnoxious to intolerable: 'You're fired, Gary! I don't trust you and I've had enough of your shit! You're out of the band.'

'What the fuck are you talking about?' Gary snorted. 'You can't fire me. Go lie down and sober up.'

When Gary told me about his crazy confrontation, it was definitely a red flag. Rita had seemed pretty level-headed when we brought her on board. I knew she drank too much, but I thought she had her shit together. We started watching her more closely and found out that not only did she like to party but she also had quite a healthy libido and slept with just about anyone. One night she hooked up with two guys from the road crew—at the same time. Well, good for her. This was rock'n'roll. I couldn't fire her for being horny. It wasn't my idea of time well spent, but that's me. Then she started fucking up.

When we were in Germany, a gig promoter went apeshit. 'Your fucking road manager just gave me the clap,' he shouted. She denied it, and I couldn't prove anything, though I have to admit, the accusation made me question her judgment a little more. The tipping point came when we were in Ohio. Rita hooked up with someone who said he worked for the venue. The next morning she was late to breakfast, and when she finally arrived, she lacked her usual swagger. She sat down looking as uncomfortable as someone on a terrible first date.

'I think I made a mistake,' she hesitantly said. 'I had someone in my room last night, and I think he stole some money.'

'What do you mean?' I asked.

She told me we had been paid $15,000 in cash for the gig, and that she had the money in her purse, and, in the passion of the moment, left it on her dresser. When she woke up, it was all gone, and so was the thief. That was the end of Rita's tenure as road manager for Gentle Giant.

When we finished touring *Free Hand*, we were tired of being on the road and ready to go home. So, did we take a well-deserved break to recharge our batteries? Of course not. We went right back into writing mode for our next album. We were never slowed by alcoholism, drug dependency, or the other stereotypical vices that trip up bands. Workaholism, however—that was a habit we couldn't kick.

We came up with some good songs, but no matter what we did, it felt like it was becoming harder to naturally evolve. We had spent more than five years feeding our creativity and developing the Giant into a fully formed being. And, like the Giant, we had grown up. We were no longer kids with the youthful hunger to destroy boundaries and succeed at all costs, and I think, for the first time, I started to understand why Phil had left the band. It was no longer just about us. There were greater concerns. We were all either in serious relationships or questioning our next steps in life.

While we were still heavily invested in the band, exhaustion was starting to set in as we all became more heavily invested in our personal lives. By not taking a six-month break, we accepted that we would forego further growth and continue from where we had left off with *Free Hand*. From a lyrical perspective, I didn't have anything new and revelatory to express, so I decided to create a concept album that restated what we felt we were and why we did what we did. There used to be two music papers that came out every week in England that covered us regularly, *Melody Maker* and *NME*, as well as other monthly music magazines and daily papers that were also interested in Gentle Giant.

Having to fill so much space in every issue was a challenge, and there was great competition from other titles, so the editors of these publications made their articles as scintillating as possible, often at the expense of the truth. To keep the material fresh and retain their readers, every six to twelve months the British music papers found a new scene or movement to champion, which often meant abandoning the last music movement they'd glorified. The catchphrase was to 'build them up and knock them down,' which seemed to us to be a terrible way to treat hard-working musicians. Bands were criticized not because they weren't good anymore but because they were deemed no longer fashionable.

No matter what we did, the new breed of UK journalists insisted on using words like 'self-indulgent' and of course 'pretentious,' yet they chose other, often more complimentary descriptions when writing about many of our peers whose music was equally challenging. It reeked of hypocrisy, and the crazy thing is that these publications that were writing negative reviews of our shows and taking pot-shots at us were still obliged to interview us since we were popular and their readers still wanted to know what we were up to. In that respect, our next release, *Interview*, was a big 'fuck you'—a concept album about the types of questions we were being asked by a biased, uninformed music press.

Three of the songs included brief interview snippets that we staged in the studio but which accurately reflect our interactions with the media. It's worth pointing out that we didn't hate journalism as a whole; some of the interviews we did were lively and enlightening, and sometimes we learned more about ourselves as we carried on conversations with experienced professionals. Too often, however, these interviews were with people who didn't like our music, didn't take us very seriously, and treated our exchanges as an excuse to be witty and sarcastic.

The spoken segments we included on *Interview* were meant to be both funny and indicative of our relationship with the press. When asked to describe our music, we all talked at the same time, making it impossible to make out what anyone was saying. To those kinds of journalists, our attitude was 'Just do your homework. If you don't know about us, don't ask about us.' Subliminally, however, we were making similar statements to ourselves: *Don't ask the same question. Come on, let's talk about something else.* What we were saying was, *Hey, let's do something different. Sure, we're popular, but that's not all we want to be.*

If we had an MO as Gentle Giant, it was to go against the grain and make music that was meaningful to us and didn't cater to anyone else. That's probably why we never had mainstream hit singles like Genesis or Yes. We wanted to be more like Jethro Tull and succeed or fail on our own terms. By the time we did *Interview*, we were getting tired of the people running the music business too, so the lyrics also echo our frustrations about industry protocol: 'What are your plans for the future now? / And can you say who does the writing then? / How did you get, who gave the name of the band?'

At the same time, the largely self-imposed pressure we were under was gradually causing band fatigue, though we refused to acknowledge or even recognize it. So, we kept driving ourselves nonstop, relentlessly touring, writing, and recording. We had a day off here and there, but a week off was like an unplanned vacation. I'm still proud of *Interview*, and I stand by every song, but in retrospect, I think we could have made a better record if we had taken a breather and found a new path to walk.

CHAPTER FIFTEEN

UNLIKELY CONNECTIONS

What's odd about the position we were in after *Interview* is that there were no warning signs to indicate that we needed some time away from one another. We were getting along great, we were performing as well as ever, and we felt like it would be a bad idea to stop and risk losing momentum at a time when we could see that prog-rock was becoming less popular but we still had our diehard fanbase hungering for new material from us. As grown adults, we were also aware that we had mortgages, car payments, and other bills to pay, and we needed to keep making money to support ourselves. That knowledge instilled in us an urgency to put out an album or two every year. Gentle Giant released eleven albums in ten years, plus a live album and countless BBC session recordings; by today's standards, that sort of output is unheard of.

We always made money on tour. We weren't drawing the crowd numbers we had for *Free Hand*, but we were headlining large venues and playing to our biggest fans. We played what they wanted to hear—and what we loved to perform—and everyone left happy. It didn't fuel our creative hunger or propel us to new levels of experimentation, but by that point we craved stability more than tremendous growth. And we had more than ourselves to worry about. We were all in, or wanted to be in, serious relationships, and we needed to have houses and family to come home to. John had married his girlfriend, Carole, even before he joined the band. Ray met his future wife, Barbara, in 1975, and they became inseparable right away. Gary met his wife Judy around then too. Kerry was dating his future wife, Lesley, who he married in 1976. And I was about to meet the love of my life.

Back in the early part of the twentieth century, a few years before my grandfather left Poland, his brother fled a pogrom, and that side of the family wound up in the US. Soon after the band started, my mom told Ray and me that we had a great uncle named Morris Laufer in Dallas. She always encouraged us to look him up when we were in America, if we had time.

Sure, like we ever have time, I thought. Eventually, though, we did. On the *Interview* tour, we had two or three days off in Dallas, so I said to Ray, 'Hey, let's be good Jewish boys and look up this Morris guy.'

We flipped through the phonebook and called a couple of Laufers, but nobody answered. I have no idea why we didn't get discouraged and give up. I guess it was like a challenge for us to try to find this guy, so we went to the next name in the book. I dialed, and somebody with a heavy Polish accent picked up the phone.

'We're looking for a Morris Laufer,' I said.

'Laufer? My name's Leo Laufer,' said the person on the other end. 'But I *knew* a Morris. Oh, my goodness, you must be family!'

We told him who we were and about our grandfather's brother, and he was thrilled that a couple of guys who might be family members from England were calling him out of the blue.

'Okay, I'm going to come over to where you are, and you're going to go back to my house for bagels and lox.'

'Sounds great,' I replied, not sure what I was getting us into, or what if anything we would talk about.

Leo drove to our hotel and picked us up, and we went back to his house to meet his wife, Shirley, and his youngest daughter, Lisa. After we ate, Leo told us his life story. He was a survivor of Auschwitz and had been interned in various concentration camps for five years. His situation at the camps became increasingly dire until a stroke of incredible luck saved his life. During the death march at Ohrdruf, Germany, he fled into the woods and amazingly escaped recapture. Most of his family lacked his good fortune. The Nazis killed both of his parents and seven of his siblings. He was desperate for family, and, by crazy coincidence, he knew my great uncle

Morris. They shared the same last name. Apparently, the name Laufer in Poland is like Cohen in America. Both Morris and Leo were from Lodz in Poland. They just happened to meet at a party in New York and got along well. Leo told Morris he didn't like living in New York, so after Morris returned to Dallas, he called Leo and told him there was a job there for him in the dry goods business. Morris was the best man at Leo's wedding.

At that time, I was going out with a girl from Canada named Orna. She had gone to Israel for a bit, and I planned to visit her there after the tour. I mentioned this to Leo during our conversation.

'Well,' he replied. 'If you go over there, look up my daughter, Rita. She's at Hebrew University in Jerusalem. She'll be pleased to meet someone else from our family.'

When I went to Jerusalem to see Orna, she was visiting some friends at a kibbutz, so I had some downtime. I gave Rita a call.

'Oh my God, you met my dad?!' she spouted, and then she laughed. 'I hope he didn't bore you to death with stories about the old days.'

I assured her he hadn't and told her he'd brought my brother and me the best bagels and lox we'd had in ages. We agreed to meet for lunch, and we got along well.

'This is crazy,' she said. 'When are you going back to England?'

I told her I would be in Israel for a couple more days and then, when my girlfriend went back to Canada, I was going to New York for a short while.

'Well, when you go back to New York, I've got another sister there. Her name's Sharon. You two should have a drink or something.' Rita scribbled a phone number on a scrap of paper and handed it to me.

Soon after that, I was in New York to meet our agents, Frank Barsalona and Barbara Skydel at Premier Talent, about an upcoming tour. I had a day or two off, and I had this phone number in my wallet, so I called it.

'My sister wrote me a letter and told me about meeting you in Israel,' Sharon said after I introduced myself. 'She said you guys had a nice time.'

'Look, I'd be happy to meet with you too while I'm in town, if you want to get together for a coffee …'

Sharon agreed to meet me, and she was so interesting and easy to talk to that I asked her if she wanted to have lunch the next day. She smiled and said yes. She was a social worker, and I could tell right away that she was caring and giving. We talked about art and creativity. She loved music but didn't know too much about progressive rock. I prattled on about touring and the lifestyle. She listened and didn't judge, and I began to see in her someone who could potentially be supportive of all my neuroses and help me become a better, more giving person. Of course, I wasn't thinking about those things while we were together for that brief time. I just thought about how beautiful and delightful she was and how I didn't want our date to end. I guess I was smitten almost immediately.

So many other girls I had been with were primarily concerned with themselves and having their desires fulfilled. Sharon was more fulfilled when she was helping others. At the end of the meal, I told her I would be going back to England soon but I'd like to see her again.

My relationship with Orna had become iffy, to say the least, and I could tell I would be far happier with Sharon. Orna came to England to visit me for a while, and it didn't work out—maybe in part because I had met someone I cared for more. Right after Orna and I broke up, I contacted Sharon, and we started seeing each other. We felt a cultural connection right away, and we shared many of the same values. Education was important to us. We both had the same values, and I knew right away that there was something special between us. But, most of all, I was blown away by her courage. Sharon worked for an agency that connected the Jewish community in the US to dissident Jews in the USSR called Refuseniks. There were several times when Sharon was sent as a 'student' to contact them, and whenever she went, I always wondered if one day she would 'disappear.' Thankfully, she did not.

After I returned to England, Sharon and I sent friendly letters back and forth and then started talking on the phone. I frequently thought about her when we weren't communicating, which was calming and comforting. Our friendship was growing at a slow, steady rate. Then, one day, she told me she was thinking of moving for good to Israel. My heart lurched, and I told her I'd love to see her in New York before we started our next tour. It was 1977, in the middle of a summer heatwave, and one night there was a power outage. Sharon was living in an apartment on the West Side on 85th Street, between Broadway and West End Avenue, and she didn't have air conditioning. We spoke on the phone soon after I arrived back in the city, and she told me how miserable she was, so I invited her to stay in my hotel, which had electricity and an air conditioner going at full blast. Thanks to the power outage, our relationship jumped from platonic to wildly romantic, and I convinced her not to go to Israel.

There are so many things a guy will try to do to impress a girl. Maybe it goes back to the days of the caveman clubbing the biggest sabertooth tiger to death and laying it before the feet of his favorite cavewoman. It's almost instinct—a subconscious urge to present oneself in a way that creates desirability. While I was in New York, I wanted to take Sharon out to eat food she had never tried. Being from Texas, she wasn't familiar with Indian food, which is very popular in England. I loved Indian food, so I made reservations at the best Indian restaurant in the city and ordered the hottest food on the menu. I was scooping up forkful after forkful and sweating profusely from the intense spiciness but trying not to give away how much I was suffering. Sharon tasted it and looked at me in shock.

'Can you eat this?' she asked.

I took a big gulp of water. 'Oh yeah,' I said. 'I love Indian food. We eat it all the time.'

'I can't do this, I'm sorry,' she replied. I thought for a moment she was talking about dating me, and my heart almost burst. Then I realized she was talking about the food.

'There are things on the menu that aren't as spicy,' I said, feeling foolish for thinking she would be impressed by seeing me eat unbearably spicy food. I called the waiter over, and we ordered far milder dishes—bland ones, by Indian standards—like shrimp korma and tandoori chicken, and she enjoyed the food. But what we both enjoyed far more was talking to one another, being intimate, and knowing we were building a real relationship.

When I left New York with the band, I felt glum about being away from Sharon. At the same time, I was excited to know that she wasn't moving to Israel, and that soon we would be spending a lot of time together. A year later, we were married.

I don't know if anything is 'meant to be.' I think you create your good fortune, or at least open the door for the possibility of it to benefit you. But there are so many things that had to happen for Sharon and me to find one another. If Gentle Giant hadn't been playing Dallas or staying over in the city; if Sharon's dad hadn't picked up the phone or shown an interest in meeting two young adults who might be distant family members; if Rita in Israel hadn't suggested I look up her sister in New York; if I hadn't decided to stop seeing Orna and date Sharon; if Sharon had gone to Israel as planned and not stayed in the States, where we kindled our relationship; if New York hadn't had a blackout on the night I innocently invited her to stay in my air-conditioned hotel ... there are so many intangibles, so many factors that had to come together in just the right mix for us to connect that it's sometimes hard for me to wrap my head around them.

A lot of guys in bands wouldn't care about meeting possible relatives while they were on the road, and they wouldn't go out of their way to look them up, even if their mother wanted them to. Who knows? Maybe that's why I was rewarded in such a wonderful way. Ray and I weren't wild rockers. We were family guys who loved music. In that respect, we set the entire series of events into action. Unfortunately, Morris Laufer had died about eighteen years before we met Leo, but meeting Leo was a gift. Even if the appointment didn't create a circuitous path to my wonderful marriage, we would have chalked up the encounter as a big win. He may not have been a blood relative, but Leo was a delightful man with an amazing family. And now we *are* related.

During the tour to support *Interview*, Gentle Giant recorded three concerts—September 25 in Munich, October 5 in Paris, and October 7 in Brussels—and used the best takes for the live album, *Playing The Fool: The Official Live*. (We also recorded a show in Düsseldorf, but those recordings didn't sound as good, so they were never used.) We didn't have to rehearse extensively for the shows or focus any harder than usual because we were always an incredibly consistent and solid live band. Maybe someone hit a stray note once in a while, but rarely anything the audience would notice unless there was an equipment malfunction, which occasionally happened, and which we usually dismissed with a joke.

The main reason we did the live album was because we hadn't done one yet, and our live shows were more improvisational than our albums. The records were meticulous and sonically pristine. The live show was more playful, and we wanted to demonstrate that side of the band to those who hadn't experienced it. Also, doing a concert record seemed like a good opportunity to make money without writing new material, since other bands at that time were having great success with live albums. *Frampton Comes Alive!* was the best-selling album of 1976, and *Wings Over America* did extremely well. *Shit,* we thought, *if they can do it…*

Playing The Fool did very well for us and gave us more time to formulate our next move. We toured the album and hired one of Ray's school friends, Jeff Altman, to spruce up our stage show with video footage from backscreen projectors and other eye candy. Usually, hiring lighting, props, and effects for a live show is laborious and expensive and involves working with big corporations. With Jeff's help, we simplified the process to a grassroots level that was infinitely more affordable and enjoyable. For the tour, we hired four more friends from Portsmouth, which was great because it was fun to be with people we knew, and we paid them well. Somehow, they were able to find more friends and fans who helped them build our stage sets. Ray or I would come up with something, and we'd say, 'Okay, now go build it.' And they did. They made a neon Gentle Giant sign and even a neon violin for Ray, but it never worked—the neon interfered with the electric pickup, and so when we plugged in Ray's violin, it buzzed and made horrible feedback. We had to remove the neon and just have the sign behind us, which also made the violin hum a little, but we were able to deal with that.

When we finished touring the live album, we all did some soul-searching to decide what we wanted to do for the next era of the band. It was the best worst thing to happen. Bands and music genres move on. The live album was the stamp of where Gentle Giant were, but the future was unwritten and uncertain. Seeing other bands who had been on our level at one point, then absolutely blew up—especially Genesis—affected us in a profound way. It was a major wake-up call. If we wanted to remain successful, we needed to do something different. That's the point we started from when writing our ninth studio album, *The Missing Piece*. Suddenly, we were under a new kind of pressure.

Maybe it came from me, the music industry, or the other guys in the band. Maybe it was all three. Bands of our ilk were either going downhill and breaking up or having hit singles and becoming bigger than ever. Radio had changed, and if you weren't willing to change with it, you were history. We were fine with some changes if they came without pressure and on our terms. At the same time, we felt the evil presence of punk breathing down our necks. In the UK, we had entered the era of the Sex Pistols, the Damned, and The Vibrators, and they were metaphorically howling, 'Hey, all you old farts get the fuck out of our way before you get run over!'

Almost overnight, we were competing for chart position with kids who were wild in the press, swore on TV, and were useless live. At one point, we visited our good friend Chris Thomas in the studio. He had worked with us as a Moog programmer back in the day and went on to become a respected producer who worked with Pink Floyd, Procol Harum, Roxy Music, and tons of other big bands. Malcolm McLaren had hired him to work on singles with the Pistols, and he subsequently ended up in the studio with The Clash.

'Come hang out with me and see this band,' he said to us one day. 'Everyone's talking about them.'

We went over and watched The Clash in the studio, and they were so fucking awful that we were amazed that they had generated such a huge buzz. They couldn't play three chords without having to stop.

'Chris, are these guys really going to make an album?' we asked, incredulity dripping from every word.

'Look,' he replied. 'This is going to be big.'

And it was. And somehow those guys learned to play together and became a damn good band that made some interesting, innovative albums. At the time, however, we were completely confused by what we were seeing, and I think they were strung out when they were playing together. There was a dog in the studio with them, and it took a shit on Joe Strummer's boots while he was playing. He didn't notice. We were looking at each other with amazement, cracking up as we watched this group trying to play a three-chord song and failing miserably. Of course, they had the last laugh. Punk was taking over in England, and bands like Gentle Giant and Jethro Tull were being shooed away as ancient and unworthy.

Disenchanted by what was happening in England, I spent lots of time long-distance commuting to New York for weekends with Sharon, who I knew would be my future wife. If it hadn't been for Laker Airways, I think I'd still be paying off the credit card debts.

When Gentle Giant were together, we realized we needed to write an album that was more commercially palatable and provided us with an opportunity for some strong radio play. We never worried about sacrificing our integrity, since integrity shone through everything we did. The real challenge was to combine that authenticity with a new songwriting approach that took us outside of our sphere of influence.

Since I was now the band's manager as well as the frontman, I was wearing two hats, and no one looks good with two hats on their head. I'm not sure if I wore one better than the other; maybe I lost out on both. I became more aware of where Gentle Giant were positioned business-wise, instead of just musically, and I strategized about what we needed to do to modify our sound for a new era. It was a necessary evil, and I went into it with Ray's assistance and support. At the end of the day, I was the captain of the ship, he was my first mate, and it remained that way until the end of the band.

Without changing our core sound, we strived to write hits. We had released numerous hits when we were Simon Dupree & The Big Sound, so we certainly know how to write and play songs that were simple and melodic. We looked at Genesis as the standard bearers of what we wanted to do without being sonically influenced by them. They had recorded their 1976 album *Wind & Wuthering* at Relight Studios in Hilvarenbeek, Holland, so we went there for three weeks to work on *The Missing Piece.* I thought it would be like a vacation in the bucolic countryside and that the new location would be inspiring. What a mistake. It was fucking awful. Never mind that we were always comfortable recording in London and liked being near home, Hilvarenbeek was in the middle of a giant field in southern Holland. When we weren't recording, we were looking at cows and watching people occasionally pass by on bicycles.

When we finished in the studio, we went back to the hotel, where there were no amenities—not even a working TV. We still enjoyed being together, just not all day, every day in the middle of nowhere, with nothing new to talk about. We were away from our loved ones. We were lonely. It was worse than being on tour in the French countryside. After John had recorded his drums, he had nothing to do, so he'd start drinking. He was still a great player, but he became an annoying drunk.

Ray and I stayed sober, so we kept working on music even when John and Gary were done. Staying in the studio was preferable to doing anything else in that damn town. I started to resent that by midday we were the only ones in the band doing anything, and my aggravation and anxiety went straight to my gut. I needed an ulcer flare-up like I needed my larynx ripped out. Everyone was relieved when Ray and I told them we were done with Holland. We packed up our shit and returned to Advision in London to finish up.

We emerged from the studio with an album that met all of our objectives and that we really liked. It was straightforward, only mildly experimental, and full of ebullient choruses and cool rhythms. Capitol loved it and planned a campaign to work the singles 'I'm Turning Around,' 'Two Weeks In Spain,' and 'Mountain Time' to radio. They shot videos, set up promotions, and prepared for the record to be a big hit. They were wrong. *The Missing Piece* came out in August 1977 in the UK and September in North America. No matter what they did, they couldn't get the music on the radio, and the only ones who heard it were our devoted fans, some of whom were disappointed that it wasn't *The Power And The Glory* or *Free Hand*, though those of them who realized we wouldn't ever make the same record twice praised the strong songwriting and catchy hooks.

Maybe we never had a chance at having a Genesis-style breakthrough. The name Gentle Giant provoked a negative knee-jerk reaction from radio programmers. They wouldn't even give our records a spin because they had already decided they would be too far out of step with the music of the moment. We toured like usual, but it wasn't the same. Our fans loved the shows, but many of them sat down when we played the new songs. We were now a specialty band with a devoted crowd. At least they were devoted, which enabled us to sell enough tickets to fill the seats—and which was a godsend, since the rest of the world was still revolving around punk rock and the energy, rebellion, and imagery that abounded in that era. Everything now was about attitude, and attitude is something that's blithely marketed, not painstakingly composed.

We started the *Missing Piece* tour with headline shows in Europe. During that cycle, the hanging neon Gentle Giant head had gotten beaten up, and the circuitry broke. Fortunately, our team was able to fix the electrical problems and bang out the dents so that the Giant again glowed high above the stage. We also convinced a roadie to wear a rubber Giant mask and stagger around the stage carrying a liquor jug. The shows were fun to play, but the ones in England were more sparsely attended than our previous shows. Some of that was due to the punk explosion, yet it felt personal, and it reminded us, yet again, that even though we were from Portsmouth, we received a better reception from the rest of Europe than we did from our home country. Those dates would end up being the last UK shows we ever did.

For the US leg of the tour, we invited Dr. Feelgood along, hoping they would help endear us to some of the mainstream punk crowd. That backfired, and when our fans heard Dr. Feelgood's primitive, sloppy rhythm and atonal vocals, they booed them as viciously as Black Sabbath's fans had jeered us. So, Dr. Feelgood dropped off the bill, and now we had to contend with some of *their* disgruntled fans, who heckled us onstage. You expect that as an opener, not as a headliner. It never feels good.

We had hoped that US radio would pick up on our latest single, 'Two Weeks In Spain,' while we were on tour. Adventurous American rock bands including Styx and Kansas were ripping off our songs left and right (violins and all), and they were all over the radio and on the verge of commercial breakthroughs. That was both frustrating and motivational. Naively, perhaps, we figured that if they could break the mold, so could we. It wasn't to be.

Our lack of breakout success didn't brighten my mood, and neither did the new wrinkles that complicated our traveling protocol when we toured *The*

Missing Piece. I had grown close to Sharon, Ray was in love with Barbara, and we both wanted them on the road with us. We knew full well that, for rock bands, bringing wives or girlfriends on tour is frowned upon almost as strongly as taking a shit on the bus (which you never do). It almost always creates friction. We already had a rule that it was okay for wives and girlfriends to come out on the road for a few days at a time, but extended stretches were a problem because they inevitably became a distraction. Everybody in the band has a job that requires being on tour. That's hard for wives and girlfriends, but touring is a major part of the job, and it's not *their* job to be there as well, let alone to inject themselves into the creative process. Ever since the days of Simon Dupree, I'd seen it happen so many times, but I figured we weren't like other bands, so it wouldn't be a problem.

It wasn't long before Barbara started whispering to Ray. She was a big fan of Bowie and T. Rex, and she thought we could take a fashion tip or two from them. I loved Ray and was thrilled he'd met someone he cared about. At the same time, Ray and I had always been a team. We confided in one another before anyone else, and now that paradigm had shifted for us both.

I wasn't exactly jealous, but I was mildly annoyed that my little brother's new girlfriend thought we had an image problem. I guess I was also a little taken aback that we were no longer Team Shulman 24/7. As much as I loved Sharon, we were more independent than Ray and Barbara. Sharon had a job in New York, so she was only on the road with me for short stints since she had priorities of her own. Barbara was a hairdresser with a flexible schedule, so she could take two or three weeks off at a time to go on the road, and that altered the balance of how Ray and I had functioned for almost twenty years. Ray was so enamored with Barbara that she became instrumental in influencing his taste and lifestyle, and she was even credited as the sleeve designer for *Giant For A Day!*

At the same time, I have to give Barbara credit for introducing Ray and me to the Granati Brothers, friends of hers from Beaver Falls, Pennsylvania, where she grew up. They were a Hall & Oates-style R&B band made up of four brothers and a cousin. Barbara made plans to see them with Ray in Pittsburgh, and he cajoled me into coming along. I loved them. They sounded great and looked amazing. With my new manager/businessman/industry advisor hat on, I approached them after the show and said, 'I bet I can get you guys a deal.'

'Really?' said one of the brothers. 'That would be incredible. We've been wanting to put a record out for a long time. But we don't know that many people.'

I talked to an A&R man I knew at A&M named John Anthony, and he liked the Granatis as well. They looked punky but played power pop, so they could fit in well with Joe Jackson or Elvis Costello. A&M signed them to a very good deal. I produced their album with Ray and got them a management deal with Premier Talent agents Barbara Skydel and Frank Barsalona. We were able to get them on tour with Van Halen—you can't do better than that for a new band.

This was a real wake-up call for me. Even if I wasn't in a band, I could still be involved in music.

With the glow of the Granatis experience still in my rear-view mirror, Sharon and I decided to get married in grand style. June 18, 1978, is a day the Dallas Jewish community will never forget. We had almost four hundred guests at the wedding, many of whom were recent Russian immigrants Leo and his wife Shirley had helped find jobs for—much the way Morris had helped Leo years before. I didn't have a clue who was attending. Sharon's parents took a cue from their daughter and got involved with the Russian Jewish community as well. Ray was my best man, and he came with Barbara, our mother, and my sister, Eve. Aunt Rose, my mother's sister from San Francisco, flew in for the festivities, as did Aunt Frieda, my father's half-sister from Glasgow. I thought the Granati Brothers might get a kick out of attending a conservative Jewish wedding, so I invited them as well, and they were happy to be there. For me, there were no panic attacks or second-guessing this time, since I knew I had found my lifelong partner. I was delighted to have my family there alongside all the guests I didn't even know, but as long as Sharon was there to hold me, smile with me, and celebrate our marriage, everything was right with the world.

During the ceremony, I looked out at the gathering and felt kind of like I was at a gig, which isn't far from what it turned into. The music began after the wedding when we all danced the Hora, and then the band we hired started playing traditional Klezmer/Jewish songs and the crowd started dancing. That's when Ray came up to me and said, 'Let's take over.' Brilliant idea! The Granati Brothers were fine instrumentalists, so I walked up to the leader of the Klezmer band and asked if we could play a song or two. It turned into a full-scale show.

We played 'No Woman, No Cry' by Bob Marley, then launched into some Rolling Stones songs and finished with 'Hey Jude.' Everyone in the audience joined in at the end: 'Na, na, na, na, na, na, na / Na, na, na, na / Hey Jude.' Even the Russian Jews, who didn't speak a word of English, figured out the lyrics. It was one of the best gigs I've ever played.

GIANT STEPS

CHAPTER SIXTEEN

THE END OF AN ERA

If Genesis's commercial template inspired *The Missing Piece*, our next album, *Giant For A Day!*, was a product of the supernova success of musically challenging radio rock bands. Our old peers Yes, Pink Floyd, King Crimson, and ELP had broken through, as had the aforementioned American bands inspired by Gentle Giant, to say nothing of Rush. As the band's manager, it was an easy call.

'We'll do an album that's even catchier and more direct than *The Missing Piece*,' I said one day. 'No more *Pretentious—For The Sake Of It*,' I added, referencing the title of our compilation album. Through the eyes of a future record label exec, it made sense. Everyone realized prog rock, in its purest form, was a withering beast, and only a select group of serious musicians, math nerds, and nonconformists were still clinging to genre. So, we wrote a pure pop-rock album and abandoned our former reliance on contrapuntal arrangements, convoluted rhythms, and folk sensibilities. Each of the ten songs was good. I'll never deny that. They were creative and catchy. They were well-played, and the production sounded good. They just weren't Gentle Giant. I had let my role as manager interfere with my innate musical instincts.

The high level of commerciality we injected into the songs couldn't turn us into a successful pop band because we were never that. It was the first time we wrote an album that wasn't one hundred percent us, and no matter how much we worked on the material, it was destined to flop. When you *try* to do something as a band instead of playing what comes naturally, you're doomed to fail. It was a catch-22. We couldn't be what we once were because it was no longer 1974. At the same time, we couldn't become a platinum rock group. We could still get good gigs at three-thousand-seat venues, but the days of six-thousand and ten-thousand-seaters seemed to be behind us. We were desperate to get that back, but we couldn't. As much as we wanted to turn our career back around by going with the status quo, it wasn't going to happen.

We gave the hit formula thing a shot; it didn't work, but I don't regret making *Giant For A Day!* As an artist, looking back with regret is one of the worst things you can do. Nothing we did was a misstep or even a compromise. They were efforts to reach a certain goal. We had a valid reason for making every song on the album, and if some of those moves turned out to be missteps, that was okay. If the reason we did something was wrong, we had to accept it and find our way again. But we couldn't regret anything.

Our fans hated *Giant For A Day!* We didn't tour the album, which was ultimately important for our personal growth. Instead, we spent the time reassessing our priorities as a band and as individuals. For most of 1978, all of 1979, and the beginning of 1980, Gentle Giant were out of the public eye. We were offered tours of Europe, but we refused to play any shows. We received invitations to play big summer festivals, but we said no. We spent the bulk of our time with our loved ones, trying to steal back lost time.

The years we went without writing anything new for Gentle Giant—which would have previously been unthinkable—reinvigorated our love for the band. We all wanted to make another album, and this time the goal would be to create great rock songs, whether they were commercially marketable or too experimental for widespread appeal. We wanted to go back to making an album solely for ourselves, and we wanted to make it great. We didn't care about critical acclaim or mainstream popularity—we wanted to be Gentle Giant entirely on our own terms, at least one more time. We could smell the bloom of the rose, and it was exciting, inspiring, and a little scary. We wanted to turn the bloom into a full, glorious rosebush and create the roots to sprout a full garden, thorns and all. We wanted to start fresh—again.

When enough time had passed, I met with our guy at Capitol, Rupert.

'We have an option with you, so I wanted to ask you when we can start the next album,' I said.

'We're not going forward,' he responded without a pause. 'We're going to drop you.'

That was a slap in the face. I left feeling dejected, but then I got angry and determined. I returned to the band. 'Okay, fuck Capitol. Let's find another label and get enough funding to make a new album.'

Everyone was on board and excited to get started. I got a haircut, shaved, donned my sharpest manager outfit, and flew to Los Angeles. I spent six weeks hunting down a new deal, and by the time I met with Columbia, it didn't take too much convincing for them to sign us. They knew we had been dropped, which is never good, but we still had a strong following, not to mention fans who hadn't seen us for years and were hungering for another tour. Columbia knew that we would be profitable and that any money made from the album would be gravy. They gave us a sizable advance, and I convinced my bandmates that we should make the new album in LA, which I had gotten to know and enjoy during the time I spent shopping for a new deal there.

Ray, Kerry, Gary, and John met me at LAX with their wives and girlfriends, and we spent quality time exploring the city, visiting restaurants, and watching shows—partly to reconnect as a family but also to soak in some of the vibrant energy of the city with the hope it might cast some sunshine on the album. On some level, I wanted the record to mark a full circle and to summon the kind of excitement, impulsiveness, and determination we had put into albums like *Octopus* and *Free Hand*.

I called Geoff Emerick, who was there with us when we started our adventure as Simon Dupree & The Big Sound, and asked him if he would be the engineer. He said he'd love to, so I flew him to LA. It was the perfect way to bookend our recording career. Geoff was in the room when, as teenagers, Ray and I auditioned for a slot on the Parlophone roster, and he was strongly in favor of signing us. Now, he would be there to end our legacy. We didn't know for sure that *Civilian* would be the last *Gentle Giant* album, but we had some idea. We wrote and recorded the album at the legendary Sound City in Van Nuys and did overdubs at Bijou Studio in Los Angeles. I enjoyed the process immensely, and I felt like Gentle Giant had rediscovered our path. Ray, who was always full of creativity, also felt invigorated. Gary wasn't a big fan of LA, but as long as he was working on music he loved, he would have been content practically anywhere. Not so Kerry and John. For them, LA was too bright, warm, fast-paced, and fashion-focused, and they hated it. They felt uncomfortable and out of their element. John hit the bottle to cope with his unhappiness, while Kerry just moped. But they were professionals, so they coped. Any time either of them complained, I reminded them of our misadventures recording *The Missing Piece* in Holland, and they stopped griping.

Having developed a solid understanding of the music business at major labels, I knew we had to have some kind of 'in' with someone in radio to kickstart the airplay. Once that happened, the label would pour more money into promotion and marketing. I knew a guy named Lee Abrams, who was a consultant to seventy-five or so AOR radio stations. He was a big progressive-music fan, and he loved Gentle Giant. He knew what radio was looking for in these uncertain times, and he felt like he could help us make music that was just hooky enough to entice radio. Since Lee was a friend, we bounced ideas off him to find a way to make a record that was completely us but would be accessible to the masses. His greatest piece of advice was to approach the music from many angles but keep the tempos constant, which made it easier to listen to from front to back. He didn't come into the studio the whole time, so he was more of an adviser than anything else, but there's no question that he helped guide the sound and feel of the album—and even less question that he deserved credit in the liner notes.

We produced *Civilian* ourselves, and we were thrilled with every track. The album gave Gentle Giant a facelift. We sounded younger, more alive, and more contemporary. It's not at all prog-y, so it's very different from *Octopus* or even *Free Hand*, but, like those records, it rocked like hell, and it proved that we could write great songs in a format that was mainstream and accessible while retaining our essence. Even though it was a more difficult album to write and record—partly because we were perfectionists about every note we played, and partly because half the band hated LA—

we nailed our every objective. In that respect, the album had the same weird atmosphere as *In A Glass House*. The two were milestones: The former was all about Phil leaving, and the latter, while I didn't know it at the time, was the band's last gasp.

That said, when Columbia released *Civilian* on March 3, 1980, radio wouldn't touch it. Seeing Lee Abrams's name in the credits, program directors thought it would look like nepotism if they played it. It was almost as if we'd subconsciously signed our own death sentence, as we did in a different way with Simon Dupree. None of us wanted *Civilian* to fail, and everyone at Columbia liked it almost as much as we did, but because of our connection with Lee, it was dead in the water as far as radio play was concerned. We were fucked.

In some ways, this was the best thing that could happen. There's a saying that it's better to die quickly than wither on the vine, and we were at a point, creatively, personally, and artistically, where it was time to say goodbye to Gentle Giant. *Civilian* was much better than our previous two records, and many critics have theorized that had we continued in that vein, *Civilian* would have been the springboard for Gentle Giant to evolve further and possibly break through with a mass audience. As they say, hindsight is 20/20.

Before the album was released, we had lined up a big tour of North America. Looking at the scheduled dates and the travel arrangements made my heart race and my stomach ache. I took that as a sign. I was living in LA with Sharon and our baby daughter Yael, who was born in 1979 in Culver City, and I wanted to be with them as much as possible. I had flashbacks to my dad being absent most nights of my childhood. I loved my father, but his late-night gigs robbed us of years of precious time, and I refused to subject my kids to that. I think I had started to feel quite similar to the way Phil had when he left Gentle Giant. Back then, I dismissed his needs and reacted with youthful anger, which I later regretted. We probably could have handled that whole period of our lives better, but we were all young and stubborn. I'm so glad we eventually mended fences.

There were other signs that touring was a bad idea. We were selling fewer records than ever, and I didn't want Gentle Giant to become a parody. I didn't want to turn into a band that only played the old stuff on tour. The thought of regurgitating the same music that to us already belonged in the history books would be soul destroying.

During a band meeting before the tour, I presented my thoughts.

'Guys, this is as far as I want to go,' I said. 'After this album, I'm done touring. As far as I'm concerned, it's up to you to do what you want with the band.'

'I'm done, too,' said Kerry, whose daughter was also born in 1979. Ray wasn't about to go on with the band without me. I'm not sure Gary and John agreed with our decision, but what could they do? In 2008, Gary formed the band Three Friends with Kerry (who left shortly after) and Malcolm Mortimore to play Gentle Giant songs, replacing Ray's violin parts with synthesizers and samplers. Ray and I never took the stage again.

Knowing that our days were numbered was a relief. We decided to launch a triumphant farewell tour that would bring our best music to our fans one final time. We had been off the road for two-and-a-half years when we launched our last tour of North America. At that point, our popularity in the UK was at an all-time low, and due to the hostility we received from the media there, we decided not to play anywhere in England. In the end, I also refused to play anywhere else in Europe (as much as they wanted us to), since I couldn't bear the idea of being that far away from my family; again, I thought of Phil and the tough decision he made after *Octopus*.

We launched the *Civilian* tour on May 7, in Rensselaer, New York, at a club called the Hullabaloo. It was a smallish place but we sold it out and the vibe was great. At one point, I forgot the lyrics, and at another, the band flubbed an instrumental line. In the old days of the band, such missteps would have caused lengthy backstage reprimands, but we just laughed it off and the crowd went along with it. When we left the stage, the fans cheered so loudly that we felt obliged to come back. This happened numerous times, and we wound up playing several encores. It was a great way to start the final hurrah.

A few days later, we were back in Montreal, one of the first North American cities to champion Gentle Giant. We played two shows at The Theatre St-Denis, which held about fifteen hundred people, so we had a total crowd that day of three thousand fans, which wasn't bad. Everything was copacetic until the night after a show in Buffalo, which—if this was a Hollywood biopic—could have foreshadowed the final days for the Giant. The driver of the truck carrying much of our gear to our next show in Upper Darby, Pennsylvania, got into an accident on the New York State Thruway near Syracuse and the truck flipped over. He was uninjured, and most of our gear was fine. The only casualty was our neon Giant head, which was completely crushed.

Worse for us, personally, was a stomach-churning incident in Miami. On the day of the gig, we stopped for burgers at a fast-food joint. By the time we got to the venue, my stomach was roiling. I dismissed it as pre-concert jitters, intuitively feeling that this might be the last great run for us, so I wanted to make it great. As we took the stage, a wave of nausea washed over me, and I began sweating profusely. I struggled to make it through my vocal parts, but I somehow succeeded before running off—sometimes mid-song—to vomit into a trashcan at the side of the stage. John was anchored in place behind his drums and couldn't leave the stage, so he expertly and repeatedly puked into a bucket throughout the show without missing a beat. Bravo.

We ended the *Civilian* tour on June 16 with two sets at the venerable venue the Roxy in West Hollywood. Knowing it was our last American show, our fans were lined up down the block. By the time everyone had gotten in, there were a couple of thousand people there, which was likely a fire hazard, but it was a hell of a way to end the tour. During the second set, we tossed Gentle Giant masks and T-shirts into the crowd and staged an impromptu awards ceremony. We honored everyone in the crew by giving them makeshift awards: a gold-plated food mixer trophy for our soundman, a gold-painted lightbulb for our lighting guy. We were playing up a storm but enjoying the silliness, and we finished the set laughing.

The next day, in a very emotionally resistant English way, everyone said farewell. There were no tears, no long goodbyes. We were completely at peace with our decision as we parted ways to go to our respective homes. Sharon and I stayed in LA for a little while. We were in good shape financially because the farewell concerts had sold well, and there was money left over from the Columbia deal. We were offered tours in Europe, but we turned them down and gave the Giant a dignified burial. I got offers from labels and groups for production jobs, and some musicians approached me about singing with them, but I didn't follow up on any of the invites. My life as a recording and touring artist was over, and I had made peace with that.

Gentle Giant never reunited. We went out on such a high note that we didn't want to do anything to jeopardize our grand finale. We knew there was still demand for our music, and I somehow knew we would re-release our albums at the right time and comb through all of the concerts we had recorded for special editions and box sets. We never could have known that a wide range of future heroes from the emerging hip-hop world and young musicians viewing the band on YouTube would discover and be inspired by Gentle Giant, or that many of them would sample snippets of our songs for their own singles. If I had a crystal ball, I would have been elated to know the spirit of our music would be reborn, decades down the road, and our stamp on the music scene would be deep and clear.

At the time, it was beyond satisfying to say, *We're done. That's all you're going to get from us. Enjoy what we've put out into the world and maybe use it to enrich your own lives and careers.* It was the best move we could have made. Our final chapter was fantastic, but now the story was over. The book was closed, and we were determined not to reopen it.

It's hard to believe that Ray and I would never play together after that. Maybe we had said all we could as musicians together. Of course, Ray wasn't close to being done with music. Like me, he went on to even greater success in the music business. He became a renowned producer, discovering and working with The Sugarcubes/Björk, The Sundays, and Echo & The Bunnymen. He then created music for video games such as *Privateer* and *Azrael's Tear*, and, as a tech wizard, he became the 'go-to' music remixer & producer for 5.1 and Dolby Atmos remixes for bands including Queen, Jethro Tull, Steven Wilson, Gentle Giant, and many more. We celebrated one another's achievements as if they were our own and we remained close as brothers until the day he died.

GIANT STEPS

PART THREE

FINDING A NEW PATH

CHAPTER SEVENTEEN
PLAYING THE GAME

Sharon and I didn't stay in LA for long after Gentle Giant came to an end. Yael was now almost two years old, so we thought it would be a good idea to be close to Sharon's family. We moved to Dallas, where her parents were delighted to help take care of their first grandchild. By then, the euphoria of Gentle Giant's grand curtain call had faded, and I started wondering what was next. There was no way I wanted to continue as a working musician. I had been there and done that with the best players in the world. But I had no Plan B. Having managed the band, I figured I might be qualified for a job at a record label or management office. I just wasn't sure if I wanted to do something like that so soon after ending my career as a musician. It was a difficult time, during which I made countless calls to Ray, who was also searching for a new role in life. I also phoned various industry contacts I had made at labels Gentle Giant had been signed with or bumped into on tour.

I was sitting on the couch reading the newspaper when I got a call from Dan Young, who I knew from Gentle Giant's time at Chrysalis. He knew I had managed the band and how hard I had worked with different departments at the label to make sure we received as much support as possible. He told me that he had been hired as the international manager of PolyGram Records and asked if I might be interested in a job at the company.

Over time, PolyGram would become a powerhouse label for pop, rock, singer-songwriters, and metal bands, but back then it was a strange new hybrid partnership between the Dutch company Phonogram and the German corporation Polydor; they were trying to make inroads in America, but they lacked the leadership, so Dan and his co-workers were looking for people who were knowledgeable about both music and the business of music to guide the label's different departments.

I told Dan this sounded like a good opportunity, and he had me call Jerry Jaffe, the head of the new rock department, who had been working with bands since 1974. Jerry was receptive to my call, partly since Dan had recommended me, but also because I knew bigtime radio consultant Lee Abrams (who had worked with me on *Civilian*) and radio consultant/ former KCFR music director Jeff Pollack, both of whom were Gentle Giant fans.

Jerry felt that since I had worked as a band manager, fronted two bands, and negotiated deals with agents, managers, and several labels, I had a de facto master's degree in music business, even though I had never officially worked for a record company. He asked if I would fly to New York for a meeting. We discussed how my experience had exposed me to the business of music as well as the music business, which meant I could relate to signed musicians better than people who had never played in bands and work with them to maximize their public exposure without them feeling like we were from different worlds.

Jerry offered me a job, and in 1982 I relocated to New York. That was the moment when Derek Shulman, for better or worse, was reborn in a whole different light. I was now a record executive—the director of the rock radio promotions department, which, on some level was ironic and a bit absurd. I had gone from being the singer in an experimental band who didn't like dealing directly with most of the people at record labels to taking a job for the very machine against which I had raged. I was like Luke Skywalker becoming Darth Vader. I was going to the dark side. It was the most bizarre period of my life, but one that would lead to many great discoveries in music, as well as a life of self-sufficiency—something that was never a guarantee as a touring artist. If I could go back now, I wouldn't change a thing.

I got a three-month rental deal on an apartment on the Upper West

Side and lived there while Sharon stayed in Dallas. I felt awkward about abandoning her, but I knew that once I had established myself at PolyGram, she could move to New York City as well.

I started at PolyGram with a salary of $40,000 a year, which wasn't a lot of money, but at least it was steady work, and there was room to grow. On my first day in the office, Jerry introduced me to the other people in the department, and right away I realized there was a hierarchy in the company. Some of my co-workers were angry that I had jumped the line or felt threatened that I was in an executive role and had the power to overrule them and even let them go. They had a point. I hadn't paid my dues. I wasn't just inexperienced—I was clueless about standard protocol at the company and how to do my job in a traditional way. So, over time, I made up my own rules.

I had only worked on my own music before, and I found that it was difficult to promote other people's music with a team of staffers from different departments, all of whom had their own agendas. Even the people in my department had their own motivations. Some loved radio promotion and wanted to be in the department for life, others saw it as a means to an end—the beginning of a trek up the corporate ladder. And a third group of employees were celebrity gazers who felt alive when they rubbed elbows with famous folk.

I was introduced to everyone in the rock department, and I smiled and joked around with them, but I felt like I was being judged as soon as our eyes met. I couldn't tell if *they* thought I was an imposter or if *I* was the one who felt like a fake. By the end of the day, I felt ill. I was way over my head and would rapidly sink as everyone realized I didn't know how to run a fucking rock radio promotion department.

When I got home after my first day, I called Sharon. 'I've got to get out of this. I need to quit tomorrow. I'm a musician, not a salesman.'

Always the voice of reason and still the rock that keeps me anchored, Sharon talked me down from quitting and reminded me why Jerry had hired me. He didn't want someone who would go through the motions, he wanted someone with strong instincts who would shake things up and improve the system. She pointed out that I had steered Gentle Giant through rough business waters time and again and insisted that all I needed was a little bit of self-confidence to make PolyGram's rock radio department shine. 'They hired you because they want *you*.'

I went back on the second day and started going over the acts on our roster with the rest of the team. Some of the guys were cool with me from the start, and a couple even knew about Gentle Giant. But the more offices I visited in the sales and marketing departments, the more I realized that the music business wasn't about music, it was about business. To a lot of these people, the records weren't works of art, they were *product*. Seeing how many people came from that school of thought was unnerving.

I got along much better with people who had tried to make it in music. Maybe they had been in bands or worked as stage techs or radio DJs, but for one reason or another, they couldn't make a living that way. But they still loved music and wanted to stay in that world, so they got jobs at record companies. I came from the other direction, and now I was determined to learn how to navigate the *business* of music and put as much emphasis on the music and musicians as possible.

That approach has been immensely beneficial to me and the companies I've worked for, and it has allowed me to see the business world through a different lens than my contemporaries. It has enabled me to approach my work with a vision that others lacked because they didn't have my experience outside of the label world, and it made me a hell of an A&R man and record guy.

Far more irksome to me than the people who just saw music in terms of dollars and cents were the ones who weren't especially passionate about music *or* business. They just wanted to enjoy the rock'n'roll lifestyle. Working in music was an open invitation for them to hang out with celebrities, indulge in drugs and alcohol, chase women (even if they were married), party all night, and run up the company credit card (sometimes with discreet payments to dealers and escort services). As long as they came to work every day and got the job done—often with the aid of recreational stimulants—conventional wisdom dictated that they could be as irresponsible, immature, and self-destructive as they wanted to be. And a lot of the label guys I met who lived fast did, indeed, die young.

That was a rude awakening to me. In the same way as when Gentle Giant toured with Black Sabbath and others of their ilk, I was a fish out of water compared to the coke-sniffing industry execs and their extra-curricular pursuits. Or, at least, I was swimming in a different pond. Soon, I would understand that all the hedonism and indulgence was analogous to power. It seemed like the president of each department at the label sat behind a big desk and reveled in the importance of the title on their door. I wanted to learn what to do and what *not* to do, and I quickly figured out that the best thing to do when you don't know anything is to shut the hell up and listen.

One of my first realizations was that if these were the kinds of people promoting albums on big labels, no wonder Gentle Giant never reached the mainstream. No matter how many times we were told we were a label priority, we weren't an easy band to promote, and these kinds of people wanted easy projects that reflected well on their balance sheets. For us to be a major priority at places like this would have required employees who were disciplined, persistent, and dedicated. They would have had to forge and foster strong relationships with people and pull favors to get them to play our challenging music. When I realized that, I made a mental note that when I reached a position where I was calling the shots, I would make sure I worked with people who shared my goals and vision and weren't just working for a paycheck.

I had to learn the ins and outs of the promotion game and how to make it work without selling my soul or becoming a drug addict. I was determined to use my skills as an artist and businessman to turn PolyGram into one of the top rock labels. To that end, I watched everything that went on around me, assessed the information I was privy to, applied whatever knowledge would benefit me, and discarded or avoided anything that might be harmful or problematic. I was a fast learner, so I knew it would just be a matter of time before I could start making some big decisions and turning things around. But first, I had to follow orders.

Since I was English, I was immediately assigned to promote bands from the UK. Jerry Jaffe figured my accent might encourage radio stations to give The Jam some love. I wasn't particularly a fan, but I feigned enthusiasm and pushed their 1982 album *The Gift* to music programmers across the country. When the band came to New York, I had to babysit them and take them to radio station interviews, which was unpleasant, since Paul Weller was difficult, to say the least, and his father/manager was even worse. I don't know if he knew I came from the same side of the industry as he did, or if he knew Gentle Giant. If he did, he certainly didn't mention it, and he never talked about anything but himself. I doubt he even acknowledged my English accent. He was more obsessed with complaining about why his latest single wasn't #1 and why we weren't spit-polishing his shit to make it shine like a diamond.

The higher-ups put plenty of resources into breaking The Jam in America since the record was their most melodic and had topped the charts in the UK. They could have stapled $100 bills to every album sleeve that went to a record station, and it wouldn't have made a difference. First of all, The Jam didn't like America, and, more significantly, they didn't like Americans. Their music was incredibly English, and their lyrics were directed at working-class British kids who worked in shops or factories and probably wouldn't ever leave their hometown. American kids couldn't relate to that. Like too many UK bands, The Jam thought people would love them for being snotty and snarky, and they answered interview questions with a sarcasm and cynicism that didn't endear them to radio.

Aside from the band being unpleasant as people, The Jam's music didn't fit the demands of the American market. It wasn't Joe Jackson. It wasn't Elvis Costello. It wasn't even The Clash, who had a playful side, and whose approach to punk rock was more accessible. And they thought they could book eight shows in major US cities and call it a full tour. They didn't realize that breaking the States requires an insane amount of touring in all kinds of markets. If their quintessentially British music didn't ensure their obscurity in the US, their attitude and approach to the industry did.

While I was working The Jam, I learned some important lessons about radio. Music directors know more about bands, scenes, and styles than anyone else at the station—certainly more than their program directors or general managers, who often only care about generating the most listeners so they can sell ads at the highest rates. Yet, the music directors were the ones who chose the songs for a station's playlist. Since they often loved all kinds of music, many of them were familiar with my past life, and they were the ones who were most likely to take me seriously when I pitched a band. In addition to getting many of them to play The Jam, which was a priority, I got them to listen to acts like Rory Gallagher. Since I was the resident Brit, I worked with Tears For Fears on their first album, *The Hurting*, and played a part in getting radio stations to spin 'Mad World' and 'Pale Shelter.'

Another highlight of my early days at PolyGram came when I worked with the German band Scorpions. I was introduced to them by Dan Young, the guy who first told me about the job. Soon after I met them, they told me they were big Gentle Giant fans and that we'd had a big influence on their early progressive material. At the time, Scorpions were relatively unknown in the US and wanted to work as hard as they could to become more recognized. This was 1982, and we were working their 1982 album *Blackout*, which contained the sure-thing radio rocker 'No One Like You.' At first, radio stations were reluctant to play this foreign band, but once they agreed it had the potential to reach a mass audience—and it did—it helped grease the wheels for the band's 1983 breakthrough, *Love At First Sting*, which featured the hit singles 'Rock You Like A Hurricane,' 'Big City Nights,' and 'Still Loving You.' Those were all sure things at radio and didn't require much work at all, but I'd like to think we made radio programmers more receptive to the new songs by breaking them in the US market first. Lead guitarist Matthias Jabs was so grateful he gave me his Gibson Explorer as a thank-you present. It sits happily in my guitar closet.

KISS were on Mercury when I was there, and it was fun working with Gene Simmons and Paul Stanley, in part because they both have incredible memories and are whip-smart. It probably has something to do with not drinking or taking drugs. That was something we saw eye-to-eye on and that they respected me for. I had first met them long before I started at PolyGram. In 1975, KISS and Gentle Giant had played at the Temple Theatre in Philadelphia on the same night (we played the early show, they played the later show). Gene and Paul remembered that almost ten years later, and when they saw me at the PolyGram office, Gene did a double take.

'Wait, are you the same guy we were introduced to in Philly? What the fuck are you doing here in a suit?' he joked. 'What are you doing at a record company, for God's sake? Are we going to have to work with you?'

I set them up with all kinds of radio interviews and worked their *Animalize* album, which rebooted their career with the hits 'Lick It Up' and 'Heaven's On Fire.'

When I wanted to win over a radio station, I first relied on the music I was working on, then on my personality. If those didn't work, I moved on. I never promised anyone front-row tickets or exclusive party invites. I never sent care packages of whisky and records. I knew there were people in the same position as I was in—at PolyGram and other labels—who offered programmers expensive gifts and even money in exchange for airplay. If that worked for them, fine, but it simply didn't fit my code of ethics. Besides, whatever I did worked well enough to keep me on the payroll, and bands kept asking to work with me, so I must have done something right.

Being at Polygram was a real eye-opener. I worked hard and paid attention to everything around me in every department at the label. I was polite to everyone and became good friends with many of my co-workers. I wanted to get started signing bands as soon as I could, but I didn't shortchange the radio department in any way. And I strongly felt that before I moved to A&R, I needed to help bring an artist over to the label.

My first toe-dip in that pool came when good old Gerry Bron called me. He was managing Uriah Heep but had been unable to get an appointment with some of the higher-ups at the company, so he appealed to me to help the band out. It was a terrible time in their career. They had no label and were clutching at straws to stay afloat. I felt bad for them since Gentle Giant had done many shows with them when they were in their prime.

At the same time, I knew they were no longer in the public eye, and some of their old fans didn't even know they were still around. They would be a hard sell.

'Would you like to hear the new album?' Bron asked, a pleading glint in his eyes. 'It's out in Europe, and I think there are a couple of songs here that could be hits. Maybe if you like it, you can set up a meeting between me and Jerry.'

'Well, I'm not sure if that's my job per se,' I said. 'But you know what? Let me hear it.'

Gerry played the album, *Abominog*, and on the whole, I thought it was just okay. The artwork depicted this ferocious-looking demon with razor-sharp teeth, which suggested it would be an aggressive metal record, but the only real teeth on the album were on the cover. At the same time, they had gotten Russ Ballard—a former member of Argent who had become a major hit songwriter for artists like Roger Daltry and Santana—to write one of the songs, 'On The Rebound,' and it had done well in England. Another track, 'That's The Way That It Is,' sounded like a decent AOR ballad.

'Look, Gerry,' I said, 'I can't promise anything, but let me play just those two songs to some people and see how they react.'

Skipping over all the stinkers, I was able to convince Jerry Jaffe to bring up the band at the next A&R meeting. He told me to come with him and help sell the album.

'We've got a good shot here to get a deal for a small amount of money,' I explained to the team. 'These two radio songs are good, the band has a history, and they're going to tour here. It seems to me that the potential reward far outweighs the minimal risk.'

Everyone agreed, and PolyGram signed Uriah Heep to a relatively tiny deal, which they knew was the best they would get. We put out the record, and 'That's The Way That It Is' went into the Top 20 at AOR, giving the band a reboot that no one expected. It was a major moment for me at the company, and it put me in a position of scouting and helping sign bands. It also made me realize the value of engendering multitiered support—not just from my team but from the entire label—

for a band I thought was worth signing. I used that approach many times, playing a song or two by relatively unknown artists to people in business affairs or marketing to help bring them onto the team. It sounds simple, but it was a revelation for me. A lot of record label departments work independently from one another, and as a result many good bands never saw the light of day.

That team-building lesson helped me about a year later, when I wanted to make a major move out of radio and into A&R. The whole department had expanded, and I figured I could grow with them and build my reputation at the company.

GIANT STEPS

CHAPTER EIGHTEEN

DESIRE

In 1983, I moved out of radio promo and into A&R. I was thrilled to be in a position to help decide which deserving artists got record deals. By then, Sharon had joined me in New York, and we were able to buy a three-bedroom apartment in the area where I lived. At the same time, I had a lot of catching up to do, since some of my peers had been signing big-budget bands for more than ten years, and all I had on my résumé was an inexpensive deal with Uriah Heep. My inexperience clouded my confidence, and I started to feel overwhelmed. I felt like I wasn't learning the ropes but clutching at miles of loose, greased string and frantically trying to keep it from slipping between my fingers and out of my hands. I had been in similar positions before, however, and I had always prevailed. Once again, being in the dark was illuminating. I had to follow my intuition to make things happen instead of adhering to an established set of practices.

Many business-oriented individuals at record labels hold a magnifying glass to sales charts, scope cities to discover scenes, and explore those hotbeds to unearth potential trends. I wanted to discover new talent on my own, not follow the flock of A&R lemmings from one bidding war to the next. I wasn't into fads or feeding frenzies. I wanted to find good musicians who wrote great songs, help them spread their wings, and sign them to a fair record deal that was a win/win for them and the label. Having played with hundreds of bands from various genres and seen firsthand what worked for them and what didn't, I looked for artists with talent, charisma, strong melodies, and something that separated them from their peers, be it looks, attitude, or another element entirely.

Some of the acts I approached didn't specifically know Simon Dupree & The Big Sound or Gentle Giant, but they knew I had been on their side of the business and understood how hard it was to write songs, record albums, tour, perform, self-promote, and survive on less money than many households allocate for pet food. That put us on the same team, more or less. Many of the bands I worked with appreciated that I didn't come from an Ivy League college, didn't have an MBA in marketing, and didn't ascend the corporate ladder through family connections. I wasn't a bean counter, and I didn't think of artists as assembly line workers with products to sell.

About two weeks into my A&R gig, I was listening to a new Long Island-based rock station, The Apple WAPP FM 103.5, when I heard a song called 'Runaway' and couldn't get the chorus out of my head.

'Did you hear that?' I asked Jerry. 'Do you know this song?'

'Not sure,' he replied. 'I wasn't really paying attention.'

I called the radio station and found out the song was by a kid from Sayreville, New Jersey. His name was John Bongiovi, and soon, after he changed his name, everyone would know who he was. But that was a way down the road. First, I had to bring him into the PolyGram fold.

The story of 'Runaway' exemplifies John's drive and determination to be a star. He wrote the song in 1980 and recorded it in 1981 at the Power Station, a New York recording studio where he swept floors and took out garbage in exchange for late-night recording time. 'Runaway' was one of eight tracks on *The Power Station Demos*, which was recorded with studio musicians and produced by John's second cousin, Tony Bongiovi.

John sent *The Power Station Demos* to numerous record labels and management companies, most of whom threw it in the trash. So, he took another path. He told the story in 2018, during his induction into the Rock & Roll Hall Of Fame:

'I thought, *Who is the loneliest person in the music business? The DJ*. There was a new station in NYC called WAPP. It was so new that there wasn't even a receptionist, so I was able to walk in and get the attention of

John Lassman and the DJ, Chip Hobart. I told them about the songs on the cassette and the frustration of not getting any label to listen to it. Chip did listen to it, and he told me he thought it should be included on their homegrown record of local original music.'

In addition to 'Runaway,' the compilation album *New York Rocks: The Apple WAPP FM 103.5* included homegrown songs by Twisted Sister, DC Star, and seven more obscure artists. Hobart and Lassman liked 'Runaway' so much that they put it on the air, first late at night, then throughout the day. The station's listeners responded well to it, and before he had bandmates or a group name, John Bongiovi had a regional hit.

I heard the song a few times on the radio and it always caught my ear, but I didn't do anything about it. Then, one day, the head of our business affairs department, Ted Green, came into my office.

'Derek, there's an attorney from Philadelphia that's called me a couple of times. He wants to speak to you.'

'What about?' I replied. I was never terribly excited to talk to lawyers.

'He's working with these guys to put a band together. They have a song on New York radio or something and a demo, and he wants to know if you're interested in giving it a listen. You gonna talk to him?'

I had dealt with plenty of lawyers, agents, and labels in Gentle Giant, so I thought, *What the hell?* I knew I needed to establish myself in the A&R department, and that meant signing bands. I might as well see if this kid has got what it takes. No one told me the name of the musician, and I probably wouldn't have recognized it. I might not even have remembered the name of the song I had already heard and liked on the radio.

I called the lawyer, a guy named Arthur Mann, and asked him to swing by my office with the demo. When he arrived, I inserted the tape into my office stereo and turned it up, not at all sure what to expect. Right away, that unmistakable keyboard line interjected with short, sharp blasts of guitar and drums burst from the speakers. Then the melodic hard-rock vocals kicked in.

'Wait, this is that song I heard on the radio,' I said. 'The "Little Runaway" thing.' The lawyer smiled and told me a talented eighteen-year-old kid wrote it, then recorded it with some local guys, but wanted to up his game and get a record deal. He asked me if I wanted to hear three more songs on the demo. I did, and they were all pretty good.

'Well, what do you think?' Arthur asked.

My poker face still needed work. 'I think this is great,' I said with a big smile. 'I just love that song "Runaway." I think that's a hit. Radio will go crazy for it.'

I wasn't ready to sign Bongiovi yet, but I saw a lot of potential in the music, and I wanted to help get him in fighting shape for a record deal. I went over to talk to his second cousin Tony, who'd produced the track and owned the Power Station, which was on 10th Avenue and 53rd Street in Midtown Manhattan. Today, the area is full of prime real estate, but in the 80s it was a shithole. There was no public transportation, so you had to drive there, and, after dark, you had a good chance of getting mugged on your way back to the car—if your car hadn't been stolen.

Tony was an unlikeable egomaniac who lived in the studio where John swept the trash and rocked out. The cousins may have been in business together, but it was clear they weren't close. Rather than sing John's praises and encourage me to sign him, Tony talked down John's contributions to the music, especially 'Runaway.'

'John wrote it and sang on it, yeah, but it was a mess until I fixed it,' he boasted. 'I had to rearrange a bunch of stuff and coach John through his vocal takes. I did that with Aldo Nova, too, and almost everyone that comes in here.'

Since John and Tony had signed a contract to work together, and Tony had supplied the musicians on the demo, I was obliged to put up with him. He and John wanted a record deal, and he was going to produce the album, he said. As much as he rubbed me the wrong way, my hands were tied, and he seemed like a competent enough producer. I called Arthur and told him to come to my office again, and this time to bring John. I wanted to know what he was like before I committed any more time and energy to his career. Strong frontmen with sour personalities have wrecked many a band.

A few days later, Arthur swung by with John, and as soon as he entered, a wave of electricity washed through the place. He was incredibly good-looking—baby-faced, with soft features and hair that wouldn't quit. All the young women he passed turned their heads in unison like they were in a choreographed video. This was something special. We went into my office, and I closed the door.

Most young artists are understandably intimidated when they're in the presence of record label guys. Sometimes they hardly talk and sit there like department store mannequins. Other times, they're fidgety and loquacious, like an extrovert on blow.

Without saying a word, John dominated the room, and if he had the jitters, you'd never know it. His grin was warm and genuine. He had confidence and star power, and he was utterly charming. Part of me wanted to hug him as if he was an old friend.

'I've been talking to some musicians for the band,' he said. 'I've got a guitarist now, but I'm getting someone else. His name is Richie Sambora, and I think he's really great. Tico Torres from Frankie & The Knockouts is drumming. And Alec John Such, who was in Phantom's Opera, is on bass.'

'Great,' I said. 'You've got this song on the radio. Are you getting out there? Are you playing any gigs?'

'Not officially yet, but we're setting some stuff up,' he said. John was eager to demonstrate the new lineup, so he started to put together some shows and invited everyone he knew, including some local radio guys. 'We're doing a few songs at the Copacabana in Midtown Manhattan next week if you want to come see us.'

Curious to see whether he could win over an audience with his poppy hard-rock songs and good looks, I went to the club to check him out. His group played between two other bands, neither of whom are worth mentioning. I was tired and thinking of going home. As soon as John and the band stepped onstage and started working the room, but I was wide awake, and they had my full attention. Musically, they weren't particularly great—no better than a lot of other bar bands without record deals—but they already looked like rock stars.

This was Richie Sambora's first gig with the band, but he and John already had an amazing chemistry onstage, playing off one another like Steven Tyler and Joe Perry. Just from looking at him, it was clear that John needed validation and adoration, and he wouldn't stop until he got it. He had one radio-ready song. All he needed was more experience and more tunes, and then he could be a hero.

After the show, John and I were casually chatting, and he said something that struck me hard.

'I want to be bigger than Elvis.'

I looked at him and smiled. I thought he was kidding. He didn't smile back. He was deadly serious. At eighteen years of age, he already had this incredible drive to be the best. He didn't have a clear musical direction yet, and the songs didn't all flow together—one would be hard rock, the next would be kind of metal, and then there was stuff in between—but he had this presence, and everyone around him felt it. Having been in successful rock bands for twenty-plus years and having socialized with everyone from David Bowie to Ozzy Osbourne, I could tell the rock stars from the wannabes. I had no doubt John was the former. He exuded this very rare, almost intangible energy. It's a combination of elements—a superpower, if you will—that you come across once every ten years or so and go, *Wow, who is this?*

I started to plan. If John and the band could put together some other songs as good as 'Runaway,' he could be one of the greats. His music was loud but fun. It wasn't angry but it had edge. It was hard rock that could appeal to fans of AC/DC or Aerosmith, but it also had a vulnerability and heart that could appeal equally to men and women. If he could make all of those elements click with consistency, he would be the biggest New Jersey export since Bruce Springsteen.

I saw another show, and by that time, John and Richie had developed an even more memorable onstage rapport. Richie provided just the right combination of talent and friendly competition—a formula for success I knew from Gentle Giant ('You, you think that's not good? Well, I'll show you'). In many ways, John's band reminded me of the drive to succeed that Gentle Giant had when we were first finding ourselves. There was so much room for him to grow, and I wanted so badly to help him succeed.

I told John that I wanted to schedule a showcase for the rest of the team at PolyGram.

'So, we're gonna get a record deal?' he said with a hint of swagger.

'That's the hope,' I said. 'We'll see.'

We booked a show at SIR Studios and four other staffers from PolyGram's rock department showed up. Bongiovi and his band played five songs. To be honest, I was glad they kept the set short. I don't know why I expected them to suddenly be good enough to win over four jaded label staffers who would rather sit at the bar and down vodka tonics than stand up front and watch a band. I had confidence in Bongiovi, but as they played, it felt like the floor had started opening up. It was a hole of disappointment. 'Runaway' sounded good, and John and Richie looked as cool as ever. But they weren't quite arena-ready.

My boss, Jerry, was skeptical. He realized John had potential, but so did lots of other bands, and not many of them get signed. I could tell why Jerry wasn't as gung-ho as I was. John was wearing pink leather pants and shaking his ass in a way that you couldn't tell if he wanted to be Rex Smith or David Lee Roth. I realized the band was not yet totally cohesive, but, to me, there was still no question that this was going to work. I was as determined to break the band as John was to be a star.

'What did you think?' I asked Jerry after the show.

'Well, he's definitely pretty,' Jerry replied. 'I think they're okay, but they're not really my thing. If you think it's going to work, then go for it. Go ahead. Do your thing.'

I appreciated Jerry's vote of confidence. A lot of guys in the industry are either too arrogant or insecure, or have such a narrow set of parameters regarding what's good and what's not that they won't consider giving someone their blessings for something they don't quite grasp. When 'Runaway' started to get national airplay from some major stations, I started working with Arthur Mann to put together a deal to sign the band. Before we worked out the terms, Bongiovi played a show opening for Scandal and invited PolyGram and other labels to attend. I could tell that if we didn't pick him up soon, someone else would swoop in with an offer. With a radio hit as validation, there was nothing to prevent another label from pulling the trigger—though, at the moment, we were still the only ones courting the band.

I wanted to sign John because I knew he would be successful, but also because I liked him. He was charismatic but not a show-off. He was polite and friendly, and he treated everyone he met like he was interested in what they had to say. He made people feel good about themselves—another great trait for a rock star. Lured by the major label cache of the Midtown Manhattan skyscraper in which we were located, and excited by the opportunity to raid the label's closets and pick up our latest releases on LP and cassette, John started swinging by the PolyGram office to hang out, and I enjoyed his company.

'Derek, can I ask you something?' he said one day. 'What's it going to take for us to get signed?'

'Well,' I said, choosing my words carefully. 'You've got "Runaway." Getting Richie was a good move. You guys look great together. What else have you got? Are there more songs I haven't heard yet?'

John said he and Richie were working on some new stuff and invited me to come to New Jersey to watch the band in their practice room and meet his parents. It was a strange offer, but it had a certain charm. Most label guys only courted artists who they were trying to win over from other bidders. Otherwise, bands sent them music and, maybe, met them for lunch. But I didn't want to play by the rules. I wanted to have a real relationship with the artists I signed. So, I went to suburban Sayreville, where John grew up. This town of forty thousand people seemed to me to be a microcosm of the middle-class American Dream. It made me think of the John Cougar Mellencamp song 'Jack And Diane,' though Mellencamp was from the Indiana heartland, which is a far cry from Jersey. Still, Americana is Americana.

Sayreville is located on the banks of the Raritan River and was full of family-style restaurants, videogame arcades, and movie theaters. As pleasant as it is, a keen nose could discern two distinct smells: desperation and aspiration. John clearly exuded the latter, and I immediately understood his desire to be bigger than Elvis. What he and his bandmates wanted to do was to break out of their hometown and discover life outside of New Jersey. They were proud of being from Sayreville but absolutely determined not to get stuck there. Having grown up in Portsmouth, I understood the sentiment.

It was also interesting for me to see the dynamic of a (fairly) regular American family. John was close to his parents, who always supported his music career. His mom, Carole, was a real character—a former marine and ex-Playboy bunny—and his dad was a hairdresser who had done wonders with John and his friends (remember, this was the eighties, and long hair was nearly as important to rock'n'roll as hit singles).

I enjoyed meeting John's parents. Immensely proud of their son, they were warm but wary. They knew that unscrupulous individuals often took advantage of musicians, and they were protective of John. After spending a short amount of time with me, however, Carole could tell I had integrity and good instincts (devoted moms can sense these things), and she wanted me to keep him from making decisions he'd later regret.

'Please look after him, will you?' she said. 'He's a good kid, but he doesn't know about the business side of show business. I don't want him to get hurt.'

I was honored that John's parents entrusted me to be his counselor and friend. I told John's mom I'd help steer him in the right direction, and, in a way, I took on the mantle of the patriarch. On my advice, Bongiovi agreed to be managed by Doc McGhee, and John and the band scheduled another big show for his growing New York-area fanbase, which was still loving 'Runaway.' For some reason, other managers came to the showcase, including David Krebs and John Scher. After the show, which was wonderfully energized and uplifting, these big-time managers were schmoozing with John. By then, Krebs had developed a reputation as a hot-shit hard-rock manager, having worked with Aerosmith, AC/DC, and Def Leppard. But to me, Doc was the right guy for John.

While McGhee was new to the scene, he had incredible charisma, he was easy to talk to, and he made everyone feel good. I met him when I was transitioning from promotion to A&R. He dropped by the PolyGram office to represent Pat Travers, and I was impressed by his style. He went from one office to another. In each case, he shut the door and stayed in there for a little while. Each time he left someone's office there was laughter, a confident exit line, and a firm handshake. He made everyone feel like they ran their department, even if they were new to the company.

Left Jon Bon Jovi, me, and Tom Keifer of Cinderella, hanging out at PolyGram Records, 1987. A rare quiet moment during a very loud era. **Below** The Polygram Records rock department at our Florida retreat, 1985.

Left Welcoming Bon Jovi with the Polygram staff in 1986.

Top With the ATCO Records staff signing Enuff Z'Nuff, 1989. **Above** Ahmet Ertegun and Doug Morris welcome me as president of ATCO Records, 1989—a milestone moment in my second career. **Right** My ATCO Records headshot, 1989.

Left Jon Bon Jovi attending my son Noah's bar mitzvah, 1996. **Below** Being interviewed on camera in my ATCO Records office, 1992.

Above With Dug Pinnick of King's X (*center*) and Matthias Jabs of Scorpions (*right*) at NAMM, 2017.

Left Catching up with Corey Taylor of Slipknot at NAMM, 2017.
Below Me, Tony Kaye of Yes, and Billy Sherwood, Los Angeles, 2010.
Bottom With Phil Anselmo of Pantera at NAMM, 2017.

Top Backstage with Ann Wilson of Heart at *The Tonight Show*, 2017. **Left** At Madison Square Garden with Elton John, reminiscing about the early days and how far we'd both come, 2022. **Above** Meeting Questlove at *The Tonight Show*, 2017.

Left Playing Paco De Lucía's guitar at his former residence in Toledo, Spain, 2024. A quiet, unforgettable moment. **Below** Playing my Fender Precision bass at home, 2024. Some things you never put down.

Above Taking a walk in Riverside Park, New York City, 2025. **Right** Remixing 'In A Glass House' with Eber Pinheiro in Brooklyn, New York, 2025. Revisiting the past with new ears.

When Doc entered my office, we both knew Pat Travers was a hard sell and that he'd have to work on me to get anything out of the interaction. He knew I wouldn't be lured by the promise of hookers and blow, so that was never a selling point. Instead, he made small talk about family and music before explaining what Pat wanted to do and how PolyGram could help him. Then, he made a playfully manipulative move.

'Derek, I got this place in the Cayman Islands that would blow your mind,' he said. 'You know, if you and your wife Sharon would want to go down to see it—you know—when you go to see Pat Travers in Florida, you're more than welcome to stay there.'

I knew he was trying to play me, and he knew I knew he was trying to play me, but that didn't sour me on him. In fact, I respected him for it. His offer was sincere and tempting. And I'm sure the offers he made to other staffers—whatever they might have been—were equally inviting. Some folks took him up on his enticements. I never did, he knew I never would, and we understood each other's position. I felt that if Doc was that good at making every PolyGram staffer feel like an executive, he could surely pull off the same magic with artists who loved having their egos massaged. He could make John feel like he was on top of the world, and then he would help him get there.

I met with John to talk to him about his management options and once again told him that Doc McGhee was his best bet. 'Look, David Krebs has experience working with AC/DC and Aerosmith, but Doc's gonna sell you like you're the only singer on the planet. I really think you should go see him.'

John agreed, and, sure enough, Doc won him over. Krebs was flabbergasted that I would recommend McGhee, a newcomer, over him. For years, he told me that I fucked him out of working with Bon Jovi. I'd laugh and say, 'Maybe, but it didn't work out too badly for John, did it?'

With Doc on the team, I was ready to offer John and the band a record deal. For a young guy without any business experience, John had good instincts for the machinations of the music industry. He was funny, knew how to be humble and gracious, and was personable to radio DJs and journalists, who instantly took to him. I wouldn't say any of that was a ruse. From the start, John was a genuinely nice guy. He was fun to be around and eager to learn everything he could. But, in truth, his drive to be the biggest included being the biggest asshole when he felt he needed to be.

John was never an arrogant shithead like so many artists whose heads inflate like parade floats when they suddenly rise to stardom. At the same time, John instinctively knew how to play hardball. In some respects, he was a shark, and I didn't understand that side of him because I've always tried to treat people fairly, even if it meant less acclaim or money for me. On the other hand, I've seen so many artists in this industry get fucked over that John's sometimes predatory nature was somewhat admirable.

'So, I want a deal, but I don't want my band signed,' he said to me when we were discussing the details of his contract. 'I want it to be me, and then they'll have their own deal.'

Of course, that meant more money for John and less for his bandmates, which was a hardcore move—especially since Richie had proved he was crucial to the band and the songwriting. Having seen so much of John's friendly side, I was taken aback that he didn't want his bandmates to have the same deal as him. It felt like an underhanded maneuver, and it was something I never would have considered when I was in Simon Dupree or Gentle Giant. We were a band, and being in a band was supposed to be like being Musketeers: 'All for one, one for all.'

I tried to talk John out of this. 'Look, if you separate yourself from them like that, they'll resent it,' I said. 'And I promise you it will cause problems down the line.'

He didn't care. He stuck to his guns and said it was the only way he would sign with me. So, I gave in and we signed the band separately. It wasn't fair, but that's what John wanted. He was incredibly ambitious and tenacious, and he almost always got his way. I was starting to think I didn't need to heed Mrs. Bongiovi's request to take care of John. He was doing pretty well on his own.

Once we'd agreed to a deal, we started discussing band names. John really wanted to call the group Desire, but I knew that wasn't the way to go, so I tried another approach that I knew would appeal to him. I stole a move from the Van Halen playbook, partially because I knew John loved Van Halen.

'You're John Bongiovi,' I said. 'Why don't you call the band Bon Jovi? It has the same kind of ring as Van Halen. You can be John Bon Jovi. That way, people will think of you when they think of the band the same way they think of Eddie Van Halen when they think of Van Halen.'

John liked my idea, and we had a deal. Unbeknown to me, however, he also had a deal with Tony Bongiovi, which would cause some wrinkles in the contract. When John was working at the Power Station, he and Tony had made an agreement that was completely unfair on John. Once John started putting out records, the contract stated, Tony would earn a predetermined percentage of royalties that would last for the duration of John's career. I got angry when I saw that. As a family, you should be happy for your relatives' success. If you helped, you deserved to be paid for your contributions, but it's greedy and rude to ask for a lifelong commitment in exchange for what was, at most, a couple of years of work.

'That's gotta be changed before you sign the deal,' I said. Doc and John's lawyer agreed. John was relieved. 'Let me talk to the business affairs office at PolyGram to negotiate a more equitable deal.' Anything was more equitable than giving up a percentage of your wages for life.

Tony played hardball. He insisted he had legal rights to John's future earnings. I wasn't about to let that fly. Ted Green and the lawyers at PolyGram found some holes in the contract and pointed them out to Tony.

'Here's the deal,' he said. 'You can get an expensive lawyer and try to make your unfair contract stick. If you do that, we will get a bunch of more expensive lawyers, and if you file a lawsuit, it will drag out and you will end up paying your lawyer a ton of money. If we go to court and you lose, you'll have to pay your legal fees and our legal fees, and you'll be in debt for life. You won't get to produce the album, and your name will be shit in this industry. Or you can compromise, produce John's album, and move on with your career.'

Tony caved. In the end, he and John signed a contract that entitled Tony to two percent of the earnings from the first album, which he would produce, and one percent from the second. That was more than fair. Some people felt John shouldn't have had to pay Tony anything, but to play the devil's advocate, John's original deal was with Tony, and Tony was the one who gave John his first shot. Tony hired the session musicians, put in time in the studio with John, and helped groom him for the big time. So, Tony certainly deserved something for his efforts, and he got it—even though it wasn't what he had bargained for before anyone knew who John was.

After the settlement, the relationship between John and Tony got ugly. Tony was still bitter about the deal and continued to hold a grudge. Luckily for John, when Bon Jovi achieved major success, it was with their third album, 1986's *Slippery When Wet*, after his financial obligation to Tony had expired. That album would sell twelve million copies and springboard his and the band's careers. No one could have predicted that when Bon Jovi's first album came out, but since there was so much to focus on now, the crappy contract he made with his second cousin was soon forgotten. It was time for him to put all his energy into working with the band, recording hit records, touring, and becoming a huge rock star.

Jon Bon Jovi was a rock star long before he stopped using the first name John. He oozed charisma and knew when to smile, who to flatter, and exactly what to say to everyone, including record label folks, radio station personnel, journalists, and fans. The girls loved him, and he loved the girls. He had all the right ingredients to cook with, and he could turn up the heat with a tussle of his hair.

Jon was pleased that 'Runaway' was doing well, but he made it clear to me from the start that he wanted a gigantic hit. I assured him that everyone at the label had high hopes for him and would throw their support behind him and his band. But an album recorded at the Power Station with one standout song wasn't going to make him a superstar. He had forward momentum, which was great, but now he needed to build his following by exposing himself to the masses.

Doc and I put our weight behind the band. Instead of booking them with poppy hard rock bands, we put Bon Jovi on tour with Scorpions and KISS. It might seem like a mismatch (like Gentle Giant touring with Black

Sabbath), but there was a method to our insanity. We wanted Bon Jovi to earn a following without simply going through the motions.

'What the fuck?' Jon said at one point. 'These aren't our biggest fans, the ones calling radio stations and requesting our songs. We're lucky if they know "Runaway." What the hell were you guys thinking?'

'Jon, when the guys in these other bands are onstage, I want you to watch them,' I told him. 'They're not shaking their asses. They're not playing to the girls, 'cause the crowd is mostly guys who want to see musicians that rock and shake their guitars. They're not even thinking about your ass.'

Jon soaked up the advice, and soon he'd stopped shaking his ass in favor of more masculine rock poses, which went over well. His backing band followed suit and started dressing more like bad boys and less like pretty girls. That toughness infiltrated the sound of the music, and Jon had the band to pull it off. When he got a little gritty, Richie, Alec, Tico, and keyboardist David Rashbaum took a cue from his newfound pretty-boy toughness.

Without much else to work with on the first album, in May 1984 PolyGram released the single 'She Don't Know Me,' the only song written by an outside songwriter, Mark Avsec of Wild Chery ('Play That Funky Music'). The success of 'Runaway' incentivized radio stations to give it a chance, but it didn't move listeners. In October, we put out the last single from the album, 'Burning For Love,' which was primarily written by Sambora. That did slightly better, but not by much.

Before we ended Bon Jovi's first album cycle, we wanted to get the band over to Europe and see how they would fare with crowds that didn't know them. PolyGram was a mutt-like hybrid of two European companies, so it wasn't hard to convince them that the band could win over European fans who liked Def Leppard, Scorpions, and Billy Idol. Touring in the States had turned Bon Jovi into a solid, spotlight-seducing rock band. They worked their asses off and gave the audience their all, even on the rare occasions when crowds stood cross-armed shooting daggers from angry eyes.

Bon Jovi didn't blow up in Europe, but they didn't bomb either, and by the time they headed back to the States, plenty of the continent's hard-rock media and fans, impressed by the band's chemistry and theatrics, would be keeping an eye on them to see what they did next. Despite Jon's unusual financial arrangement with his bandmates, Bon Jovi was a tight, unified force, and the outstanding relationship between Jon and Richie created an onstage focus for the band for many years. Over the decades, layers of tension would develop between the two until their marriage was no longer sustainable, but while they had the same shared drive, goals, and love for music, their performances eclipsed their problems. And, as with many other great vocalist/guitarist teams—Lennon/McCartney, Jagger/Richards, Plant/Page, and so on—the friction fueled their creativity.

I worked closely with Doc to maximize every opportunity to push Bon Jovi further up the rock'n'roll hierarchy. We were able to rally every department at PolyGram. At staff meetings, we emphasized how the timing was right for the band to break through, and that *Bon Jovi* needed to be the label's number one priority. We followed the axioms of Machiavelli, discouraging certain staffers from downplaying the album and vocally supporting those who showed a serious interest or were willing to play ball to benefit their future at the label. We threatened no one, but we certainly provided vocal incentives. In the end, we had more than one hundred national and international offices around the company intently focused on Bon Jovi's success. The company pumped much of its promotional budget into the album and provided the band with healthy tour support. We were putting our bets on a winning horse that just needed a little nurturing before the triple crown.

The tours went well, and radio stations continued to play their music—mostly 'Runaway.' That was fine, but not quite enough. *Bon Jovi* went gold (and eventually platinum), which most bands would be ecstatic about. None of the bands Bon Jovi toured with had gone gold on their first album. Yet, considering how hard PolyGram worked to break the band, we expected more, and we needed Bon Jovi to rise to platinum-plus status in order to justify our expenses. We knew we had to get a second album out right away to keep the wave of support growing and that meant putting together new songs and getting into the studio.

Around the time Bon Jovi were preparing to start work on their second album, my son Noah was born, and I invited Jon to come to my house and celebrate the bris with us. Jon knew that a bris was a Jewish tradition, but I think he thought it was a just celebration of a baby's birth. He didn't know what he was in for. He arrived, took a look at Noah, and congratulated me. He kissed my wife, told her how beautiful Noah was, and then mingled a bit and sipped champagne. A few minutes later, the *mohel* took Noah in a blanket and walked to the center of the room. I'm sure Jon thought the man was like a rabbi; he'd say a few prayers and then everyone would continue to celebrate.

In the Jewish faith, a *mohel* is a specialist who performs circumcisions on newborns. I could see Jon smiling as he watched the *mohel* say a prayer in Hebrew and lift Noah. When the doc slipped the blanket off Noah and pulled out a knife, Jon's smile disappeared, and his face turned white. The *mohel* flicked his knife, Noah cried, and Jon looked like he was going to throw up, faint, or both. When the baby was bandaged, wrapped in a blanket, and stopped crying, Jon seemed to regain his composure, but I could tell he had been enlightened in a way he didn't expect.

There's a saying that a band have their whole career to write their first album and less than a year to create the second. It's what separates the one-hit wonders from the career acts. Bon Jovi weren't quite ready to follow up their debut that quickly, but they did the best they could and wrote some pretty good songs, including 'In And Out Of Love' and 'Only Lonely,' which were solid singles. Richie had co-written four songs on *Bon Jovi*. This time he co-wrote six. As far as I could tell, the process went smoothly, especially considering how little time they had to throw everything together.

Once Bon Jovi got into the studio, their circumstances changed. The most affordable move would have been to go back to the Power Station and record with the same gear used on the first album. For obvious reasons, that wasn't going to happen. So, we hired Lance Quinn, who had engineered the first album, to produce the new one, with Obie O'Brien as engineer and peacemaker, and booked time at a studio called the Warehouse in Philadelphia, which was cheaper than any decent New York-area studios.

I went down to Philly to oversee the recording, and right away it was clear that the anxiety level within the band had risen exponentially.

Spending all their time on the road and in the writing room had taken its toll. Jon was short-tempered and stressed out, and he and Ritchie hardly joked around anymore. The band's goal, it seemed, was to quickly record the songs and get the fuck back home. However, their path was strewn with obstacles. Everyone thought that having the familiar face of Quinn to walk them through the second album would be a good idea. No one realized he wasn't a good producer and didn't collaborate well with bands. He and Jon were soon locking horns like angry rams. Having released one album, Jon wanted to call the shots in the studio, but Lance treated him like a student in a remedial class. They both had big egos, and while truthfully Jon wasn't ready to steer the ship, Lance should have looked at him as an apprentice, not an underling.

The biggest problem with Lance was that he had worked with Tony, and that immediately soured him to Jon. Also, Lance would interject if he didn't like something the band played, but he lacked the creativity or the people skills to help massage ideas that were close but not there yet. Jon was great at coming up with riffs and melodies, but he hadn't mastered the art of cohesively combining them. Tony Bongiovi had been able to work with rough ideas and blend them together, which is why the first album sounded good. Lance didn't do that so well—he simply shot down anything that didn't sound right to him, which infuriated Jon.

After one shouting match too many, I had had enough.

'Lance, this isn't working. You're off the project,' I said sternly.

'You can't do that,' he shouted. 'You can't finish it without me.'

'We can and we will,' I corrected him.

His response? He turned around, dropped his pants, and flashed his ass at me.

'Wow, okay,' I responded. 'I'm impressed. Did you learn that from Tony?'

After a few moments of silence, and with the temperature rising, he told me to go fuck myself and left.

With Lance out of the picture, the songs on *7800 Fahrenheit* still weren't as cohesive as they should have been, and it was too late to erase the tracks that were already finished. We had to defer to Obie O'Brien, the main engineer, to finish recording the album with the band. Jon got along far better with Obie than Lance, and Obie made everything *sound* good. In the end, the album wasn't bad. It wasn't a sophomore slump. Jon sang his heart out, Richie played his ass off, and so did everyone else in the band. There were some good songs. Maybe they would have been better with a different producer, but the band still rocked when they needed to and tugged at the heartstrings at just the right moments. When I heard the final mix, I put my hand on my chin and wondered, *Hmm, is this going to work or not?*

Bon Jovi hadn't been away for long, and they still had a lot of momentum. Their live shows had improved, and they held their own opening for Ratt, Dokken, and even Judas Priest. Interestingly, their fans weren't just male anymore. A sizable number of girls started showing up, and not just with their boyfriends. MTV started playing the videos for 'Only Lonely' and 'In And Out Of Love,' which boosted the band's reach considerably. Everyone at the label was aware that *7800 Fahrenheit* wasn't as good as the debut, but we could all see the band was still drawing crowds, and the singles were performing—if not well enough to catapult album sales then at least sufficiently to put asses in seats.

Doc and I knew we had promised the moon and delivered just a few stars, which made the record a minor disappointment to the label (even though it eventually went platinum). The question was, what do we do next? Instead of doubling down and waiting for lightning to strike, we tripled our efforts and helped create a thunderstorm.

Jon and Richie were a good writing team, but they were still young, and while they could compose strong hooks, they didn't always know how to use them in a song in the best way. Doc and I thought it would be a good idea to have an established hit songwriter work with the band. I did some homework and discovered that KISS had worked with Desmond Child on their single 'Heaven's On Fire' and two other songs.

'Who's this Child guy?' I asked Gene and Paul. They told me that Desmond had been in a group called Desmond Child & Rouge in the 70s. KISS discovered him on Capitol and asked if he would work with them. One of his gems, the 1979 disco-tinged hit 'I Was Made For Lovin' You' from KISS's *Dynasty*, helped resurrect the band. Child had also worked with Billy Squire, Cher, and Bonnie Tyler.

I called Desmond, who said he was open to meeting Bon Jovi. Then I told Jon what I was thinking. 'You and the band are great, and you and Richie work well together,' I said, buttering him up. 'You're about one step from being huge. What would you say to the idea of working with another songwriter for the next album? There are a lot of other rock stars out there that hire incredible, well-known hitmakers, and we think that would be a great move for you.'

If someone had come up to me in the early days of Gentle Giant and said that I should hire someone to write hits for me, I would have told them to fuck off. Having dealt with hundreds of artists, I've learned that's how most people would react—but not Jon. His desire to be a star outshined his ego.

'Look, if that's what other bands are doing and you think it will work for us, then yeah, I'm open to it,' he said.

We met Desmond in a little garage somewhere in New York, and he played us three or four demos he had sketched out. Immediately, I could tell this was the right move. Jon's eyes opened wide, and he smiled. It seemed like he was picturing himself singing these songs, or similar ones, to giant crowds. Jon and Desmond talked for a while about music. They were influenced by many of the same artists, and their personalities clicked. It was a match made in heaven—or as close to heaven as you can get in the Tri-State area.

Having landed the perfect co-writer, we needed the right production team. Tony and Lance had been nightmares. Fortunately, the label agreed to pony up for someone more established. I had heard about producer Bruce Fairbairn and his engineer/protegee, Bob Rock, who made their names working with Loverboy. Bruce also produced albums by Blue Öyster Cult and Krokus, and he and Bob had just worked with melodic hard rockers Black 'N Blue.

I figured the dream team of Richie, Jon, Desmond, Bruce, and Bob was a sure thing. Everyone was pumped, except maybe Bruce, whose initial reaction was, 'I'm not going to do anything with them until they've got great songs.' Fair enough. I sent him six songs. Four were by Desmond, including a demo of 'Livin' On A Prayer'; two were by Jon and Richie, including 'Wanted Dead Or Alive.'

Bruce called me, fighting to hold back his enthusiasm. 'Okay, I want to do it.'

I got Jon and Bruce on the phone. Then, Bon Jovi flew to Bruce's studio in Vancouver, Little Mountain, and began work on *Slippery When Wet*. I wondered how the change of venue would affect the band's mood. Maybe I was projecting, since back in the Gentle Giant days I had hated recording outside of London, and Vancouver was far away from the East Coast environment the band members were used to. There was no reason to worry. From the start, Jon and Bruce blended like peas and carrots. And Bruce, Bob, and their team had a superb work ethic. Everyone was meticulous about working on every song until it was perfect.

I visited them in Vancouver five times while they were working on the album, and each time it was clear that everyone was excited, dedicated, and in great spirits. When they finished, they screened the album for four or five people from PolyGram. Played in its entirety, it was clear that this thing was going to be huge. There were hit singles on there, but that wasn't the only selling point. Everything flowed in the same direction, and nothing was lacking from any of the songs—no missing parts, no hastily constructed segues, nothing to interrupt the listening experience. It rocked, it grooved, it was poppy, it was infectious. Everything about it felt right. It's very hard to describe the overwhelming state of euphoria I felt, or how I absolutely knew that this was going to be one of the biggest albums of all time. I would have bet my career on it. I knew *Slippery When Wet* would move mountains. And it did.

Radio programmers went crazy as soon as they heard it. MTV played the video for the first single, 'You Give Love A Bad Name,' non-stop, and the song and album shot straight to #1. Then came 'Livin' On A Prayer,' which became the longest-running #1 song on the *Billboard* Hot 100, and 'Wanted Dead Or Alive.' And the band kept going.

Jon was a gorgeous, instantly recognizable rock star, Richie was a big-shot guitar hero, and Bon Jovi sold out arenas and stadiums across the world. *Slippery When Wet* was the top-selling album of 1987 and to date has sold more than twenty-eight million copies worldwide.

I was immensely proud to have been a part of Bon Jovi's gestation and evolution. At the same time, the victory was bittersweet since I knew my days as a creative force for the band had peaked. *Slippery When Wet* was the last Bon Jovi album that really rocked, and it served as the missing link between Jon the rock star and Jon the pop icon. From there, the band branched out further into the pop world, and my role in their career became less significant. I had done what I could to make Jon a star, and I had fulfilled my obligation to his mom to look after her boy. Now, Jon was a man, and he was calling all the shots. I was getting ready to move on too, to explore different paths and make new discoveries.

CHAPTER NINETEEN
POP GOES THE WORLD

Having discovered, developed, and signed Bon Jovi, I rapidly moved up at PolyGram and landed other big artists before anyone else knew who they were. Not long after Bon Jovi came on board, a manager in Philadelphia named Larry Mazur came to my office to plug another new band. We shook hands, and he handed me a demo tape that had at least sixty songs on it. I didn't have the time or patience to make it through the whole thing, but even though the songs weren't fully fleshed out, I could tell right away that the vocalist, Tom Keifer, had a fucking amazing voice.

'Okay, this guy sounds really good,' I told Larry. 'When the band plays another show, let me know, and I'll try to make it.'

Around the same time, Jon told me he had seen this melodic metal band at the Empire Rock Club in Philly and they'd blown him away. Both Larry and Jon were referring to the same band, Cinderella. Ever since Elton John introduced me to the music of Spirit—and maybe even before that, when all these legends at the Abbey Road café turned me on to British Invasion bands—I knew that when a musician you admire tells you to check out a band, you should take them seriously.

I went down to The Trocadero to see Cinderella, and the crowd was decent. As soon as they hit the stage, it was clear that my instincts were right about their singer, Tom, who was also a guitarist. He had the looks and chops to be a star, and the bassist, Eric Brittingham, was also talented and had a strong stage presence. But the second guitarist and the drummer, Michael Schermick and Tony Destra, weren't very good. They were dragging the band down. I knew Tom could rise to great heights, and I wanted to be there when it happened. But this wasn't the lineup for him to do that.

'So, what do you think?' Larry asked me backstage after the show.

'Honestly, Tom's great, and Eric's great. But I can't sign them because you've got half a band here.'

Larry took me over to meet Tom. When we started talking, I asked him what he wanted as a musician. Tom wasn't like Jon. He didn't tell me he wanted to be bigger than Elvis. He was more humble than that. He told me how much he loved Muddy Waters and Buddy Guy and wanted to be in a cool, bluesy rock band. I love that stuff, too, but that's not what I wanted to hear from someone when I asked them about their goals. I wasn't sure he wanted to be a rock star badly enough.

I told Tom we should stay in touch and to keep sending me any new music. I guess he might have been hungrier than I originally gave him credit for. Over the next year, he sent me another hundred songs, and they were considerably better than the first batch. To my relief, he fired Schermick and Destra in 1985. The two formed the glam-metal band Britny Fox, who eventually wound up on CBS; tragically, Destra died in a car accident two years later. Larry helped Tom put together a better band featuring guitarist Jeff LaBar and drummer Fred Coury and invited me to see another one of their gigs. Everyone in the band looked prettier than *Sports Illustrated* swimsuit models, making them, perhaps, the prettiest of all the pretty boy bands. They were better with makeup than most women, and from the back, many people mistook them for girls. More importantly, though, they rocked hard.

I signed Cinderella to a development deal and called the producer Andy Johns, who agreed to record four songs at the Sound Factory in Hollywood. They came out with the single 'Shake Me' and three other tunes, all of which sounded like the soundtrack to a roaring party. It was good-time, down-and-dirty, bluesy rock'n'roll. There was no question that Tom had evolved to star level, and his new band had the attitude to back his performance. I immediately took a major interest in them, offering them a deal for a full album, as well as working with Tom to co-write one of their biggest hits.

One of the songs Tom sent me had a solid beginning but then shot off in an uncomplimentary direction. It didn't have a strong pre-chorus or a chorus. It was just blah.

'Tom, this is a great start for a song, I love it, but the rest of it doesn't hold together,' I told him over the phone. 'How would you like to try writing the rest of it with me? I've got some ideas I think you'll like.'

'I'm open to it,' he said. 'Let's give it a try.'

The ideas I had for the song came from working with other hard-rockers making lighter-raising ballads at PolyGram. We had just worked with Def Leppard on their breakthrough melodic single, 'Bringing On The Heartbreak.' It had a similar kind of rhythm to the song Tom sent me, but it had an undeniable B-section that led up to a rousing chorus. To be honest, it had producer Mutt Lange's signature all over it.

'Listen to this,' I said. I played the song for Tom. 'Now, let's try to emulate the section that leads into the chorus.' We both messed around with a couple of ideas and then finessed them into the perfect part (thank you, Mutt), which Tom and I put our own spin on. The song, 'Nobody's Fool,' became one of Cinderella's biggest hits. The band didn't credit me for my writing contribution, but that was fine. I was making a good salary at the label, and I had plenty of songwriting credits on my résumé. I was just pleased to know I'd helped them take off.

With a combination of surefire radio hits and raucous rockers to work with, I put the band back in the studio with Andy Johns to record a full album. He wanted to work at Bearsville Studio in Woodstock, New York, so the band drove out there from Philadelphia to find Andy in full-on rock'n'roll mode. He's a hard-living, indulgent English producer who had worked with The Rolling Stones, Led Zeppelin, and Van Halen, so we were lucky to have him on our team. But when he was in the zone, he went into method-rocker mode, ingesting as many drugs as his peers, downing anything that would keep him flying, and injecting every ounce of unstable creativity into the production. He had brilliant sensibilities, but he was as volatile as crypto coins, which frightened the hell out of Tom.

From the start, it was clear that Cinderella's drummer, Fred Coury, wasn't cutting it. Either he didn't know the songs or he was intimidated by Andy. Whatever, he was off the beat, and he couldn't match the energy level of his bandmates.

In the middle of one song, Andy walked over to the kit and started punching the snare and kicking the bass drum. He yelled at poor Fred and practically tore him away from the set.

'You're ruining everything,' Andy shouted. 'You're fucking up the band!'

Fred was kicked out of the room and Andy called in session drummer Jody Cortez, who had toured with Boz Scaggs. Cortez wasn't a metal drummer, but he could hit hard and kept a steady beat, which galvanized the rest of the band. With a new, reliable rhythmic pulse, Cinderella were playing like seasoned professionals. Now, in the middle of a banging session, Andy started screaming with delight.

'Man, I love this so, fuckin' much I'm going to cut my wrists and use my blood to write *love* and *hate* all over the speakers!'

Tom thought Andy was using some kind of English euphemism, so he laughed and raised a fist in the air. Then Andy grabbed a razor blade he was using to cut tape, slashed his wrists, and did exactly what he said he would do.

I wasn't there at the time, but my phone rang and I saw it was Tom, so I picked up.

'He's killing himself!' Tom cried. 'You have to come over!'

'What's that?'

'It's Andy. He's hurt himself, and I think he's bleeding to death!'

I rushed over to the studio, and when I got there Andy was still in a manic state, his wrists wrapped in wet white washcloths stained red. His eyes were bulging.

'Derek, I love this so much, I'm giving my blood!' Andy exclaimed.

'Wow, okay,' I said. 'Just stay in control, mate. Don't go overboard. We'd hate to lose you.'

If Andy's studio behavior was psychotic, his production was anything but. Every instrument had its place in the mix, Tom's vocal performance was insanely good, and the energy level was intoxicating. *Night Songs* sounded unbelievable and was everything I hoped it would be. Not only did Tom's heartfelt vocals and penetrating guitar ooze with charisma, but he imbued Cinderella with a sound that was missing from the rock and metal world. His blues influences—the same ones that initially made me second-guess his ambition—crackled through the mix, giving the band a vibe somewhat reminiscent of AC/DC, which hadn't released an album in a while. In a weird way, Cinderella filled that hole, combining bluesy riffs with simple arrangements and a great vocal.

Jon Bon Jovi and Richie Sambora, who became good friends with Cinderella, sang background vocals on 'Nothin' For Nothin'' and 'In From The Outside' and appeared in the video for 'Somebody Save Me,' which lured in the MTV music programmers. The station put Cinderella into rapid rotation, and *Night Songs* debuted at #3 on *Billboard. Slippery When Wet* was at the top, beating out Bruce Springsteen's *Born In The USA*. I had signed bands with the #1 and #3 albums in America. Bon Jovi was the new Jersey sensation, topping the old Jersey legend. I could live with Cinderella taking a back seat to Bruce, and they were fine with it as well. It was their first album, after all. We were all off to the races.

Connections are everything in the music business, and I'll always owe a nod of gratitude to Doc McGhee. Of course, I was the one who convinced Jon Bon Jovi to go with him instead of David Krebs, but Gene Simmons introduced me to Desmond Child, so it has been a symbiotic relationship. And I would never have discovered Cinderella if Bon Jovi and Larry Mazur hadn't mentioned them to me.

My experience with another rock success, Kingdom Come, also began with a tip-off from Mazur. Their original vocalist, Lenny Wolfe, had been in the German band Stone Fury, who were on MCA when they broke up.

'So, Lenny is great,' Larry told me. 'He's managed by this guy Marty, and they're putting a new band together.'

Larry played me Stone Fury, and man, Lenny had a striking, multi-octave voice that was pitch perfect. With Larry's help, he assembled a group of musicians that included drummer James Kottak, who consistently played a hair behind the beat in the vein of drummer John Bonham, giving the music a propulsive sound. (Kottak would later replace Herman Rarebell in

Scorpions and stayed with them until he died in 2024.) Lenny's tendency to sound a lot like a combination of Robert Plant and David Coverdale only cemented the comparisons to Led Zeppelin, but they sounded like a *great* Zeppelin (in contrast with the multitude of bad ones). And, in the absence of an active Zeppelin, I viewed that as a positive.

I asked Bob Rock if he would produce the Kingdom Come album. This would be his first big solo production gig, preceding his legendary work with Mötley Crüe, Metallica, and others. Kingdom Come flew out to Little Sound Studios in Vancouver and knocked out their self-titled album, including the ballsy, swaggering 'Get It On,' which helped propel the album to #12 and cement its gold status. Before the label released the song as a single, Bob convinced us to print up vinyl copies without any writing on the record or jacket and send them to radio. Many radio programmers and disc jockeys thought it was Led Zeppelin, which is what we were hoping for. It reminded me of when Simon Dupree did 'We Are The Moles' and it was mistaken for The Beatles.

Kingdom Come came out and went gold that same week. However, our calculated tactics were problematic for the band. Lenny was a prideful creature who was melodramatic on the surface yet insecure deep down. He didn't want to appeal to us for guidance, and he didn't understand what he needed to do to get people to align themselves with him. Everyone compared Kingdom Come to Led Zeppelin, which caused a backlash. Lenny could have dealt with it by telling the press he was influenced by Zep—he loved them, and he was flattered that his band was being compared to the legends. That would have ended most of the media snark right away. But he didn't do that. He became defensive and insisted that Kingdom Come weren't trying to be anyone but themselves. He threatened to shut the band down and became abusive whenever anyone asked him about Led Zeppelin. The press fed off the negativity, became even more spiteful, and left Kingdom Come facing an uphill battle. The first album was still getting strong airplay when they toured, and they landed an opening slot on a great bill, the 1988 Monsters Of Rock package tour that also featured Metallica, Dokken, Scorpions, and Van Halen. Kingdom Come's second album, *In Your Face*, came out in 1989, after I had left PolyGram. It had some decent songs and was initially well-received, but the band broke up before heading out on tour.

Although I was never a huge metal fan, I had my greatest success at PolyGram signing hard rock and metal bands. Those weren't the only kind of artists I worked with, however. I also signed Dexys Midnight Runners to the label and pulled a 180 by bringing the quirky Montreal new-wave band Men Without Hats into the PolyGram family for their third album. The group had a huge, wacky hit in 1982 with the synth-pop novelty 'The Safety Dance.' By 1986, they were out of the mass public's consciousness, but they were silly and fun, and I liked them. One day, multi-instrumentalist and vocalist Ivan Doroschuk brought a bunch of demos to me. One of them had a quirky instrumental keyboard riff, which I loved. But that's all it was. It was called 'Pop Goes The World,' and, as with Cinderella, I suggested to Ivan that we work on the song together to turn it into something special.

I thought he might be resistant until he told me he was a massive Gentle Giant fan and was excited to co-write with me. I wanted the song to be silly and funny but also have commercial appeal. Without dampening the joyous main hook, I added a structured verse, and we worked it into the fun part, which became the instrumental chorus.

'Pop Goes The World' became the title track of the band's third album, and it revived their career, going platinum in Canada and hitting the Top 20 in the US. The single had a long life, reaching #1 in Austria, #2 in Canada, and #3 in South Africa. Again, I received no songwriting props, but helping out a fan of my former band was its own reward.

During this time I was hyper-focused and working around the clock on this new career. I was incredibly lucky that Sharon and my kids supported me, but there were more than a few times when my anxiety peaked and I wondered whether I was abandoning my family as my father had done. When I brought up my fears with Sharon, she talked me down and said I was ensuring the security of the family, not cavorting all night with my drinking buddies. We bought a bigger apartment close to where we were living, and I was able to purchase a weekend cottage in Putnam County, where the whole family could be together away from the city.

By the time my contract at PolyGram was nearing the end of its term, I was in demand as an executive. I had discovered and signed three of the biggest rock acts on the label and risen to the role of senior vice president. Now, I decided, it was time to run a label. Instead of directing the guy steering the ship, I wanted to be the captain behind the wheel. I scheduled a meeting with my attorney, Nick Gordon, to discuss my options before I made my wishes known to the company.

'I want to make it absolutely clear that your contract is ending. So, why don't you see what the folks who sign the paychecks want to do?' he suggested. 'I bet they offer you a blank check and let you fill in the amount.'

It wasn't a farfetched notion. I was riding one hell of a winning streak. I had signed Bon Jovi, Cinderella, Kingdom Come, and Dan Reed Network, as well as rebooting the careers of Men Without Hats and, to a lesser extent, Uriah Heep. But at PolyGram, I had climbed as high as I was going to get. They could have made me an executive, but I wanted to go somewhere that could give me the kind of autonomy that didn't exist in a company where everyone had to confer with a committee of departments staffed by people with their own agendas.

PolyGram offered to make me the president of Mercury Records, which the group had obtained in an umbrella deal along with Phillips and Phonogram. It would be a European and US-based company that I would run, but in effect, it would be more of the same, since I would still have to report to other people, and after my seven-year apprenticeship with PolyGram, I wanted to launch a new venture.

I let it slip in the right circles that I wanted to run a new company in a new way. As I expected, big-time label heads who had seen how successful I was at PolyGram wanted to charm me into working for their companies. They asked me to join them for meals at five-star restaurants, accompany them on first-class flights to visit their European offices, or take a weekend to visit satellite offices in exotic foreign lands. I knew I was hot shit, but it was funny how much everyone bent over backward to bring me on their team when, a decade earlier, I had had to struggle, compromise, and practically beg to get Gentle Giant a deal with a label with staffers who thought outside the box. I was still a square peg, and I wanted to find the right round hole to squeeze through.

David Geffen, who I have great respect for, flew me to LA to meet with him. He was a convincing, powerful leader and a straight shooter with a finely tuned bullshit meter and amazing ears. The first thing he told me when we sat down was that if I came over to Geffen, I would work closely with John Kalodner, who was one of the best A&R guys in the business, having signed deals with Aerosmith, White Zombie, Madness, XTC, Jimmy Page, Whitesnake, Nelson, Damn Yankees, and others. David added that he was also working with Tom Zutaut, who signed Mötley Crüe, Guns N' Roses, and others. Knowing how I wanted to run my own company, he told me he could offer me a splinter label and I could hire anyone I wanted to work with. David was even-keeled and persuasive. I met with him three times, and he always shuttled me around in limos, put me in the best hotels, and even offered me a piece of the company, which was extremely tempting. I told him I would let him know, while continuing to explore other offers.

I sat down for several meetings with Tommy Mottola, the US head of CBS Records. As established as the company was, and as much as it had to offer me, the world Tommy and his staffers inhabited was almost as foreign to me as the comedy of Yakov Smirnoff. The company executives were all dressed to the nines and acted like support characters in *The Godfather*. I guess they were too busy cow-towing to the boss to learn anything about me; when I sat down with them, only one of them knew who I was or what I had done. It was surreal to me that none of them knew anything about Gentle Giant, who ironically had released three albums on Columbia. Nonetheless, the label had big guns and made an enticing offer. Tommy said I could take over Epic or Portrait Records, the former of which had a great history.

My next meeting was with Tommy, CBS Records president and CEO Walter Yetnikoff, and Don Ienner, the president and future chairman of Columbia. There were big lunch spreads in the upstairs executive suite. We didn't talk music. Their biggest pitch was, '*Look, you know, we'll give you a huge salary.*' It was fascinating to see how hard all these top executives tried to woo me, and it was good for my ego to take these meetings and hear what they had to offer. What amazed and baffled me was how many times I was offered the finest cocaine—as much as I wanted—and beautiful escorts to serve my every desire. More than one exec would tell me, 'Blow and babes. They're all yours.' They were that up front. I was laughing about it because it was so absurd to me, but they were serious. This huge international corporation wasn't even subtle or discreet about telling me that cocaine and prostitutes were fringe benefits of working at Columbia...

Over at Atlantic, I met with Steve Ross, the COO and future CEO of Time Warner. After a friendly, informal discussion, he said, 'I'd love you to meet with Ahmet. I want him to show you what you could do with his Atlantic group of companies.'

I had met Ahmet Ertegun before, and I knew about his legendary contributions to the music business as the founder of Atlantic and the man who signed The Rolling Stones, Led Zeppelin, Aretha Franklin, CSNY, and loads of other legends.

'You're the hottest person out there,' Ahmet said. 'Obviously, the Warner Music Group would love to have you, and I'll have your back,' he added, which was assuring. Then, he said something unlike anything I had heard in a meeting with a top music exec. 'You just have to know that one day I'm not going to be here, so you better have people around you that will support you. You're on the top of the world and things are going great right now. But sometime in the future, you won't be. So, make sure that you hire people that will know what's going on—and will tell you.'

This was very sage advice—and advice that he didn't have to give me. I was impressed. Ahmet sold me hard on coming over to the Atlantic family of labels. After wooing me with the promise of running my own company with my own team and making big money, he made a generous, unusual offer. 'Derek, you're a hard worker. You need a little time to unwind. I want to send you and your family over to Turkey for a vacation at my villa. I'll be there to show you around.'

It was an offer made without conditions, so I accepted. Ahmet's people arranged for his private jet to fly us to Istanbul and for us to stay at the Hilton. He was there with his second wife, Mica. I went with Sharon and our kids, who were still quite young. After we finished sightseeing, we all had dinner at an incredible restaurant, where Ahmet was treated as royalty, a king with subjects who fawned over him like Solomon. In Ahmet's case, with great power comes great indulgence.

After dinner, Sharon tended to the kids in the corner while Ahmet and I talked shop. 'When the wives have gone home, we'll go out somewhere special,' he told me in confidence.

It was getting late, so Sharon took the kids back to the hotel. I told her that Ahmet wanted to speak with me privately and that I'd be home later. Ahmet's limo driver picked us up, and as soon as the doors closed, we were whisked away to a private disco. I'm sure it had a name, but the only applicable term I can come up with is the Whore's Club. There were beautiful girls of all nationalities wearing practically nothing. Ahmet introduced me, and within seconds these girls were throwing themselves at me like I was Sean Connery in his early Bond days.

'You're such a handsome man,' one blonde woman said, licking her lips. A brunette grabbed me and said, 'I hope you're having a great night. I can make it even better.' An exotic Asian woman slid two fingers down my chest. 'Relax and let me take care of you.'

My eyes shot around the room seeking an escape. If I wasn't happily married, maybe I would have rolled with it . . . but nah, paying for sex—even with someone else's money—was never my style. As it was, cheating on Sharon wasn't even an option. The situation was completely surreal. Ahmet had gone from Solomon to Caligula. He was surrounded by women who were clearly intimately familiar with him and chatting away as they rubbed oil over his bare torso.

'Wow, you know, I've got to get up early in the morning for a meeting,' I feebly sputtered. I walked over to Ahmet and thanked him for a great time and his incredible generosity. I told him I was still jetlagged and exhausted and I needed to get back to the hotel.

'Derek, it's just us,' he cooed. 'You, me, the girls. Let's have some fun. If you want, we can have Sharon and Mica come over and join us.'

Ahmet seemed to be suggesting that if I wasn't okay with just being with him and these girls, maybe our wives could be driven over to take part in some kind of wild orgy. Maybe Mica would be okay with that, but it wouldn't have flown with Sharon, and it wasn't anything I could fathom. I stuck to my story about being jetlagged, adding I had an upset stomach, which wasn't far from the truth. Ahmet shrugged as I left and was driven back to the hotel. I checked in on the kids, who were sleeping, hugged my wife, and we went to bed with our arms wrapped around one another.

My lack of interest in polyamory didn't sour Ahmet on hiring me, and he acted as if nothing had happened. In actuality, nothing did. He took us to his boardroom and set up a two-day tour of Turkey for Sharon and the kids. Then he took me to his villa in Bodrum, where his chefs prepared an amazing dinner for us. We were joined by former ABC News anchorman Peter Jennings and his wife and kids. I had a good time with Peter. We spent more time than was necessary talking about cricket, but we laughed and enjoyed one another's company. Ahmet put us up in a guest house, which was like a palace, and after dinner, Turkish music performers played at an amphitheater outside of his estate. I don't know if Peter was being offered the same amenities as I was, and I didn't mention anything. When he wandered off, however, Ahmet said, 'When the guests have gone, we can go to another special club.'

I don't know if Ahmet was bisexual or if he wanted to intimately know the people working for him. It was beyond anything I could comprehend. One of the female guests brought over a silver appetizer tray. She opened it, revealing a huge mound of cocaine. Someone else offered me Turkish hash. Again, I had to wriggle out of the situation. For a second, Ahmet looked at me perplexed. Maybe he thought *I* was gay, or maybe a narc or a former addict. I was a high-stakes player in rock'n'roll, and I was turning down top-quality drugs and wild sex? For him, that didn't compute. He was doing his best to win me over by offering me things he valued, and I kept turning them down.

I think Ahmet figured I would enjoy the booze, drugs, prostitutes, and untethered hedonism because these indulgences were byproducts of wealth and power, and almost every other record executive reveled in the opportunity to indulge. He was a brilliant man, and he wasn't about to question my personal quirks.

'I understand,' he smiled, even though he didn't. 'I will have my driver take you back to the hotel.'

We flew back to New York. Sharon and the kids returned to their daily lives, and I ping-ponged back and forth between corporate label offices as I weighed my future. There could never be enough meetings, and all of the top executives competed to outdo one another. 'Well, what did they offer you?' was a phrase I sometimes heard from execs willing to outbid their competitors. It reminded me of wealthy people at an auction paying top dollar for a rare painting, and it wasn't too different from the way some of these guys battled to sign the biggest bands in the hottest genres. I'd learned the game at PolyGram. No matter what was on offer, I knew not to say yes or no. I listened and heard what everyone had to say, as well as what they could promise, and how the job would fit the next step I wanted to take with my career.

Back at Columbia, we were talking about that subsidiary label I told them I might want to run. Walter hired a private jet, and we went to New Orleans to see some great Cajun music, enjoy some of the local cuisine, and talk over the possibilities. Once again, Yetnikoff pulled out the old hookers-and-blow playbook. Unbelievable. The music business had accepted straight-edge artists for decades, but a clean and sober record company executive? Out of the question!

Having spoken with numerous insiders, I found out that Doug Morris, who had been President of Atlantic Records since 1980, was having a run of bad luck and was scared shitless of me coming in and taking over the company, which I had zero interest in doing. He didn't know that, and even if I told him, he wouldn't have believed me. He came from the cutthroat world of high-stakes business, where employees routinely stabbed one another in the back to get ahead. I have always found that kind of duplicity pathetic. It takes far more courage to be a team player than a saboteur.

I had another meeting with Steve Ross.

'So, how did it go with Ahmet Ertegun?' he asked me.

'I'll say one thing. He's a real character.'

'Yes. Yes, he is,' agreed Ross. He had one more shot at seducing me to join Atlantic. 'Honestly, though,' Steve said. 'I think this could be the place for you. You won't have to answer to Ahmet. You don't even have to see him if you don't want to. And this is Warner Music. You'll have the weight of Warner, Elektra, and Atlantic behind you. You can build your own team, and you're the perfect person to revive ATCO Records and turn it into something great.'

ATCO was founded in 1955 and had released albums by Bobby Darin, The Coasters, Sonny & Cher, Buffalo Springfield, Vanilla Fudge, Pete Townshend, and many others before becoming a mostly dormant Atlantic offshoot. Steve Ross wanted to revive it as a competitive rock label. I liked the idea of being a part of the Warner Music family, which had great acts and lots of cache, and I was impressed that Steve wasn't trying to sweeten the deal with fringe benefits. During a silent moment in our meeting, I pointed under his desk at a basket of promotional goodie bags that each contained a straw doll, a rattle, and some candies.

'What are those for?' I asked.

'We have a retreat in Jamaica, and we hand out these dollar souvenirs to people when they come in. Do you want one?'

As bizarre as it sounds, that little gesture of offering me a one-dollar doll made a huge difference in my perspective. Steve wasn't offering me babes and blow, private jets, or a key to the executive washroom. He was asking if I would like a silly little doll. He didn't say, 'Oh, take the whole basket.' He wasn't treating me like an executive he wanted to win over—more like a dad he bumped into who might want a little knick-knack for his kids. That was enough for me to decide I would accept the ATCO job. As long as I was answering to Steve, who seemed to get me and my 'non-rockisms,' this Warner Music Group family was right for me. So, that was it. They offered me a joint venture contract, which was unbelievable from a business standpoint, and we signed the deal.

I gave my notice at PolyGram, went over to 75 Rockefeller Center, and started putting a team together. I needed to make sure everyone at the label was like-minded so we wouldn't have anyone with conflicting interests or agendas. The people I liked working with best at PolyGram weren't egomaniacs or hedonists, they were music lovers who wanted to be part of a creative team. I knew I had to build the team quickly and start signing artists that would make a dent right away because Warner Music Group had poured a lot of money into ATCO's resurrection. I had to perform, and the pressure was on.

I brought in some great people I had worked with at PolyGram. Harry Palmer, who was the head of marketing, became my General Manager, and Ted Green became my head of business affairs. I also brought over some marketing people I trusted, and I hired a guy from Chicago named Craig Lambert, who was at Capitol when Gentle Giant were on the label. He was a total whack-job, tall and crazy, but he had so much energy. And more to the point, he got Gentle Giant on the radio in Chicago at a time when getting our music airplay was next to impossible.

Some of my industry friends told me I might want to think twice about Craig, telling me he was a bit of a loony, but I thought a loony would work at the kind of asylum I wanted to run. The only problem was that I had to lure him over from Capitol, and as far as I knew he was happy there. I called him up.

'Craig, I don't know if you remember me, but I was a PolyGram for …'

'You're in Gentle Giant!' Craig interjected.

'Right. We broke up ten years ago and I became the vice president for PolyGram and now I'm at ATCO, which is part of the Warner Records family,' I said. We're looking for a radio promotions …'

'Wow, yeah, I'd love to work for you!' he enthused.

It was a done deal. I had my team. Now it was time to let the lunatics do their thing. I told Harry, Ted, and Craig to hire the people they wanted to work with and that they didn't need to run them by me first. That was the secret. I knew I had to delegate, but I didn't want to manage. I wanted ATCO to be a team that could pursue a joint vision and celebrate our success together. Now it was time to sign some artists.

GIANT STEPS

CHAPTER TWENTY

BLACK-TOOTHED GRIN

One day toward the end of my tenure at PolyGram, I was talking to a little-known lawyer out of New York named Jules Kurtz. He was working with a band from Texas called Pantera, and he was contacting every label around to try to help them get a deal. He showed me a videotape of a live show that they'd shot soon after they hired their new vocalist, Philip Anselmo. After checking it out, I compared it to one of the three albums they had self-released with their previous singer, Terry Glaze, and the new guy was a huge improvement. I found out he had been doing shows with the band since 1986, and he was on their latest self-released record, 1988's *Power Metal*, which was a huge development and far heavier than their previous releases.

I was familiar with Pantera as I had seen their name in fanzines and on flyers when I was living in Texas. There was a big buzz about them around Dallas, and their guitarist Diamond Darrell (who would change his name to Dimebag a few years later) was being called a cross between Randy Rhoads and Eddie Van Halen. They played shows all the time, but no record company would touch them.

'Jules, I'm really interested in this band,' I told him, shortly before I exited PolyGram. 'But please don't tell anyone because I'm moving labels, and I'd like to at least see if I could do something with them.'

I felt in my gut that Pantera had the potential to be a huge metal band, and I thought I could make them a priority at ATCO the way Bon Jovi had been at PolyGram. At the same time, I didn't want to hold up their career while I was putting the label together. I told Jules not to wait for me if he got another offer, but that once I was on staff at my new job, I wanted to look closely at Pantera and see if I could make them work with the rest of my roster. Strangely, however, I might never have gotten around to signing them if my new boss hadn't asked if I would hire his son to work for me.

This wasn't a condition of me getting the job, it was a favor that Steve asked for, and I was happy to help out. Mark Ross wanted to be an A&R man, so I met with him and immediately found him to be smart, knowledgeable, and friendly. He had already worked in various capacities at Warner Music Group, but since he was Steve's son, no one took him seriously. They thought he was only working in music because of his dad, or that he was a spy sent to make sure everyone he worked with was loyal to the company. It was a shitty position for him to be in.

'Mark, I don't give a damn who your father is,' I told him during our meeting. 'I'd like to hire you, and if you work hard and things go well, we all win. But I'm not going to give you any special treatment.'

Mark was grateful for the job and excited to help bring bands to the label. I sent him out to Houston to see a band called Tangier. Hurricane Hugo had just swept through the northeastern Caribbean, causing extensive damage, but the airline didn't think it would progress as rapidly up the southeastern United States as it did. Mark's plane took off, but it had to be rerouted to Dallas to avoid the storm. When he landed, he called to let me know the Tangier gig was a wash and ask me if there was anyone in Dallas worth seeing. I told him he should check out Pantera and gave him the contact number I had for the band.

Mark called, and their drummer, Vinnie Paul, answered the phone. Mark said he was from ATCO and would love to check out the band's show that night. Pantera didn't have an actual show booked, but Vinnie told him they were scheduled to play at some girl's birthday party at a Mexican restaurant in Fort Worth. He told Mark to show up if he was interested and gave him the address.

At about 11:30 that night, my home phone rang.

'Derek, this is Mark! I'm sorry to call you so late, but I had to let you know that I saw Pantera, and they were the best band I've ever seen in my whole life!'

I told him I was happy to hear it. I hoped his enthusiasm confirmed my thoughts that these guys were ready for a deal and I should strike before other labels came sniffing around. At the same time, I had some reservations. Mark was a rookie, and his effusiveness could have come from his excitement about being on his first real scouting assignment.

The next week, I flew to Texas to see Pantera at a club in Arlington. Within three songs, I had become a fan beyond a fan. Phil was such an incredible frontman, and Darrell had that X-factor that could never be scientifically manufactured. He was a whizz on guitar, and his sound was so thick and heavy, with a crunch so vicious I thought the speakers in his amp would burst. He loved playing, and it showed. As aggressive as the riffs were, and as wild as his solos could be, he injected joy into every note. He wasn't just a guitar hero, he was a petroleum-fueled character, and his outrageous personality rang through his fingers and out to the world. He was a star.

The strong connection between Darrell and his brother, drummer Vinnie Paul, kept the music fist-tight, and Phil brought an untamed, sometimes unhinged quality to the band. They had grown and become more aggressive and exciting than they were when they formed as a glammy metal band who worshipped Van Halen and Ratt. Now, they were more like Metallica crossed with Judas Priest, but with a meaner Southern bite. I knew they would only get meaner and better. So, we signed them.

The band wanted Ozzy Osbourne producer Max Norman to work with them on their first major label album. Max flew to Texas to see a show and felt they had promise, but before he had already accepted a gig to produce a new album by ex-Dokken guitarist George Lynch's new band, Lynch Mob, and he couldn't do both records at the same time. We didn't have the budget to match the offer George made him, so Max had to back out of the Pantera gig.

This turned out to be the best thing that could have happened. Darrell liked the guitar sounds on a pair of albums by Overkill and Metal Church that were both produced by Terry Date, so we gave him a call. It worked out perfectly, and they would end up going back to Terry for every album until they made their very last one, 2000's *Reinventing The Steel.*

Terry was cheerful, easygoing, and open to any ideas the band had about improving their sound. Pantera were obsessive about being as heavy as a tub of mercury yet having each note ring out with lethal clarity. Having played hundreds of club shows over the years, they knew how to set the dials to maximize their sound, and Darrell was a master of his gear, setting his amps with lots of high and low tone but practically no midrange ('scooping the mids,' as it's known) to achieve a devastating rhythmic crunch as well as a piercing quality that made his guitar leads stand out at any volume.

Aside from honing their sound live, Darrell and Vinnie had spent plenty of time learning the ropes with their dad, country artist and producer Jerry Abbott, in his studio, Pantego Sound. Before they started working with Terry, they sent me the demos for 'Cowboys From Hell,' 'Walk,' and some other tracks, and they sounded great—incredibly tight, galvanized, and well-mixed. It was a great starting point.

Terry recorded *Cowboys From Hell* with the band at their dad's studio, fine-tuning their demo sound to make them street-lethal. After recording a take, he'd sit down with Darrell and bassist Rex Brown, slowing down the analogue tape and listening to the playback to make sure every drum beat, bass note, and guitar riff were perfectly synchronized. If they weren't, they'd do it again. They were that consumed with becoming the most precise metal band ever.

Considering how much they loved drinking, smoking weed, and partying hard, it's amazing that Pantera were able to resort to muscle memory and make their recordings so tight, even when they swaggered and grooved. The band's wild streak went hand-in-hand with the rowdy, raucous music they made. Whether they were tracking a song, inventing mixed drinks, making weird sci-fi videos, or taunting poor Terry (who responded incredibly well to their devious pranks, even when they stole his rental car to tear up and terrorize the neighborhood, then returning it severely damaged), Pantera were filled with childlike glee and impish joy. I told Terry that as long as they remained dedicated, productive, tight, and musically exceptional, and didn't kill anyone, I didn't care what they did for fun. I'd even foot the bill for a few trashed rental cars. But I had seen too many bands destroyed by their own indulgences, and I made it clear that in no way would I put up with Pantera's shenanigans if it impaired their performances. I urged Terry to make sure they were clean and sober when they recorded. As precise as the music was, I can't guarantee it was all recorded sober. But that's rock'n'roll.

Some of Pantera's pranks were overblown and even dangerous, but they weren't mean-spirited. They loved to 'bust a nut,' as they put it, and if that meant daring crew members or other musicians to consume used cigarettes in their beer, paying unwary friends to eat everything on a deli tray that had been pissed on, drawing penises in Sharpie on the faces of revelers who passed out, or throwing firecrackers at other musicians asleep in the bunk, it was all part of the revelry. They were absolutely authentic. What you saw was what you got.

I loved Pantera, and I was also their label head, which meant checking in on them in the studio and hanging out with them backstage. Knowing their reputation for tomfoolery and hearing their aggressive music, I was a little nervous about socializing with them. I figured I would be completely out of my element on the party front, and I didn't want to be held down and have to slink home with Sharpie penises drawn on my face. I hoped to talk to them about music and touring, which I felt was an important part of exposing them to new audiences. While bands like Nirvana, Soundgarden, Pearl Jam, and Smashing Pumpkins were starting to pave the way for a changing heavy music scene, MTV and radio still weren't exactly gung-ho about thrash metal. But that left an opening for a rowdy, bombastic sound kids weren't hearing elsewhere.

I went backstage after a show in New York to hang out with the band, and the party was already raging. Darrell and Vinnie were passing around shots of Black Tooth Grin, which I later found out was a Darrell invention consisting of Seagram's Seven with just a splash of Coca-Cola (they later upped the formula to Royal Crown when they got some money). They greeted me with warm handshakes and handed me a shot. Figuring it would help ingratiate me with the band so I wouldn't be seen as a corporate teetotaler, I downed the drink. My throat was on fire. Darrell handed me another. I finished that as well. When I regained my ability to speak, I told them how great they were onstage and how well their sound would carry in a huge venue. Vinnie slapped me on the back like I was a high school buddy. I felt included, but as the alcohol went to my brain and I started to get lightheaded, I thought, *If I carry on like this, I won't be around tomorrow. I'll die right here!*

The next time I saw the band, I made sure Mark Ross came along. He was younger and a bit of a drinker, so he did enough revelry for both of us. When I was handed a drink, I leaned against a wall, and when no one was looking I splashed the booze onto the floor. Another maneuver I developed was to feed Black Tooth Grins (dozens of them, over time) to potted plants and shower vodka cocktails over railings and onto hotel balconies and sidewalks. When we were at the bar, I made sure to order a club soda and lime that looked like an alcoholic beverage and then drink it like I was relishing a fine cocktail.

Despite the differences in our drinking practices, the band and I got along well and became great friends. They were fantastic, brilliant people, and I loved them to death. They had that effect on people. They enjoyed having a good time and made sure everyone around them was equally entertained, amused, and/or wasted. They all had such different personalities and interests, which made them fun to be around and musically unstoppable. It wouldn't be too farfetched to call them the heavy-metal Beatles. You have to have a certain level of friction meshed with airtight camaraderie to be a great, airtight band. In the best moments, something comes out in the music that stems from that friction, that contrast. And it's those differences that make great bands exceptional. I could see that in Pantera.

Phil Anselmo was full of anger, listened to hardcore, and loved boxing. He viewed life as a struggle, and while he could be a great guy, he didn't want to get too close to anyone. When he was in a bad mood, it was best to leave him alone. He was the darkest member of the band, and he endured many dark nights of the soul long before he got hooked on narcotics and almost destroyed the fragile chemistry of Pantera toward the end. Vinnie was the pragmatic *let's get it together and do this* guy. He kept things moving. Dimebag was the biggest party guy and a happy drunk. 'Hey, c'mon Phil,' he'd growl. 'Let's do some shots!' Phil would go along with it and laugh along with Dime, but then he would go off and party with his own people, who were a little more volatile and less positive about life. Then there was Rex, the quiet, creative bass player who drank with his buddies but would just as often be in the corner drinking by himself. Pantera had the perfect combination of creative forces to make them about as heavy as a metal band could be.

When Terry finished *Cowboys From Hell*, it sounded modern and savage, mixing elements of thrash, traditional metal, and something newer and more forward-thinking, which set the bar for the new wave of American metal bands like Lamb Of God, Slipknot, and Machine Head. Between Metallica-inspired riffs and shredding solos, the rhythms abounded with Southern groove and brimmed with attitude. As a record executive, it was clear this was a great album with a batch of classic songs. Now that I had it in my hands, I had to figure out what to do to attract the uninitiated. My first thought was, *I can't believe this is so fucking good*, followed by, *How the hell am I going to break this?*

MTV was at the end of its AOR period, and the glam era was fading. Grunge and alternative were starting to sway programmers. Where MTV went, radio followed. And radio wasn't playing much hair metal anymore. The closest they were getting was Guns N' Roses and Pearl Jam. They'd still have a soft spot for a hooky Journey song, but something as rooted in thrash and bursting with exuberant rage as Pantera—that seemed like the last thing anyone would put into rotation. I realized that to break into an environment that was growing hostile to metal, Pantera needed a good manager.

I called up Walter O'Brien, who I knew from Concrete Marketing back when we were both doing radio promotion, and invited him to my office. We exchanged pleasantries, and then he tried to get me to sign the Seattle band Metal Church, who had lost their label deal following several good, heavy albums.

'Well, Walter,' I began. 'I would love to talk about Metal Church. But right now, I'm thinking about something bigger. I want representation for Pantera, because they just did a really great record, and I believe they could blow up on a mainstream level. I think you're the right person to manage them.'

Having taken tons of metal bands to radio, Walter spoke Pantera's language as well as anyone. I brought them together, and they clicked right away. He agreed that outside of the few metal radio stations that existed, it was going to be hard to get Pantera airplay. We decided the best way to build awareness was to put the band in front of audiences to do what they were best at—tearing up the stage. We put a ton of money into touring and put them on the road with everyone we could think of: alt-metal, funk-metal, thrash—all were fair game.

Throughout 1990, anyone who needed a support band, big or small, Pantera opened for them: Prong, Suicidal Tendencies, Exodus, Mind Over Four, Sanctuary, Fates Warning. We reached out to journalists and radio folk in every market and comped so many tickets at every show that the clubs were always packed. No matter how mismatched the bill might seem, Pantera were consistently unbelievable. Phil climbed PA monitors and amplifier stacks and leaped back to the stage like an Olympic athlete. Rex and Vinnie locked into one another's playing with unerring precision, and Darrell soared above it all, striking metal poses, making rock faces, and flying through solos that wowed audiences every night. They were young, but having played so many shows in their teens, Pantera were already veteran performers, yet they played with the hunger and energy only young, ambitious, and slightly dangerous bands can generate. I was sure Pantera's live shows would make them legends.

A year after *Cowboys From Hell* was released, Pantera were opening for Judas Priest in England. And by the time they started working on their second album, *Vulgar Display Of Power*, they were more focused and determined. Having tasted the fruits of stardom on their first ATCO album, they were writing better, more consistent songs, and fans who discovered the band from their live shows, via word of mouth, or through impulse purchases were eager to snatch up *Vulgar* when it came out on February 25, 1992. It wasn't on radio; it wasn't on TV. Only the fans knew about it, and in no time, there were tons of them; in less than two years, Pantera went from playing rock clubs to headlining arenas.

GIANT STEPS

CHAPTER TWENTY-ONE

STRAIGHT INTO COMPTON

It might seem strange that the guy who signed Bon Jovi and Cinderella and resurrected Men Without Hats would be so gung-ho about Pantera. Maybe I welcomed the challenge of doing something totally different. At the same time, I've always loved great music, and it was clear to me that Pantera were a great band headed for great things. Besides, it was hardly my greatest fish-out-of-water moment at ATCO. That came when the label signed a distribution deal with Ruthless Records, and I was jettisoned with no seatbelt into the wild world of gangsta rap. During my whole tenure in the music business, there's only one time I've felt completely out of my element and possibly scared for my life, and that was when I was meeting with the members of N.W.A and traveling around LA with their entourage.

N.W.A manager Jerry Heller and rapper Eric 'Eazy-E' Wright founded Ruthless with $7,000 in 1988, and in no time they had built up an underground empire, putting out records by the group and their members Easy E, Dr. Dre, Ice Cube, and Arabian Prince (later replaced by MC Ren). In an effort to reach a larger and more diverse audience and sell more records, they negotiated a distribution deal with the Warner Music Group, and I wound up as the middleman. For some reason, the higher-ups at the company thought I was the right man for the job.

The first time I met with Jerry and Eric was in New York, and with us as we talked was a huge hulk of a man who didn't say a word. When I asked who he was, I found out his name was Suge Knight and he was the label's bodyguard. I would never have guessed it at the time, but he already had a rap sheet longer than the label's catalogue. Soon after that, I went out to LA to meet the rest of the group. Being utterly naïve about gangsta rap, I didn't believe all the hype about gangs and guns. When Suge was standing guard at our meeting, I figured he was part of some gangster hip-hop shtick and just there to emphasize the toughness these guys wanted to get across in their music. It seemed like part of an image to help make N.W.A seem more dangerous and increase their sales—kind of like Black Sabbath did when they wrote songs about satanism.

When I arrived at LAX, Jerry and Eric picked me up in a black Mercedes. I sat in the front seat next to the driver; Eric and Jerry were in the back. I looked down and noticed a truncheon at my feet. Not wanting to make a big deal over it, I placed my hand on the armrest and saw a handgun in the compartment where other celebrities usually kept CDs, books, and maps. That's when I knew I was dealing with people who knew how to fire guns and use clubs and might already have done so against other individuals. I had read that Eric started working in music after his cousin was murdered and figured it was part of the mythology. Now, I believed it. *Oh, shit! What had I gotten myself into?* Even Don Arden and his team of thugs were small potatoes compared to the *shoot first don't bother asking questions later* ethos of LA gangs like the Crips and Bloods.

This was not a world I understood. It was a lucrative corner of the music business, for sure. Eazy-E's *Eazy-Duz-It*, the label's first release, was a huge success; N.W.A's *Straight Outta Compton* hit pay dirt and was a landmark release; and the company was about to release an album by Dre's girlfriend, Michel'le, that was sure to be successful. But I was acutely aware that being a part of this windfall of cash wasn't worth the risk of a hailstorm of bullets through the windshield. I had to concentrate to hide my discomfort and act professionally.

We drove through the Compton and Watts areas of LA to Ruthless HQ in a dilapidated and dangerous neighborhood right in the middle of the South Central ghetto. It reeked of desperation and decay, and I started to understand where these rappers were coming from and what their music was about. They were reflecting their world, which was about being downtrodden, being a minority, and having to use whatever assets and experience you had to get your message across. The shit they rapped about—police brutality, racism, guns, drive-bys, drug deals, murder—was all real. The music was part of the message, and the message was about their lifestyle. I realized their songs were art imitating life, and I started to understand why and how hip-hop became incredibly popular. It was authentic, raw, and scary, and it offered a glimpse into a crazy world that listeners could learn about from the safety of their locked suburban homes.

I first met Jerry when I was in Gentle Giant and he was a young Jewish kid just starting out in the music industry, and I was relieved there was someone there who I had something in common with. When we got out of the car, he said, 'Look, follow my lead. You have to trust me and believe me because I know this world. It's a world you want to benefit from. The music is massive, and I promise you when they present something to you, you'll be very happy, and so will they. But this is not a world you want to be part of.'

Fair enough. I didn't fit in anyway. But I had to do my job and work in this genre of music that was foreign to me, and I did my best. The first project I worked was Michel'le's album. Jerry played it to me, which wasn't bad. Her vocals were incredible, but I wasn't used to the sound of samples in hip-hop, so the beats sounded too electronic to me.

'Listen to me, this is going to be a winner,' Heller said.

I knew this was more his domain than mine, but I felt there was room for improvement. 'Don't get me wrong, I think it's good,' I told him. 'I just feel like it could sound more organic. I'd love to sit down with Dre and listen to the record with him, and I can give him some input. How's that sound?'

'You da boss,' Heller chuckled. Around a week later, Jerry came to my office with Dre and Suge, who stood in the back. Dre played the record. Not realizing Dre was the grand master of hip-hop beats (and the man who would eventually name his headphone company Beats), I suggested he rethink the mix.

'Could you maybe get the beats to sound a little more lively?' I asked him. 'I think they could be placed in a slightly different way sonically, so they're more present.'

He was very nice and took my unschooled criticism well. I'm sure he saw me as this guy from another world of music who didn't know what the fuck I was talking about.

'Uh, yeah. Yeah, man,' he said. 'I can do that.'

Dre went back to the studio and came back to present his new mix to us. It sounded the same to me. I'm not sure he even changed anything, but I wasn't about to say anything. We released the first single, 'No More Lies,' and it blew up. It was massive. Five weeks after that came out, *Michel'le* went gold.

N.W.A and Ruthless were happening in a big way, and it looked like there was plenty of money to be made with the distribution deal. But while Michel'le, N.W.A, and other acts were taking over gangsta rap, I was working on a pile of ATCO projects, and I couldn't devote the time they needed me to spend with them. I assigned one of my co-workers to oversee Ruthless, and soon after that, both companies decided the relationship wasn't as ideal as it initially seemed, so they parted ways—which, I must admit, troubled me not in the least. Another label, Priority Records, took over the distribution, and eventually Dr. Dre left Ruthless to start Death Row Records with Suge Knight.

ATCO was an artist's label, and the focus was primarily on music—or at least that was my goal—but since the label was an Atlantic imprint when I came on board, as opposed to an independent company, there was some carry-over from other parts of the Warner family, which is how we secured some of our acts. There was also a certain amount of bartering we had to do to secure the artists we wanted.

At the time, AC/DC were on Atlantic and were on the verge of being dropped. They were in a downward tumble and hadn't released a full-length original album since 1985's *Fly On The Wall*, which tanked. They could still fill venues on tour, but it looked like their best days were behind them and they would soon become a legacy band playing package tours in summer sheds. That would have been a shame, since they could still put on a great live show and were still talented artists who, I felt, still had plenty to offer. I thought they deserved a chance to redeem themselves, but the company was looking at paying them one million dollars for the next album they delivered.

'Ah, you can't drop AC/DC,' I told Doug Morris, who I tried to be as civil with as possible, even though I knew he had argued against me running ATCO.

'AC/DC has nothing left,' he said. 'And I don't see it happening in this music climate.'

'What are you talking about?' I said. 'It's AC/DC. They're legends.'

'Well, if you want to take them over to ATCO and try to get them to do something real, maybe we could trade. If you give me Pete Townshend, I'll give you AC/DC. Otherwise, I'm gonna drop them.'

'It's a deal,' I said. Pete Townshend was in the grandiose concept solo album phase of his career. In 1989, he did *Iron Man: The Musical*, which featured Pete, John Entwistle, and Roger Daltrey on two songs, as well as special guests Nina Simone and John Lee Hooker, but it still flopped. No one wanted to hear Pete Townshend doing conceptual music outside of The Who. By contrast, AC/DC were still gods of rock'n'roll. I thought that if they had the right support, they could write another hit album. It was about time. I made the trade with Doug, and I looked forward to the challenge of working with the band.

AC/DC had never allowed anyone from Atlantic into the studio before, and they were reluctant to play the record-company game. I thought having a history as a recording and touring artist might encourage them to be more open with me than some of the pencil-pushing label guys they were used to. I wanted them to see me as someone who was on their side and had done what they'd done. I hoped my insider angle would pay off, and I had some connections to them that I thought might thaw the ice. When I was in Simon Dupree & the Big Sound, we had played some festivals with the Easybeats, the band that featured Angus and Malcolm Young's brother George as well as Harry Vanda, who co-produced AC/DC's early albums. Plus, I had produced Gentle Giant albums, and I knew working closely with producers was important to AC/DC. I also knew their managers: Stewart Young, who also managed Emerson, Lake & Palmer; and Steve Barnett, who worked for Gerry Bron.

I called Stewart to talk about AC/DC moving over to ATCO and said, 'I'd love to work a little bit with Angus and Malcolm when they're in the studio, if that's okay with them.'

To my delight, they were fine with it. They were ecstatic about being off Atlantic as the guy who signed them had left the label and they no longer felt connected to the company. They were pleased that their new label head understood music—not just business—and were interested in working with me to help them revamp their sound.

Knowing that a great producer could help put them back on track, I called Bruce Fairbairn, who was excited to be asked to work with the band. (I mean, really, Bob? Who doesn't like AC/DC?) They went out to Bruce's place in Vancouver and felt invigorated working on a new record for a new label in a new environment. In a way, it was a rebirth, and suddenly they felt more inspired and creative than they had in ages.

It's so easy to be complacent about new AC/DC songs. Even the band members recognize that everything they do is going to sound inimitably like AC/DC. They'll never branch off in a crazy art-rock direction or add samples and electronic beats to their music. At the same time, while there are bands that can approximate AC/DC's bluesy hard-rock sound, no one can effectively imitate it in a meaningful way that stands the test of time. That said, it's easy to listen to a new AC/DC riff and say, 'Yeah, it sounds like AC/DC.' But it's harder to know right away if it's going to be *good* AC/DC or *classic* AC/DC.

I went to Vancouver a number of times to check on the band's progress and help with some of the song arrangements. Welshman Chris Slade was drumming for them at the time, on what would be his only record with the band. He replaced Simon Wright, who had left to join Dio. Angus Young told Chris not to play any drum fills or breaks whatsoever, just kick drum and snare. Unconventional as this was, it turned Chris into a metronome, and he kept perfect time. In most other bands, a drummer who doesn't swing or play fills would make the music sound stagnant. But as I learned by watching them in action, the rhythmic surge and punch in AC/DC came from the rhythm guitarist, Malcolm Young, and he's a large part of the reason why they were so incredible.

You don't realize it until you see the process unfolding, and it's fascinating to watch. Everyone in the band understood that Malcolm was the anchor and root of every song, and he had such a great connection with his brother, Angus, that Angus could intuitively play leads and fills on top of Malcolm's riffs and they always filled any gaps and perfectly complemented the rhythm parts. The chemistry between them was explosive, and the rest of the band fleshed out the sound. If there was a break in a song, it was followed with a resounding boom that released all the built-up tension in a rush of sound.

AC/DC perfected this formula years before they signed to ATCO. Maybe they became complacent at a certain point. But there was a new energy to the songs they worked on with Bruce for *The Razor's Edge*. The opening rapid-fire hammer-on and pull-off thing Angus does on 'Thunderstruck' is as iconic as Eddie Van Halen's solo in 'Eruption,' and perhaps even catchier. As the song builds, Malcolm turns up the heat with a funky little part, and the song his critical mass with the pre-chorus before lightning strikes in the chorus. Genius.

I have to admit that as great as that song was, I felt that 'Moneytalks' should be the first single. It surged at a mid-tempo, it was more simplistic, and I thought it contained the most accessible hook on the album. Angus and the band's managers all thought we should go with 'Thunderstruck,' so we did, and it blew up. That confirmed something I had believed for years: by far the best A&R guys are musicians. They're the ones who know their fans and the marketplace the best.

The Razor's Edge was a global sensation that hit like a cluster bomb at just the right time. 'Thunderstruck,' 'Moneytalks,' and 'Are You Ready' all became go-to radio tracks, and the album hit #2 on the *Billboard* 200 and remained on the chart for seventy-seven weeks straight. Bruce also produced the 1992 album *AC/DC Live*, which was recorded during the tour for *The Razor's Edge* and was also a big success.

I made another big trade with Doug Morris soon after I acquired AC/DC. Stevie Nicks was on ATCO, and I swapped her for Bad Company, who had been signed to Atlantic. That switch happened after Bad Company's manager, Bud Prager, told me that Doug had made it clear that he had no interest in another Bad Company record with vocalist Brian Howe, and the band would love to be on ATCO. I knew Brian from many years back. He was from Portsmouth and a fan of Gentle Giant. He could be arrogant and full of shit, but I could tell him to 'Shut the fuck up for a minute, will you?' and he would accept it from me since we had a shared background. It was a rocky time for the band, and there was grating friction between guitarist Mick Ralphs and drummer Simon Kirke, but they had written some great songs with producer Terry Thomas for their 1988 album *Dangerous Age*, which did quite well. Still, it wasn't the breakthrough Atlantic had hoped for. I thought I could help them change that, and I did. *Holy Water* came out in 1990, and the title track was a worldwide hit. The album went platinum in the US. As far as trades with Doug went, I was two for two.

I helped reboot Bad Company a full seventeen years into their career. By contrast, I signed the Boston-based group Dream Theater, who have now been together for almost forty years, before most people knew who they were.

I had just hired a friend from England, Derek Oliver, to be an A&R man, and he introduced me to the band. They had already released an album on Mechanic through MCA, *When Dream And Day Unite*, but it was mostly composed of the songs they wrote in the late 80s when they called themselves Majesty, and since the record company didn't consider it a priority, practically no one heard it. Soon after that, they were dropped, and no other labels were interested in them.

Derek liked the band and invited them to come into the office to play us some of their new songs. At that point, Dream Theater only had a four-song instrumental demo, but when drummer Mike Portnoy played the songs for us, I felt like they were very well put together. They were obviously influenced by progressive hard-rock bands like Rush, but they were heavier and more metallic. The musicianship was tight, and it was clear that these guys were talented.

I liked Mike right away. He was incredibly enthusiastic in telling me how their next album would be leaps and bounds above their first record, and how that one was actually a terrible reflection of them; they had grown so much since those songs were written, and they were searching for a new singer, which is why the demo didn't have vocals. I couldn't very well sign them to a major label deal based on four demo songs, especially since I hadn't heard their new singer. But I was intrigued. Their predicament reminded me of the situation Ray, Phil, and I were in when we were transforming from Simon Dupree & The Big Sound to Gentle Giant and looking for a new label.

'I like the songs,' I told Mike. 'And I'd like to help you out.'

I offered him a development deal, which gave Dream Theater enough money to record six full songs. I told him that if those were as good as the ones he'd played me, we could talk about a record contract. A couple of months later, Mike came back to me with six newly recorded songs featuring vocalist James Labrie, and they sounded amazing. We cut a deal with them for the album that became *Images And Words*. The musically complex album hit #61 on the *Billboard* 200 and eventually went gold. But as good as the album was, there was no way it would have received such strong radio and MTV support if we hadn't twisted the arms of the right people, or at least serviced them with phone calls that made both of our jobs easier.

The best song on the album was 'Pull Me Under,' which seemed like it would do well on radio—except it was over eight minutes long. Derek and I met with our radio guy, Harry Palmer, and we all decided the best way to get it on radio was to edit it down to a five-minute single. Some bands—especially those who consider a song to be a complete musical piece—might refuse such requests. God knows, Gentle Giant would have told the label to fuck off if they wanted to transform a fully formed composition into a bite-sized radio nugget. But I wasn't representing Gentle Giant, I was advising Dream Theater.

We contacted the band and their producer, David Prater, and they agreed to work together to edit the song down. It took them a big of wrangling, but sure enough, they got the version for the video down to 4:49 and made two radio edits, one at 6:01 and one at 5:54. They managed to cut the song down without killing it, which is a remarkable feat. MTV wouldn't consider playing anything more than five minutes long, but they loved the song, and since it came in just under the maximum length, they aired the video many times. Lots of radio stations played the six-minute version, while those that had strict rules about songs that were that long accepted the 5:54 edit. 'Pull Me Under' turned Dream Theater into prog-metal stars worldwide, and the guys were so happy we'd gone to bat for them and figured out a way to get their epic song on air.

I was also expecting big things from one of my other signings at the label. It was a band called Enuff Z'Nuff from Blue Island, Illinois, of all places. They had developed a strong following in the Chicago glam-metal scene, and their song 'Fingers On It' had featured in the 1986 film *Henry: Portrait Of A Serial Killer*. I had seen them a couple of times and heard their demos, and I thought they made some of the best good-time rock I had heard since Cinderella. They had the psychedelic charge of Badfinger, the hooky songwriting of Cheap Trick, and the sleazy swagger of Mötley Crüe. Their frontman, Donnie Vie, was pure eye candy in concert, and the band was a sheer endorphin rush. By the time I was ready to pull the trigger, they had already recorded a self-titled EP, but they didn't have a home for it yet. I contacted their manager and offered them a deal. Then, after I signed them, they recorded their first album.

We released *E'Nuff Z'Nuff* in 1989. Sure E'Nuff, the video for the first single, 'New Thing,' was embraced by MTV and went into regular rotation at lots of radio stations. The next single, 'Fly High Michelle,' did even better, hitting #47 on the *Billboard* Hot 100, and MTV played the hell of out of it. To keep the band flying and ensure our parent company continued to support them, I pushed hard to convince everyone in our meetings that E'Nuff Z'Nuff were a headline band and should play showcases at all the big music conventions.

Everyone at every record company went to these music conventions, the biggest of which were Concrete Foundations Forum, New Music Seminar, and CMJ. We got Enuff Z'Nuff booked as the headliners of the Foundations Forum. We promoted the shit out of it and told every radio DJ, journalist, editor, and video-company staffer that it would be a legendary gig.

It *was* memorable, but for all the wrong reasons. The band got fucked up before the show, and their performance was all over the place. The guitars were out of tune, the rhythms were sloppy, and the vocals didn't punch at nearly the weight class the band usually hit.

It wasn't a career-ender, but it sure didn't help us get the support we wanted from anyone at Warner Music Group. I later found out that the band members were self-destructive and couldn't control their bad habits. They could have been one of the biggest rock bands of the 90s and beyond, but drugs and poor business decisions sealed their fate. We released their second album, *Strength*, which they worked on while their debut was gaining momentum. But their time had come and gone, and the album charted at #143 before fading from sight. We dropped them after that. It's a tragically familiar tale. Chemical romance was their ticket to obscurity.

Before E'Nuff Z'Nuff snorted their way off the map, everyone who heard them believed they were heading for greatness. During that time, Pantera were taking off, AC/DC were on fire, and I was trying to suss out what everyone in the Warner family thought of ATCO and whether their goals for the company complemented mine. I was also still trying to figure out the status of my working relationship with Doug Morris. He hadn't wanted me to be a part of Warners, but now that I was on board and didn't threaten his job in the least, he seemed to have made peace with me. Our artist trades were amicable—even though they usually benefited me more than him—and I wanted to keep the peace and remain civil, but I was ever cautious.

One day, when we were casually chatting, he showed his true colors.

'You've got a lot of new releases,' he said. 'What's your favorite record coming out?'

'I'll tell you now,' I said without a pause. 'It's a band called E'Nuff Z'Nuff. It's going to be fucking massive. I love this band.'

'Yeah, you know. I think I've heard about it,' he replied. 'It's supposed to be pretty good.'

'So, Doug,' I said, in an effort to continue the friendly conversation. 'What's your favorite new Atlantic record?'

'Well, let me show you what *I* like,' he said. He brought over a blue and white alphabetized sales sheet and placed it in front of us. He put his index finger at the top line and scrolled down, stopping at a name three-quarters of the way down the page. 'That's my favorite,' he said, pointing at the biggest seller.

My heart sank. He didn't care about the music. All that mattered to him were numbers. That's when the shoe dropped and I saw what I was up against. This was the corporate *who gives a shit what it is as long as it sells* music industry, and I was surrounded by it. That was the writing on the wall.

CHAPTER TWENTY-TWO MONSTERS OF MOSCOW

One of the highlights of my career, and a high-water mark for Pantera, happened during a break from the first batch of studio sessions for *Vulgar Display Of Power*. The Soviet Union was in a state of collapse, and on December 25, 1991, Mikhail Gorbachev resigned as the president and Boris Yeltsin became the head of the new, independent Russian state. When that happened, Mark Ross, who was still fairly new to the game but clearly possessed the right genes for A&R, had a stroke of genius.

'Derek, I think it would be great if we could stage a free concert in Moscow to celebrate the new freedoms of the Russian people,' he said.

'Fuck yeah!' I replied. 'Let's do it!'

'But how to hell do we get it done?' Mark countered. 'Things are happening over there now, but there are going to be changes soon. We could do it now, but if we wait more than a month or so, it might be too late.'

It's hard enough to get the proper permits and stage a festival concert in the US in less than a few months. To get bands, managers, and labels on board, negotiate a big concert event with Russian promoters during a time of turbulence and transition, find a place to accommodate tons of people, and get the permission of the government and the cooperation of the police and military seemed impossible.

'Derek,' Mark said after a pause. 'Would you mind if I asked my dad if he could help us make this happen?'

Mark always walked a slippery slope between being a record company employee and the son of the guy who ran the company. He always tried to downplay the family connection, but this was one time he wanted to exploit it.

'If you feel comfortable doing that, it could only help,' I said. 'If he can open the doors, I'd be happy to step in and take over. And then we could work together to make it happen.'

Mark talked to his dad, and Steve thought it was a great idea. He allocated four million dollars for booking the bands, getting the show cleared, and making it happen. He wasn't just being benevolent. As a brilliant businessman and strategic capitalist, he viewed a less restrictive marketplace in Russia as an opportunity to directly import records to stores over there. He understood that introducing live Western music to a mass audience was a good investment.

We approached the biggest, most energetic rock bands we had access to—AC/DC, Pantera, and Metallica, who were on Elektra. The final band was The Black Crowes, who made the bill more diverse. Mark helped out with the scheduling and venue coordination, and I handled the more political tasks. I knew that certain people would have to be paid off to prevent the project from stalling or grinding to a halt, and I took the lead with the behind-the-scenes negotiations. I talked to a few people under the Warner umbrella, one of whom worked in the international department and had been to Russia before. He was Marty Payson, the CFO of Warner Music Group, and, like Sharon, he was involved in Jewish dissident causes.

'Whatever you're thinking Russia is going to be like, put it out of your mind, because what you'll experience is the complete opposite of what you're expecting,' he explained. 'Be businesslike but compliant. Never challenge anyone's ego or authority.'

I thanked Marty for his advice and, amid fears of winding up in a Siberian chain gang, finalized my presentation. Sharon, who had been to Russia before on a covert mission to help Jews who wanted to leave the country, came along to lend support. We flew to Paris on the Concorde and then switched to a 747 from the 70s to go from Paris to Moscow. I was expecting to see a modern, major city airport. It was more like a packed, dingy rock club. The walls were spray-painted with political slogans, the floor looked like it hadn't been cleaned in a year, and the place stank of mildew, sweat, and fear. Our Russian contacts picked us up in a smelly, beaten-up limousine and drove us to our hotel. During the ride, we looked out the window and thought this must be what it's like to travel through a heavily bombed Third World country. The highways were normal enough, but when we exited onto the regular streets, it looked like we had entered South Central. Buildings were falling apart and debris littered the sidewalks. I had assumed Russia was a powerful country with a modern infrastructure. It was so strange to drive through this sad, crumbling place. There were old women on the sidewalks selling the shoes off their feet, and merchants peddling bags of potatoes to customers lined up for blocks.

We got to the hotel and checked into a room where the former secretary of state Jim Baker had just stayed. We were advised by an ambassador for the US government not to say anything political or private in our room, since it was surely bugged. Sharon said that this was true—every time she had gone to Moscow on reconnaissance missions, she was warned about Russians spying and asking leading questions that would betray her confidants and get her in trouble. She urged me to stay quiet and listen and took the lead when we were at the hotel. From the inside, the place was nice enough. The beds were comfortable, and the restaurant was decent, but one look out of the window confirmed that we were surrounded by poverty. If that was what the infant seeds of democracy looked like, I feared Russia had a long, hard road to climb to break the chains of communism.

We met with the people who were helping us organize the concert and were advised to import hundreds of workers from Belgium, Poland, and Romania to construct the stage and the surrounding buildings. I would have liked to hire Russian workers to help them overcome their extreme poverty, but we were warned that there were too many logistical issues. Everyone who applied for a job would have claimed to be an expert, even if he wasn't qualified to build a birdhouse, and we would have been wrapped up in red tape and government work permits. By hiring workers from outside the country, we would be dealing with a smaller pool of people with proven track records for constructing stages for major events in impossibly short periods of time. And, since they weren't from Russia, the government didn't have to be involved.

With the preliminary planning wrapped up, we flew back home and scrambled to continue our work. The event organizers over there got approval to build the stage at the Tushino Airfield, an open-air military location that could hold more than one million people. By the time we had the bands booked, the place secured, and the staff in place, there were just three weeks left to make sure the facility met safety standards—not that Russia had any, but we needed to make sure everyone who flew in would be able to perform, get around safely, and leave without being hassled or hurt. That was harder to guarantee than we thought: the police and military were handling security, and, depending on who we talked to, we were greeted either with optimism and joy or pessimism and hatred. Some of the old-guard military had been raised to despise American and Western music, and we wondered if they had an axe to grind.

There was excitement and tension surrounding the whole event, which was called Monsters Of Rock: Moscow—a reference to a yearly festival in England at Castle Donnington that ran from 1980 to 1996 before being resurrected by Live Nation as Download in 2003. There was also a Monsters Of Rock tour in the United States in 1988 that featured Kingdom Come, Metallica, Dokken, Scorpions, and headliners Van Halen (with vocalist Sammy Hagar). Even though they played second on that bill, it was widely accepted that Metallica plowed through the more mainstream-sounding bands—even Van Halen—and made a mark on the scene as prominently as a cement casting at Mann's Chinese Theater. We hoped the Moscow concert would give them the overseas presence they enjoyed in the States, though we doubted they'd wipe the floor with Pantera or AC/DC.

Fans in the crumbling Soviet Union were familiar with the bands on the lineup from black-market tape trading, but they'd never dreamed of actually seeing them live, and their excitement and energy couldn't be contained. The event was free, and we expected up to a million people to show up for it. At the eleventh hour, however, the show was in jeopardy of not happening. Mark and his team were told in no uncertain terms that the concert would be canceled unless some of the people who were in charge of the event were paid off, including the mayor and heads of the army.

Mark and his team had arrived a week in advance of the show, and now they had to fly back to New York, fill up suitcases with hundreds of thousands of dollars, and return to Moscow to 'take care of' those in charge. While Mark was out of the country handling financial arrangements, I met with the head of the army.

'You know,' he began. 'We expect there to be more than a million people coming. And, let's just say, we can't guarantee their safety. We'll need more soldiers to make sure everyone is as safe as possible. And we need to, well, take care of them.'

'What's that mean, exactly?' I asked.

'Well, you know what that means,' he said, then gave me a dollar figure.

With just over twenty-four hours to go until show time, I flew back home, filled another suitcase with $250,000, and brought it back to Moscow, where I was picked up and shuttled directly to the head of the army, who gladly took the suitcase from me.

On the day of the concert, I walked around the grounds to try to calm my nerves and shake my jetlag. The bands were all there, having arrived two days early, so Sharon and I took a stroll. There was nothing around the airfield, just empty space, and there were more than 1.6 million people arriving at the grounds. There were no stores, no merch counters. When a man wheeled out his ice cream cart a quarter mile from the venue, there were lines three blocks long. That paled in comparison to the bread lines, which looked to be two hundred yards long. But bread was free. Ice cream was not. And neither was McDonald's.

There was one single McDonald's in Moscow, and it was the only fast-food outlet in town. The venue didn't have any sort of catering for artists, so Mark and his team headed out to order five hundred Big Macs to feed the bands and crews.

Even with all the bribes we had to pay, the volatile environment, the lack of food, and the less-than-leisurely accommodations, the event was spectacular. The fans were rabid, rushing the stage until they couldn't squeeze any further up.

A Russian band I had never heard of opened the show. Then the Black Crowes went on. They were treated well by the crowd, who were starved for any kind of rock entertainment. When Pantera went on, the place went mad. These kids loved metal, craved catharsis, and needed to lose their shit to loud, wild bands. There was a gigantic screen in the middle of the airfield, which was the only way most of the crowd could even see the show. You'd never have known it. Fans a hundred yards from the screen and five hundred yards from the stage were in ecstasy, screaming along to songs they'd probably only heard on fiftieth-generation cassette burns. The sound was bombastic, and the bands were beyond pumped.

Metallica were incredible, as we predicted, and they later called Monsters Of Rock: Moscow one of the greatest shows they ever played. AC/DC ended the show with 'For Those About To Rock (We Salute You),' and to see 1.6 million people screaming at the top of their lungs, with cannons blasting to the music and fireworks exploding overhead, was beyond euphoric. It was completely, ridiculously amazing.

The only thing I regret about Monsters Of Rock: Moscow is that there wasn't better crowd control. There were up to a hundred thousand army soldiers there, and a lot of them were worse than the Hell's Angels at Altamont. As kids rushed forward, a wave of soldiers with batons and riffles was there to stop them. They had been ordered to keep the fans away from the front, and in their minds that meant they had free rein to beat the shit out of them. During Pantera's set, Phil threatened to stop the show if the soldiers kept beating the fans. Knowing the entire crowd would riot and tear the soldiers apart if the music stopped, the bullies backed off. But they were just as violent during Metallica and AC/DC. I knew kids were hurt at the show, but the Russian government kept such tight reigns over the media that I didn't find out that some of them were actually killed until a decade or more after the show. When I first heard that, I felt like I was going to throw up.

I felt similarly ill after I got back from Russia, but not from a rocky flight or jetlag. I had just pulled off the impossible, staging one of the biggest hard-rock concerts ever. And my team and I did it in a place where no one thought it could be done, and in a region that needed ear-blasting escapism more than anywhere else. In a month, we had surmounted countless obstacles and put The Black Crowes, Pantera, Metallica, and

AC/DC in the minds and hearts of the Russian people. In other words, I was on top of the world. So, I think anyone can understand how upset I was to find out that while I was out of the country, working hard to change the global landscape for rock, Doug Morris was doing everything in his power to change the structure of Warner Music—to humiliate me and solidify his place in the hierarchy of the corporation. He was already the co-chairman and co-CEO of Atlantic, and now he wanted to stage a coup to dissolve ATCO.

Steve Ross had become critically ill with prostate cancer. Bob Morgado, who had been chief of staff for New York governor Hugh L. Carey and wasn't a music guy at all, became chairman of the Warner Music Group and started to flex his muscles. He had already put the thumbscrews on Warner execs Mo Ostin and Lenny Waronker, and now Doug wanted to exploit the shakeup to move up in Warner Music Group. He wanted me out of the way, so he scheduled a meeting with the ailing Ross (who died in December 1992) and convinced him to shutter ATCO and promote his assistant, Sylvia Rhone, to run Elektra Records.

Not long after I returned to the States, Harry Palmer dropped by my office.

'Hey man, are you sitting down?'

'No, I'm doing a handstand on my desk,' I quipped. 'What's going on?'

'I'm not sure, but it might be bad news,' he said, knowing full well that he was being euphemistic. 'Doug has told a couple of the staff members in radio promotion that they no longer work for ATCO. They're working for Elektra. And he told other people at ATCO they no longer have jobs.'

'What the fuck are you talking about?'

'This all happened while you were gone,' he said.

I went to see Bob Morgado to find out what was going on. Bob was strictly a numbers guy. He didn't care about musicians, art, or loyalty to staffers.

'Bob, what's happening? You're closing ATCO?' I said, barely able to control my anger.

'Doug said it was a good idea, and it makes sense to me,' he said. 'He said you and Sylvia could be co-chairpersons of Elektra. You can work together.'

This was completely out of the realms of anything I could have predicted, and it was the last thing I wanted—to work with Doug's inexperienced assistant, Sylvia, and teach her how to run a record label while we shared the credit for my work. I should have taken a deep breath and told Bob I would think about it, but I was being diplomatic.

'No fucking way!' I shouted. 'After I went to Russia to put on this huge show, to be stabbed in the back while I'm gone is bullshit! Go fuck yourself! I'm done!'

Bob could have shown me the door, but he recognized my value to the company, and he knew Sylvia was green and needed help with Elektra.

'Derek,' he said, 'just pick a record company to run, and you can work alongside Sylvia.'

That might have worked out if Doug hadn't gone already around me while I was gone. As it was, the axe was already buried in my back. The bridge was burned.

'No chance in hell,' I said between gritted teeth. 'I'm out. I'm done.'

Was it the right thing to do? Damn right, it was. Was it a smart thing to do financially? No, but I didn't care. I had revived ATCO and turned it into a profitable, artistic label. They had taken my baby and drowned it.

The situation was exacerbated by timing. I had just experienced an incredible high and then come back to a soul-ripping low. I still had time left on my contract, so we wrangled around different ideas, but none of them involved keeping ATCO going on my terms with my staff, so I refused everything. The imprint was worth about a hundred million dollars, and I owned a piece of it. I had signed a joint-venture deal. I could have fought them for the money I was owed. Instead, I used the leverage I had to justify my exit as an executive and prepare for my future.

'I don't give a shit about any other label, and if you want to keep me from going elsewhere, you better come up with a deal I can stomach.'

I stayed on for a year in a diminished capacity under Irving Azoff and kept my salary. I still made money, but it was a low point in my career. I put together a small staff and kept showing up at the office every day. I was going through the motions, acting like a record guy but feeling like a fucked-over artist. I was, as my brother Phil would have put it, licking the ass that fed me, acquiring the taste until I couldn't stand it anymore.

That year, Warner Music Group went through more shakeups that splintered more labels and left former peers without jobs. I had no more fight left. I kept playing my role and cashing my checks. One morning, I looked at myself in the mirror as I was getting ready for work. I was clean-shaven, wearing an expensive suit, and about to scurry to the office like a corporate pawn.

'Who is that guy?' I said with a frown, poking the mirror where it reflected my chin.

Later that day, I was sitting in the office with Harry Palmer, who was now the general manager of ATCO. The radio was on, and I was listening to a poppy love song with a syncopated beat, buoyant horns, and sugary female vocals.

'I've heard this before,' I said. 'I like it. Harry, do you know who this is?'

He chuckled, looked at me like I was joking, and went back to scrolling through a spreadsheet.

'No, I'm serious,' I said. 'Who is this? It's catchy.'

'What are you talking about?' replied Harry. 'It's "Sincerely Yours" by Sweet Sensation. We signed them, and it was a big hit. It's ours.'

This was an epiphany as poignant as the moment when I decided I couldn't be Simon Dupree anymore. *Okay*, I thought, *I'm doing it wrong. This is not who I am. I'm not good at this anymore, and I don't even care. This music is not for me, and maybe it never was.*

It was the first real wake-up call for me since Doug Morris pointed to a sales chart and showed me what was important to him. Not the music, the sales. And now I had learned the hard way that he would threaten and intimidate people into doing his dirty work so that his job remained safe.

The corporate game was over. Much of the old guard was gone, anyway, so I worked out a deal where I would be taken care of for the eighteen months that were left in my contract and left the company. I was still financially secure. Mentally, I was broken.

GIANT STEPS

CHAPTER TWENTY-THREE
LEADER OF MEN

After riding out my contract with Warner Bros, I took six months off to figure out what I wanted to do next. The taste in my mouth on my last day at work was like sour bile. I wasn't even sure I wanted to stay in the music, but if I did, it sure wouldn't be in a cutthroat corporate environment where artists were only as important as the number of records they sold.

I took a couple of business meetings, including one with Columbia. They were still very interested in having me work for the company, but it was the same team that offered me hookers and blow, and I took that as a warning sign that I should stay out of the corporate world. Fool me once, shame on you. Fool me twice, shame on me.

Everyone in the music business knew about the fragmentation of ATCO and my subsequent departure, so I wasn't surprised that people kept checking to see if I was looking for another job. I ignored most of them, but one that interested me was from Cees Wessels. I had known Cees from when he worked in marketing at RCA and I was at PolyGram. He seemed like an interesting guy. I had heard that he'd moved back home to Holland and started an indie metal label, Roadrunner, and I was curious about an operatic, face-painted metal artist he signed named King Diamond, who was originally in the popular Danish black-metal band Mercyful Fate. There was a time when I'd considered bringing King Diamond over to PolyGram. At the time, Cees was calling the company RoadRacer after receiving a cease-and-desist from Warner Bros, whose cartoon friend of Bugs Bunny took exception to a label stealing his name. When enough money (or ACME TNT) exchanged hands, Cees regained the name Roadrunner. I was aware Roadrunner had risen to some recognition in the underground, but I hadn't kept track of any of the bands.

When Cees called and asked if I would meet with him, I was determined not to go back to being a major label executive. But Roadrunner was an indie label with respectable clients, so I agreed to get together. I didn't realize he lived only a few blocks away from me on the Upper West Side. We met for dinner and talked shop for a bit. He told me about the history of Roadrunner, and we discussed his plans to expand the company. He was already working with a sharp A&R guy named Monte Connor, who had an encyclopedic knowledge of metal and had signed underground bands including Death, Deicide, and Obituary during the heyday of the Florida death-metal scene. He also signed the Brazilian thrash titans Sepultura, who went on to solid success at Columbia, and the artsy, gothic doom-metal band Type O Negative—the first act on the label to go platinum. Cees wanted to develop the label beyond metal and sign a more diverse and hopefully lucrative roster. While he wanted to remain independent, he was intent on signing acts to compete with the major labels. He started by buying a hip-hop label in Atlanta called Power Records and a dance label called Next Plateau, and he was recruiting electronic dance groups and new wave bands to other imprints. His intentions were good, but he lacked the musical savvy to make sure he was signing promising and profitable acts.

'We don't have a proper setup,' he admitted. 'Would you be interested in overseeing everything?'

'What do you have in mind?' I asked.

'I want you to run everything and make sure we have bands that will make money.'

I followed him back to the office to take a look at the place and the people who worked there and I immediately noticed a huge difference between the Roadrunner staff and the employees of Warner Music Group. Roadrunner's team wasn't made up of business-school majors and communications graduates moving product. They all seemed like they had worked for college radio stations or mom-and-pop record stores.

They loved what they did and they lived for the music they promoted. They were dedicated, knowledgeable music fans, and when they weren't in the office they were at shows or hanging out elsewhere with their artists and co-workers. I thought these would be great people to work with and oversee. At the same time, I noticed they were predominantly rock fans, yet they were also working with hip-hop and dance acts they didn't quite understand because they weren't part of that culture.

'Well, Cees,' I said. 'You've got the makings of a great company here. But if you want me to be involved, the first thing I've got to do, unfortunately, is to undo some of the things you've done.'

I told Cees that I felt the company could do really well, but that they were trying to tackle more than they could wrap their arms around and spreading themselves too thin. To make it work, Roadrunner had to get rid of all the other genres he had put money into—namely, hip-hop and dance music—and be really, really good at one thing. This was going to be a bit unpleasant for me, since the founder of Next Plateau, Eddie O'Laughlin, was a good friend and a talented label guy who'd signed Salt-N-Pepa in 1987. I'd have to tell him that Roadrunner was shedding everything hip-hop or dance-related, including Salt-N-Pepa, and focusing exclusively on rock and metal.

At first, Cees, who didn't like any of the metal bands on Roadrunner, tried to win me over with another approach.

'Well, how about we focus on pop?' he said. 'I like pop, and it's what radio stations and MTV are all playing.'

Cees didn't know pop music any better than he knew metal. He was a marketing guy. He took two-week trips to Europe every month and wrote down the names of all the successful pop and electronic music he heard in the hope of signing them in the US. I told him it would require tens of millions of dollars to compete with pop divisions at Warners, Columbia, and Geffen, and that he'd have to bring in an entirely new staff. His current employees were pros with rock music, but they knew very little about pop.

'Let's focus on being the best rock label in the world,' I said. 'We can work with rock and metal and make Roadrunner a household name for that kind of music. You've already got the staff for it.'

It was a golden plan with a major problem. Cees hated rock music. His world revolved around classical, and he would go to eight Wagner Ring Cycles a year. He had hired people who loved the music he despised and were successful at promoting it, so he'd built a company rooted in metal. That's what he was known for, and now I was asking him to double down. It was a good idea, but he didn't understand what he had. He had only fallen into metal because he had limited funds and the bands he brought into the fold were relatively cheap to sign and produce. He had made good money doing this for years. Type O Negative, Sepultura, and Fear Factory were all successful bands who sold a lot of albums and toured the world. They were highly profitable, and I wanted to take them—and new bands from the same world—to the next level.

'Derek, you know the record business world, and you know rock,' Cees said. 'I've done well, but I'd like to be bigger. If we put all our efforts into rock, can you oversee the company and do what you did at PolyGram and ATCO?'

It was a tempting offer. My only reservation was that he didn't have the kind of backing those labels had, so there wasn't a lot of money to throw around. We'd have to find great artists who hadn't yet been discovered by major labels. I had experience with that, and Roadrunner had done well with bands that could have been on major labels. But if I was going to be involved, Cees had to view music as art and not just a commodity. I believed in the kind of artist development that had enabled artists like Gentle Giant, Bon Jovi, and Pantera to grow and evolve. Cees didn't understand the musical references, but he grasped the marketing potential and he was all in.

I came on as president of Roadrunner in late 1997. The first thing I did was sit down with Monte and the marketing guys and talk about the bands who were already on the label and had the potential to become more popular. I wanted everyone who was there to be a part of the process and not feel like I was some big-label douchebag that had swooped in to ransack their cottage industry, take credit for their achievements, and threaten their jobs.

'I very much want to work as a team,' I said, which was probably the first thing some asshole from a corporate label would say before coming in and destroying a company. 'You guys know and understand the music you work with. You've built it into this great thing. I've been elsewhere doing other things, so I don't know everyone you've been involved with. Fill me in and let me know how you think we can grow these artists even more. Let's see what we can do to help this thing get to where we want it to be and let's focus on these bands.'

If nothing else, the meeting was meant to rally the team, to show them that we were on the same page and I didn't want to wreck their playground. I wanted to make it bigger and stronger. The first band I saw with a glimmer of going a little further was Coal Chamber. Their song 'Loco' was a crazy metal song, but it had strong melodies, and in a nu-metal scene that supported bands like Korn and Deftones, they were promising.

'I think we could take this to rock radio, not just college metal stations,' I said. 'Even though it's hardcore, it's got a bit of a chorus—even if it's a shouty chorus.'

Everyone liked the idea, and as I got to know the members of Coal Chamber and talked to them about their goals, it reinforced my hopes that Roadrunner was the right fit for me. I loved being at an independent company where I could sit down with the musicians and say, 'Look, here's what we've got, and here's what we can do for you.' They understood, and they reacted positively. I think they liked getting feedback from the label president, as opposed to hearing something some marketing guy told their manager.

I listened to all the albums with scheduled releases and met with artists. Some bands didn't want guidance and wanted to call their own shots. That was fine, and as long as they were good for the label, they kept their deals. Those who wanted to work with me usually received more of my attention and more of the company's resources. I was clear about what the company could afford to spend on them to make them bigger, and what our plan of attack was. With a strong push to rock radio and a wildly surreal video that did well on MTV, 'Loco' ranked on numerous rock, metal, and radio charts, and Coal Chamber's self-titled album went gold.

I was more hands-on working with Fear Factory, helping them to reach a larger audience. They were an extreme band influenced by thrash, industrial music, and a little death metal. But their vocalist, Burton C. Bell, had singing chops: he see-sawed between bloody-throated screaming and melodic crooning long before metalcore groups like Killswitch Engage and All That Remains came onto the scene. Burt was a star, and guitarist Dino Cazares had speedy riffs, searing solos, and great stage presence. I talked to them about writing a purely melodic song, but that didn't feel authentic to them. So, I suggested they cover a catchy tune by someone they liked. We tossed around some ideas, and they decided it might be fun to do a loud, modern take on Gary Numan's 1979 new-wave hit 'Cars.' It was the perfect choice. We got Gary to add vocals, and we included it as the bonus track on Fear Factory's 1998 album *Obsolete*. The song became a hit on radio, and a video (which also featured Numan) received heavy airplay on MTV. In the end, 'Cars' helped springboard *Obsolete* to 750,000 sales and renewed public interest in Numan.

If Fear Factory had started writing songs that were still futuristic but slightly more commercial, they might have achieved the multi-platinum success that other unconventional metal bands such as Tool or System Of A Down enjoyed. But like many of the bands on Roadrunner, they wanted to remain *un*commercial. It's an aesthetic of the extreme metal genre. Commerciality is equated with selling out, even though groups like Pantera and Slayer remained successful without even coming close to selling out. So many of these bands shun mainstream exposure and, effectively, slit their own throats. They crave attention, but they're afraid of becoming successful, as if accomplishing that is somehow a kiss of death. And then, if they're *not* successful, they get frustrated and break up. It's a self-defeating situation, and it caps these bands' success at a certain level. They taste, see, and smell fame, but they want it on their own terms. If they're happy with where that takes them, more power to them. But a lot of them commit commercial suicide after a hit and then can't figure out why they didn't make it. That was the case for both Coal Chamber and Fear Factory.

Monte and the rest of the team were infinitely supportive of finding bands that could be coached. Enter Slipknot. Monte brought the band to me and told me how great they were. When we went to see them, it was like nothing I'd ever witnessed—nine guys in masks and matching jumpsuits going completely insane. There were two crazed percussionists a furiously precise fast drummer (Joey Jordison, RIP), and a vocalist who seemed as intent on injuring himself as he was in screaming and singing. Their shows clocked in somewhere between performance art and the end of the world. It was ridiculous in an incredible way. I was similarly magnetized by them as I had been by Pantera, and the only time I looked away from the stage was to watch the crowd, which was equally spellbound. This was something fucked-up, perverse, and remarkable.

'Monte, this is crazy,' I said. 'I can't even describe it. Don't let them get away.'

Slipknot became part of the Roadrunner team, and we went into their first album all guns blazing, pairing them with maverick producer Ross Robinson, who had worked with Korn and Sepultura. The first single was 'Wait And Bleed,' and we were able to get it onto mainstream rock radio, which was no small achievement for such an extreme band. Everyone at Roadrunner worked incredibly hard, and the band's music spread like a disease. MTV came on board, the international department made it a priority, and 'Wait And Bleed' became the first gigantic worldwide hit on Roadrunner. I was so proud of my team—some of whom I'd inherited, some of whom I'd hired—for being so gung-ho about breaking Slipknot without taking any creative control away from the band. And Slipknot rewarded us by playing to their strengths, killing themselves on the road, and becoming the scariest, wildest, most unpredictable, and best fucking metal band of their generation.

That was a major turning point. I had a great team that made the label shine, which also reflected well on me. It was everything I had wanted at PolyGram, everything I had tried to put together at ATCO—and had for a short while—but on a level where no one's main objective was to throw darts at the board to see what sticks. Cees was delighted. He couldn't begin to understand Slipknot, but he didn't have to. *I* understood Slipknot, and my staff understood them even better. Cees understood the platinum records the band brought him, and that was all he ever wanted. After we helped turn Slipknot into a world-class metal band, I thought, *Man, if we can do that for such a subversive, misanthropic group, imagine what we could do for a mainstream-style band?* I would find out soon enough.

One of the A&R guys at the company, Ron Burman, was excited about music, bubbled with enthusiasm, and was eager to share his discoveries. He would regularly come into my office with six new tapes and tell me they were all great. One day, I asked him to discuss his latest gems with me, one at a time.

'Ron, is this great?' I'd say each time.

'Yeah!' he'd reply.

'Ron, are they all great?' I asked after hearing them, knowing full well that they weren't. Some were average at best. 'Which one is going to be the biggest?'

'They're all going to be!'

'No, wrong. That's not how it works,' I corrected him. 'You've got to see them, taste them, smell them. You've got to determine how something makes you feel, why it accomplishes that, and how it compares to everything else. Not everything can be the best.'

He listened intently to what I was saying, and some of it sunk in. His enthusiasm never waned, and he kept bringing me boxes of new tapes. One of them contained a grungy song called 'Leader Of Men' from an unknown rock band.

'Okay, now what is that?' I asked, my ears perking to the music.

'It's some band out of Vancouver,' Ron said. 'I think it's really good.'

'Yes,' I told him. 'There's something there. This is a really good song.'

When Ron went back to his cubicle, he was glowing. I finally liked something he played for me. I looked at the tape and it was one of three demos by a band called Nickelback. I sat at my desk and played 'Leader Of Men' over and over. I did my research, made some calls, and found out they had released an EP and a couple of albums on their own between 1996 and 1998. They shopped them everywhere, but no one wanted them. Everyone thought their latest record, *The State*, was horrible. I kept playing 'Leader Of Men' and thought it could be a hit. I'd heard their other songs, as well as *The State*, and I thought that if they had the financial support and the right team to work with—our team—they could be pretty successful.

I went straight to Dave Loncao, Roadrunner's head of radio promotion, who I had hired a few months earlier. I played him 'Leader Of Men' and asked him what he thought.

'It's a fucking smash,' he enthused. 'I know I can get this onto radio, big time.'

Nickelback's frontman, Chad Kroeger, had a great voice in a commercial Creed-meets-Bush sort of way. 'Leader Of Men' didn't have a chorus, which is not always good, but in this case, it impressed me. The song had a great build-up, and anyone who can write a song that repeats the same kind of verse four times without boring their listeners and *doesn't* need a refrain is a damn good songwriter.

I took Ron Burman to Vancouver with me to check out the band live. Ron was thrilled that I was interested in one of his finds and was excited about the trip. We saw Nickelback in a small rock club. The sound in the place wasn't great, and it wasn't packed, but the band were good, and Chad was a solid frontman onstage. I decided to sign them.

At the time, Nickelback were working with an inexperienced attorney. I asked him what was happening with the band, and he showed all his cards. Nickelback had self-released *The State* in late 1998, and it didn't go anywhere. The lawyer was trying to get the band a deal in Canada, and while they had generated a bit of interest at EMI, it seemed to have waned. I had been worried that there would be a bidding war for Nickelback, yet they couldn't even get a decent deal in their own town.

I was excited, but I held my hand close to the vest. 'You know,' I said to the lawyer. 'I might be interested. Let me think about it.'

I signed Nickelback to a relatively cheap deal. We put out 'Leader Of Men' as a single, and the band went Top 10 on radio. It happened that fast. By the time we put out *The State* in late 2000, the album had been released twice—including, as it turned out, in a limited run by EMI Canada—and we were still able to blast out three more singles and reach #130 on *Billboard*. The scene was set for the follow-up, which was recorded in the same studio they'd used for their last album. Recognizing their roots in classic rock and grunge, we hooked them up with producer Rick Parashar, who had previously worked in Seattle with Pearl Jam, Temple Of The Dog, and Alice In Chains. He clicked perfectly with Kroeger, and in just a few months Nickelback had recorded *Silver Side Up*.

Before the album came out, I heard some of the tracks, including 'How You Remind Me.' I had no doubt that the song would be a huge radio hit, and if that translated into sales, they could be the biggest band on the label. It was almost like hearing Bon Jovi all over again. That song started a wave of momentum that never let up. In October 2001, a month after it was released, *Silver Side Up* was certified gold and platinum. Less than four years later, it had gone six times platinum in the US, eight times platinum in Canada, and three times platinum in the UK.

Before we signed Nickelback, Roadrunner was worth somewhere between ten and fifteen million dollars. By 2005, the label was worth closer to sixty million. We had effectively boosted the label's profile and legitimized it for anyone who had previously dismissed it as an underground metal label. Moreover, we had done so while retaining a team atmosphere and nurturing and supporting all of our artists as they progressed through their careers.

I wanted to continue at that pace. Cees wanted to shoot for Jupiter. In his mind, he thought he was getting as big as some of the major labels and should pursue more bands that would be hugely profitable and go multi-platinum. He was more of a marketing man than a music man, and even though his label had been going for decades, he didn't realize or accept that you can never count on finding the next Nickelback. Bands that strike a chord with the mainstream and become massive stars so quickly come along about once every five or ten years. It doesn't matter if you're a huge label with endless funds or an indie that happens to strike oil (as Sub Pop did with Nirvana). It's a rare phenomenon, and I was lucky enough to have played a role in the careers of a few mega-platinum groups.

'Derek, we need to sign more bands like Nickelback,' Cees said, blinded by the green. 'What they're doing doesn't seem so unusual. There must be a hundred that are just as good that haven't been discovered yet.'

It was like he'd forgotten that Roadrunner was built on a foundation of underground music that strongly appealed to a certain demographic. By hiring the right people and signing good-quality bands, Roadrunner had become a tastemaker, and fans trusted that if a new band was on the label, they would probably like them—or at least should give them a chance.

I like to use this expression for Roadrunner: you have to build a cake first before you can eat it. The cake was built over time and finished when Slipknot broke. Nickelback were the icing on the cake. But to complete the analogy, if you put too much icing on a cake, it falls apart. Cees loved icing, and he didn't want it to stop raining down. As impossible as that was to do, he sure tried. The mandate was to bring more super-melodic, alternative hard-rock bands to the label. So, Roadrunner signed bands like Theory Of A Deadman, Feeder, and Ether Seeds, which I felt was a bad move. It's not that they were horrible bands. You just can't force lightning to strike twice.

In a further quest for another multi-platinum winner, Cees insisted on selling twenty-five percent of Roadrunner to a European pop music company called Edel. The deal fell apart and put Cees in financial jeopardy. I was upset that he wouldn't follow my advice, but in the end, he owned the company and I didn't. I had a piece of it, and I was being paid well to run it.

I kept coming to work and following Cees's direction, but I was also starting to plan my exit. Being at Roadrunner was no longer inspiring. I wanted to keep looking for quality rock artists and help them grow, just like I was hired to do. Now, however, we had less money to sign great bands, I was making fewer creative decisions, and regretfully, Roadrunner was turning into what I hated about the music business. The last thing I wanted was to see was Roadrunner adopting the capitalistic, hedonistic MO of Atlantic, Universal, Columbia, and the rest.

Cees could tell I was unhappy with the changes taking place at the label, and we scheduled a meeting to discuss the future.

'First of all, I'm really glad you brought me in,' I told him. 'And I'm happy to have been a part of building Roadrunner into a hundred-million-dollar company. I wanted to be a part of something that was primarily about the bands and the music, and we made that happen. But now I'm afraid we've become more about business than music.'

Cees explained that he was hamstrung by the deal with Edel that went sour and now felt he had to sell Roadrunner to remain profitable. When Roadrunner went down further in value, he sold it to Warners, who made the label an Elektra imprint. If he had sold it when it was at its prime, he would have made four or five times more money than he got in the end. By then, Roadrunner was in bad shape and the cash flow was drying up. The label was still selling lots of records by Nickelback and Slipknot, but Cees had brought over too many of these Nickelback-style bands he thought would make him richer, and he was spending way too much money on marketing and promotion to try to break them. We parted ways after he sold the company, and today, Roadrunner, though still a label, is no longer the indie powerhouse that helped redefine the metal and hard rock genres; sadly, now it is just an imprint of the Warner Music Group repertoire, the history and the amazing success of this iconic rock and metal label just a sad asterisk.

GIANT STEPS

CHAPTER TWENTY-FOUR

LEGEND HAS IT

Looking back, one of my strangest and funniest moments at Roadrunner took place early on, when Cees still wanted to expand into the hip-hop world and the label was looking at signing a distribution deal with Psychopathic Records, which was owned by the loose-cannon rap-rockers Insane Clown Posse. The Posse were especially interested in pushing an album by the horror-themed rap group Twiztid, featuring ex-House Of Krazees members Jamie Madrox and Monoxide Child.

I scheduled a meeting with Monte and ICP to find out what we might be getting ourselves into. Soon after we sat down in the conference room, they slid a CD into the stereo, and on came their signature song, 'Diemuthafuckadie.' As soon as the riff kicked in, Madrox and Monoxide Child were banging their heads to the beat and grooving with the song, which was underpinned by a buoyant, whimsical, and all too familiar melody. I turned to them in complete and utter bewilderment.

'Yo, yo. Listen to the chorus when we go, *Die, fuckin' die / diemuthafuckadiemuthackadie!*' Madrox said with a grin. He gesticulated with both arms, looking like a gangly puppet with tattoo sleeves.

'Yeah, man. This is the bomb!' Monoxide Child added.

I had to say something. I turned to look at the fellows in Twiztid. 'Well, do you know who that song is? I mean, the sample.'

'Well, it's something you've probably never heard of, but I tracked that shit down,' Monoxide said. 'It's this totally unknown band called Gentle

Giant. They have this song called "Spooky Boogie," but I'm sure you've never heard it, you know?'

I blinked hard and looked back at him. It wasn't just a riff they were looping—it was the whole hook of the song. I smiled. I was sure Monte was playing a joke on me and had put the clowns up to this.

Am I being punked here? I thought. *Is Ashton Kutcher going to walk in any second, laughing his ass off?*

No, I wasn't being punked. These guys were as serious as a spoonful of cooked meth. I turned to Monte, who was squirming in his seat. 'Wow, I don't know what to say. This could be interesting.'

I walked out smiling at the absurdity of the situation. A few minutes later, Monte came into my office. 'We're not working with these guys,' I told him. 'I don't want anything to do with them or their inane posse.'

As it turned out, Twiztid had released 'Diemuthafuckadie' on their own, and the song was a minor hit and a fan favorite. I picked up the phone and called my attorney. In the end, we got a nice little settlement from Twiztid and Psychopathic Records for copyright infringement.

It wasn't just that they'd ripped off our song. Kansas and Styx liberally borrowed ideas from Gentle Giant and admitted that we were a major influence. That was flattering. But Twiztid weren't influenced by 'Spooky Boogie.' They stole it. They didn't even ask for permission to use the song before they sampled the majority of it. And then they did absolutely no homework before entering a meeting with me and playing me my own music. That seemed unbelievably unprofessional at the time, but now, whenever I think about it, I can't help but laugh. The incident was so ridiculous and surreal that if Nick Hornby incorporated this scene into a novel, his editor might tell him it's too farfetched. Whatever, it kind of makes me wish we'd called *our* song 'Diemuthafuckadie' instead of 'Spooky Boogie.'

From a time even before the British Invasion, playing rock'n'roll was a way for young adults to try to rise out of the slums to a different level of society. Tons of artists never made it out of their practice rooms, but so many teenagers across the world picked up instruments and gave it a go that, based on probability alone, a bunch of them were going to make it on some level.

In the UK, the British Invasion only increased the public's interest in music and the cultural flood of new bands. Most didn't have the tenacity, talent, or luck to become local—let along national—celebrities even if they were very good. Then, there were bands like Simon Dupree & The Big Sound who moved away from friends, sacrificed relationships, lived on digestive biscuits, tea, and lentils, slept on strangers' floors, and slaved away at menial jobs for next to nothing just for the chance to break out of our humdrum upbringings and do something our parents or our grandparents would never have dreamed of doing.

For me, that's where the kinship between Gentle Giant and some groups in the underground hip-hop community begins. We all came from the same place—the gloomy slums—and turned to music in an effort to escape our environments and outrun our demons. So, I completely understand how artists such as Questlove feel a special relationship with Gentle Giant, and why rappers like Travis Scott, De La Soul, A Tribe Called Quest, Run The Jewels, and yes, even Twiztid have been inspired by our music enough to want to sample our hooks for their songs and, in effect, create a new relationship between the zeitgeists of contemporary rap and our fifty-plus-year-old music.

Gentle Giant haven't played a note together since 1980. We thought our music would live forever because it's original, well-crafted, and enjoyable for those who crave something outside the mainstream. And, on a certain level, it has. We've seen diehard Gentle Giant fans clamor for vinyl reissues, remastered albums (many of them lovingly crafted by Porcupine Tree's Steven Wilson), and box sets of unreleased live recordings. But it's tracks like Travis Scott's hit 'Hyaena,' the opening number of his 2023 album *Utopia*, that most effectively expand the reach of Gentle Giant's music and expose us to a new audience.

'Hyaena' opens with an almost thirty-second sample of 'Proclamation' from our 1974 album *The Power And The Glory*. At the time of writing, that is the most recent and most loved recontextualization of our music. When Travis performs 'Hyaena' in concert, thousands of fans sing along with the Giant intro. Many of them don't know where it came from and don't care. A select few, however—the analytical music fanatics and hip-hop producers—take a dive down the rabbit hole, and, without having to go too deep, discover that Gentle Giant have been sampled on more than a hundred rap songs, while many contemporary artists (including those listed above) have cultivated as much appreciation for our unconventional songs as I have for theirs.

When I started at ATCO and worked with Michel'le, I couldn't understand the language of hip-hop. I grasped the business side of things, and the danger of it was real enough, but the art eluded me. At first, it all seemed strange and percussive—all beat, no melody—but now I get why underground hip-hop is seen as the new progressive music movement. By focusing on hybrid songwriting and innovative performance, young artists are getting off the streets and into the studio, providing themselves with an opportunity to escape poverty and become established through the expressive language of their music. No one in the establishment is reaching out to help them succeed or even pushing for them to get ahead. This is the world they inhabit, and, as a kid who struggled to escape the streets of Portsmouth and make a name for myself on the global stage, I can relate to that.

And, apparently, it is natural for rap acts to integrate elements of rock into their music. They have been blending styles since 1973, when dancefloor DJ Kool Herc started using two turntables at the same time to loop James Brown's breakbeat in 'Funky Drummer,' and Grandmaster Flash used a crossfader to make the process more fluid when he deejayed warehouse hip-hop parties that same decade.

As it turns out, 'Diemuthafuckadie' wasn't the very first song to feature a Gentle Giant sample. In 1996, unbeknown to me, the British duo The Wiseguys recorded the buoyant rap song, 'Sweet Baby Truth,' using samples from Jimi Hendrix's 'Hush Now' and 'Aspirations' from *The Power And The Glory*. Other parts of 'Aspirations' would later be sampled by The Samurai Of Prog in 2013 and Roberto Ottaviano in 2015.

The Power And The Glory soon became a favorite among the experimental hip-hop community. 'Playing The Game' was sampled by I.G. Off & Hazadous for his 1997 track 'Hip Hop Til I Die,' and in 1999 by Lootpak, who also sampled 'Proclamation' in two tracks, including one featuring Defari and Tha Alkaholiks. Kenny Dope referenced the same track on his 2001 song 'Thoughts & Visions,' before Travis Scott made the intro into a sing-along anthem. Another big year for Gentle Giant samples was 2016. Our 1972 *Octopus* song 'Knots' was famously sampled by Run The Jewels for their hit 'Legend Has It,' which was used in a trailer for the 2018 movie *Black Panther*, and in a Lexus commercial.

For a while, I was oblivious to much of this. I first learned that Gentle Giant had scored major points in the hip-hop community in 2014 when I was running Frontiers Records, a very successful Italian independent label that specializes in melodic rock, and had bought Heart frontwoman Ann Wilson over to *The Tonight Show With Jimmy Fallon*. We went backstage and were ushered into the talk show's green room.

I have never liked green rooms; they're too much like corporate conference rooms before a big meeting, and they make me uncomfortable. I tried to play it cool, though, and Ann and I engaged in small talk while one of the director's assistants searched for the show's musical director, Questlove. This was during the first season his group, The Roots, were the house band for the show. When they'd finished whatever it was they were doing, some of the musicians filtered into the room. I introduced them to Ann. Keyboardist James Poyser greeted her, then turned to me.

'You're not the Derek Shulman of Gentle Giant, are you?' he asked.

'Actually, yes. Yes, I am.'

'Hold on just a second!' Poyser rushed out of the room.

'I don't know what that is about,' I said to Ann, and she smiled. We continued talking, and then Poyser returned with Questlove.

'Derek? Derek Shulman,' said the six-foot-plus tall drummer with a humungous afro approaching me with something resembling hesitancy.

'Yes, I'm here representing Ann,' I said.

'Oh my God!' Questlove shot back. 'I love you, man! Gentle Giant are my favorite rock group. Seriously!'

He and the other members of The Roots asked me for my autograph and took pictures with me. Poor Ann Wilson, who was supposed to be the real music star of the day, quietly sat in a chair, out of the range of the cellphone cameras. This was the kind of treatment she was used to receiving, not observing.

'Man, if you want to, send me some music stems, we'd love to work with you,' Questlove said.

I remember thinking, *Wow, these guys are on TV every night with all kinds of guest stars. How do they act when Paul McCartney is on the show?* Not that they were at all unprofessional with me. I later found out that, no, Questlove doesn't fanboy over major celebrities. Gentle Giant have a special place in his life, and we have stayed in touch over the years and maintained a strong relationship. He still posts images of us on his socials as one of his favorite bands, for which I'm grateful and humbled.

I had a somewhat similar experience in 2017, when Run The Jewels played four sold-out nights in Hell's Kitchen at the popular club Terminal 5. My son Noah and I went to one of the shows, and it was so crowded inside we could barely move, even in the VIP area. The concert was incredible, and after the show we went backstage to say hello and congratulations to rappers El-P and Killer Mike. I can only compare what transpired to an early 90s *Saturday Night Live* 'Wayne's World' skit, in which Mike Myers (Wayne) and Dana Carvey (Garth) utter their show's catchphrase, 'We're not worthy.' When Run The Jewels met me, they immediately bowed before me with exaggerated arm gestures and big smiles. It felt very odd because they had just played in front of thousands of adoring fans, and yet here they were honoring me as some sort of hero, which I've never pretended to be.

I suppose people like Questlove, El-P, and Killer Mike have their music heroes, as do we all, and when they first discovered Gentle Giant in their youth, it was a revelation for them. It's heart-warming to me, and not just because it's gratifying to receive accolades from artists I admire. More importantly, it means the legacy of Gentle Giant lives on in the hearts and minds of the next generation of underground music enthusiasts. We never achieved the mainstream popularity of Genesis, Yes, or Rush (even when we tried for it), but we remain cult pioneers whose music has struck a chord with a new breed of sonic experimentalists. I can't say why this has happened. I can only guess. Maybe it's because Gentle Giant were never trying to be a symphony orchestra. We didn't have Mellotron parts or multiple percussionists. We didn't want to be existential philosophers, spiritual healers, or space warriors. We wrote fairly intricate pieces that involved point-counterpoint dynamics and intertwining parts that were very good musically and interesting to listen to. And the uniqueness of the band seems to have appealed to the more creative members of the hip-hop community, who recognize and respect the authenticity of it—because that's such an important trait of music for them as well.

With the exception of Twiztid, I credit every hip-hop act that has sampled our music for creating an original work of art. Back in 2016, A Tribe Called Quest sampled our 1972 *Three Friends* song 'Prologue' for their song 'Mobius' and hired Busta Rhymes and Consequence to guest on the track. When I first heard our delicate, ethereal passage underneath this confrontational beat, I felt strange. It was our music, but it wasn't. The entire tone had changed, and the confrontational charge was never something we considered.

This is not our music, I thought, and, maybe, at that moment, I was a little disappointed. In hindsight, I realize that of course it's *not* our music, and it *shouldn't* be our music. Those are our notes, voices, and arrangements, but they've been recontextualized to fit someone else's aesthetic. They made it their own, which is what progressivism is about.

Today, I tip my hat to them and to everyone else who has kept our fifty-year-old-plus music alive by adapting it in a modern context that we could never have imagined. And for those who care to take the time to listen to it, study it, and compare the sampled parts to the way they were originally used, I hope they come out of their analysis with bold, new ideas to take the songs even further. For me, it's fascinating to see how the torch has been passed, because I was involved with it when it was first conceived. Now, as I look at these creative reinventions, I realize that our passages are just as real to the artists working with them now as they were to us when we wrote them.

For a guy who was part of a band that stopped writing songs in 1980—a band whose most talented member, my dear brother Ray, died in 2023; whose oldest member, my brother Phil, recently turned eighty-eight; and whose youngest member, Gary Green, was seventy-four at the time this book was submitted—it's amazing to know the music lives on.

EPILOGUE

WALKING BACK TO HAPPINESS

Sometimes, when musicians spend too much time away from the recording studio—a place where innovation, collaboration, and sometimes confrontation blend to create something bigger than the sum of its parts—the fires of invention tend to fizzle. I've had an incredible time working for more than forty years to help artists of all styles evolve and develop. The rewards of nurturing untapped newcomers into seasoned professionals are considerable, both personally and financially. It has also been hugely rewarding to take the helm of new and resurrected labels and build them into formidable, competitive entities with rosters of credible, noteworthy rock bands and solo acts.

At the same time, the decades I've spent working with other people on their music and celebrating their accomplishments yielded vicarious victories. At best—if I had played an active role in helping shape songs (as I did with Bon Jovi, Cinderella, Dream Theater, and Men Without Hats), it was a musical win for everybody. At worst, it was a fringe benefit of working a corporate job. Most often, it was a semi-creative pursuit that distracted me from thinking about what had made me happier and more fulfilled than any other job in the world.

When I was a label guy, I almost forget the enthralling euphoria of being right in there with my brothers and best friends working on tight deadlines to write, play, and record songs that represent who and what you are, how you feel, and what you have to contribute to the history and culture of music. It's a thrill that I subconsciously wrote off as a reward from the past—a one-of-a-kind sensation of pure freedom that came to an end when I parted ways with Gentle Giant in 1980.

Whenever I got melancholy about being away from the spotlight, I reminded myself that if great things lasted forever, there'd be no way to judge how amazing they were. My brother Ray and I had a great fifteen-plus-year run, which is five years longer than The Beatles were together. From the mid-60s, I was in creative environments with the best musicians and producers, and we worked together to turn magnetic tape into streams of authentic, high-concept art without sacrificing our integrity or resorting to pretension. Along with my blood and band brothers, I took a thrilling thirteen-album ride (including Simon Dupree and *Playing The Fool*) through a rock'n'roll amusement park, and I emerged sated and mostly unscathed. I figured I had accepted my fate and moved on.

That said, I have had the chance to take numerous glances in the rearview mirror to re-envision the power and glory of the past. My bandmates and I have enjoyed backward glimpses of those great times during strolls down memory lane. We were invigorated when fans fawned over us—especially those who were accomplished musicians, themselves. And, whenever we have reissued an album or unearthed old live recordings for a box set or special edition, it has allowed us to savor another taste of past lives.

Our first opportunity to hear full Gentle Giant albums reimagined and reinterpreted came courtesy of Porcupine Tree vocalist and producer Steven Wilson. He had already been creating 5.1 stereo remixes of albums by King Crimson, Jethro Tull, and Yes when he told Ray he was a huge Gentle Giant fan and would love to remix some titles from our catalogue. Ray told me right away, and then I talked to Kerry and Gary. We all loved the idea and felt it would add new luster to reissues of albums that some considered forty years past their sell-by date.

'Is it possible for me to remix *In A Glass House*?' Steven asked Ray during their first conversation. 'That's what I would love to work on most, of everything you've done. It would be exciting to get my hands on those recordings and try to do what I think would benefit those songs right now.'

We would have loved to offer him the gig. Sadly, the original multitracks of *In A Glass House* were lost. It was the only album in our catalogue that no one could find the tapes for. We looked everywhere, but no dice. They could have burned up in the 2008 fire at Universal Studios that destroyed as many as 175,000 audio master tapes from the UMG vaults. They might have been disposed of by Worldwide Artists Management out of spite after we exposed them for screwing us, Black Sabbath, and others. Or, maybe they mysteriously disappeared after WWA had to leave their offices in a hurry for legal reasons.

Steven was disappointed, but he still wanted to work with us. He started with a wonderful remix of *The Power And The Glory*, which we released in 2014, and he followed up the next year with *Octopus*, which was also fantastic. By 2024, he had remixed half or more of our catalogue and lovingly recalibrated every delicate nuance and dramatic arrangement. We've been thrilled with everything Steven has done with our catalogue and consider him an honorary band member.

I thought Steven was going to be the only producer to work with Gentle Giant's catalogue. That changed after 2023, when Paul McCartney announced that he had just finished creating a new Beatles song, 'Now And Then,' using a five-minute piano demo John Lennon recorded around 1977 on a tape recorder at home in the Dakota in New York. With the help of director Peter Jackson's production company, WingNut Films, a team of audio experts and programmers used AI to turn the vocals from Lennon's bedroom demo into a studio-quality vocal. I read about how Jackson's team used AI to separate the stems—not tracks, but excised bits of audio—to build new recordings. I was intrigued, but at the time I couldn't imagine using AI for Gentle Giant's music.

Then my son Noah, who had hired sound mixers for various video projects when he worked at Sony, put me in touch with a talented Brazilian producer and engineer in Brooklyn named Eber Pinheiro. I was impressed to learn that Eber was a Grammy-nominated engineer who had worked with Chick Corea, Gilberto Gil, Stanley Clarke, Jewel, and others. He has also mixed many television and movie soundtracks. I felt proud that Noah worked with such a talented guy. It's always amazing to see your children's accomplishments. For, me, I think the feeling was sweetened by knowing that both my kids' accomplishments were related to music. And it was even sweeter when Noah told me that Eber had asked him about Gentle Giant and the missing multitracks for *In A Glass House*.

'This guy's a big, big fan of yours,' Noah told me. 'He said he'd like to get together with you. How would you like to see if you two can do something new with *In A Glass House*, using AI to make up for the missing multis?'

I thought this was a stellar idea and could put closure on an album I had been wrestling with for decades. Not only was *In A Glass House* the first Gentle Giant record we did after Phil left the band—and long before the two of us were again on speaking terms—it was the one on which I laid my feelings bare about the way he abandoned the group and the betrayal I felt in the aftermath. When it was done, I had mixed feelings about the album. It was dark and pain-stricken, and for the longest time, I couldn't listen to it without getting upset. It was a bad period for me and the band that I didn't want to revisit. And then, as time healed over the scarred memories, I began to look at the album from a different perspective.

When we recorded it, I was still single, and I was furious that Phil would abandon his family—not just me and Ray, but the whole band—to devote his life to his wife and kids. In hindsight, I understand what a tough decision it was for him and why he prioritized his family. Of course he did. He had no choice. It was either lose the band or lose his family. It was a no-win situation—a Sophie's choice, so to speak—and he did the best he could.

Decades later, when all that had thankfully sunk in and I had accepted Phil's decision, I developed a new appreciation for *In A Glass House*. Listening to it no longer emphasized betrayal. It conjured the emotional resonance of a bleak period in my life without it feeling personal. The creativity that came out of the unhappiness was tangible. Viewing it in a new light, I could appreciate the music and not get bogged down by the message. So, I agreed to go to the Inputpost studio with Eber to test whether or not modern machinery could breathe new life into Gentle Giant.

As a band, we had always embraced advances in studio technology, so it made sense to give this AI thing a shot. We tested it on two songs, and I had no idea what to expect. Eber was able to separate virtually all the tracks on 'Way Of Life' and 'The Runaway.' Watching the process unfold and taking part in the editing was incredible. Using AI tools, he was able to take something that was done and gone and bring it back to life. When he worked with the drum tracks, Eber separated the kick drums, snares, toms, and cymbals and turned them into completely separate tracks he could strengthen with AI algorithms. He did the same thing with the guitars and all the other instruments.

Working with Eber, I was able to remix 'Way Of Life,' which made me feel incredible—young, vibrant, Giant-like. When the band first recorded it, we had used the best equipment that was available at the time. Now, Eber was using a whole new level of technology to rebuild this piece of history. It was a huge moment for me. Listening to the tracks and saying to the engineer, 'Why don't we try to subtly double track this guitar part?' or 'Can you bring this vocal part a little higher in the mix?' brought me back to the days when I was making similar decisions as a songwriter, vocalist, and co-producer.

At one point, Eber played back a track I had provided input for, and my eyes welled with tears. So many emotions informed the salty rivulets that ran down my cheeks—elation, pride, grief, nostalgia. It was more powerful musically than anything I had experienced since we broke up the band, and it brought me back to the days when my sole objective was to be a musician. Eber saw me crying and asked if I was okay. I told him I was better than okay. Sitting there in my late seventies, feeling like I was seventeen again, made me feel completely fulfilled. Eber was pleased that his work moved me the way it did. He told me Gentle Giant's music was still extremely popular in his native Brazil (which I knew already because it is home to three of the top ten cities for Gentle Giant streams on Spotify).

After the session, Eber's business partner, Mario, walked in. He was also a Gentle Giant fan, and he explained to me how our music had helped his best friend in Brazil, Xorus, out of a deep, dark abyss. After undergoing a string of awful personal issues, Xorus was about to take his life. In a bizarre twist of fate, he decided he wanted to stay alive after listening to *In A Glass House*.

I was speechless. Mario asked if would join a video call with Xorus, and I readily agreed.

'Say hello to Derek Shulman,' Eber said after Mario's iPhone lit up. Xorus was dumbfounded; he was as elated and ecstatic as Questlove had been that day at *The Tonight Show*. He smiled wide, and tears of joy sprung from his eyes. He told me his real name was Tiago, and that Mario wasn't exaggerating when he told me Gentle Giant's music saved his life. All the beauty was gone from his life, then he heard something beautiful, and it filled him with resolve.

There was so much emotion, delight, and respect between the three of us that I thought the WiFi would crash from the swarm of human energy. I know Tiago will never forget the call, but I think it affected me just as deeply. And that, coupled with the resurrection of these two Gentle Giant tracks, was almost too much to absorb in one day. To think it all stemmed from the memories and experiences three different people had from a single album over the span of decades. In a very real sense, I got to re-experience the creation of *In A Glass House*, while at the same time experiencing its re-creation. And, as we remixed 'Way Of Life' and 'Runaway,' the meaning of the entire album was further reinvented for me. It was so revelatory that I was even excited to tell the story to Phil.

To listen to these fifty-year-old tracks made new, to watch the stems being separated, to add studio effects to guitars the same way we would have done and rebuild something we feared was unsalvageable, was astonishing. I closed my eyes as I listened to the music, and I was there again with Ray, Kerry, Gary, and John, tweaking and modifying it to meet our stringent standards. Then I flashed back to the present, and I was painfully aware that Ray would never hear it. That was a fucking shame—a crime of mortality. Exercising the only option I had, I sent it to the other guys, and they loved it like I did.

It was a great metaphor for the ongoing evolution of Gentle Giant in a new digital age, but it meant even more to me as an artist. It made me stop and think about my life in music and all the roles I've played in that world, from artist to record label executive. More than anything I've done in decades it made me feel like a relevant recording artist again. For that session, I was back in Gentle Giant, and I realized that the feeling of creating something good and tangible was something I could never capture on the other side of the fence.

As a label guy, I was thrilled when Bon Jovi went to #1 with *Slippery When Wet*, and I had every right to be, since I was involved with the creation of that album right across the board. But that was a very different kind of joy than what I experienced sitting there and listening to the vocals, guitars, and keyboards of this long-lost album, and hearing them come together in a way that made it better than ever.

'Wow, we were great,' I said to Eber, and he agreed. That kind of truth is something you don't always accept or appreciate when you're in the middle of the creative process the first time around and you're caught up in all the minutiae of having to meet deadlines, plan a tour, promote yourself, and everything else that comes with being a living, breathing band constantly consumed with the crucial question: What's next?

Being back in the studio, fifty-plus years after making the album, feeling like I was a real part of its re-creation, was otherworldly. I walked out of the studio and flashed back over my entire career. Writing, creating, performing, being an artist—that was my life for just over fifteen years. Then, at a time when I felt I had contributed all I could as a musician, I went from the creation of music to the business of music. Thankfully, I was really good at both, and sitting behind a desk at a corporate music company—or five—made me financially secure and provided me with far more job security than I ever had as a frontman. At a time when I was starting a family, that was important. I always feared following in my father's footsteps—never being home at night, never being able to provide for my family. I'm proud to say I was there with my wife to raise our beautiful, creative children, neither of whom ever had to worry whether there would be enough money for food, holiday gifts, and college tuition, not to mention orthodontist bills, bar and bat mitzvahs, weddings, and an abundance of expensive creature comforts. Oy vey.

When I worked in the music business, the biggest artists I worked with or discovered all had one thing in common. They were true to themselves and had integrity. From my own band, Gentle Giant, to Elton John to AC/DC to Bon Jovi to Pantera, their music will live forever and will forever leave a legacy. These artists were never followers. They did it their way, whether with my help or on their own. What I fully understand in my golden years is that while I thankfully made a successful living helping to establish these incredible artists, in the end, it all comes back to the music and the visions of the artists creating it. That video call to Brazil reinforced this feeling in ways I had never imagined.

Now, in my late seventies, I spend a fair amount of time looking back at my life, and I have determined that when I was a recording artist in my late teens, twenties, and early thirties, creating experimental and unconventional music just for the sake of doing it, walking that tightrope and developing a fanbase of oddballs who were thrilled to take every precarious step along with us—that was the most fulfilling time in my professional life. After years of missing that and never expecting to regain it, I got to relive the experience when I worked with Eber to revisit those two songs from one of Gentle Giant's most loved albums, now with an unlimited number of tracks with which to rebuild and enhance the original recordings. Used in the right way, technology is a beautiful thing.

Back in the day, we started with four-track recorders, eventually graduating to sixteen tracks and finally twenty-four tracks. We were only limited by the gear that was available to us. Now, the only limit to creativity is narrow-mindedness, which Gentle Giant never suffered from, and which is something I've always shunned. Being back in a studio with an engineer and an abundance of artistic options made me giddy.

You know, it made me think, *this was me all along*.

Overcome by the ocean of sound coming from the speakers, the music took me back in time, and the long-dormant Giant was going through yet another growth spurt that even the hip-hop artists who loved sampling his creations couldn't match. This is not the past. It is the present in a place where time is but a construct. As old as the songs were, they were being reborn. They were transcendent and far greater than the sum of their parts. They were history. They are the present.

My father is here. Phil is here, Ray is here, and so are my brothers in the band. This is my music, my lyrics. For at least this moment, Gentle Giant are back in full force, doing exactly what we want. There are no compromises, and I'm thriving in my element. This is Derek Shulman. These are my real Giant Steps.

ACKNOWLEDGMENTS

This book is dedicated to my younger brother Ray, who passed away on March 30, 2023. He was my best friend as well as my co-conspirator in making music together for many decades.

My thanks go out to my wonderful wife and kids and all of my family who have been so supportive of me baring my soul in these pages.

Special thanks go out to 'The Boys In The Band.'

Thank you Ian, Noah, Mateo, Hilary, and especially Jon, who helped my mumbling speech appear lucid in print.

This book was inspired by a very special man, Jack Schwartz, who unfortunately passed away a couple of years ago. He was a journalist and editor for the *New York Times*. Whenever we would meet and I would relate my stories to him he would encourage me to write my book.

Jack, this one's for you.

ALSO AVAILABLE FROM JAWBONE PRESS

Riot On Sunset Strip: Rock'n'roll's Last Stand In Hollywood Domenic Priore

Million Dollar Bash: Bob Dylan, The Band, And The Basement Tapes Sid Griffin

Bowie In Berlin: A New Career In A New Town Thomas Jerome Seabrook

Hot Burritos: The True Story Of The Flying Burrito Brothers John Einarson with Chris Hillman

To Live Is To Die: The Life And Death Of Metallica's Cliff Burton Joel McIver

Jack Bruce Composing Himself: The Authorised Biography Harry Shapiro

Return Of The King: Elvis Presley's Great Comeback Gillian G. Gaar

Seasons They Change: The Story Of Acid And Psychedelic Folk Jeanette Leech

A Wizard, A True Star: Todd Rundgren In The Studio Paul Myers

The Resurrection Of Johnny Cash: Hurt, Redemption, And American Recordings Graeme Thomson

Entertain Us: The Rise Of Nirvana Gillian G. Gaar

Read & Burn: A Book About Wire Wilson Neate

Bathed In Lightning: John McLaughlin, The 60s And The Emerald Beyond Colin Harper

Big Star: The Story Of Rock's Forgotten Band Rob Jovanovic

Recombo DNA: The Story Of Devo, or How The 60s Became The 80s Kevin C. Smith

Neil Sedaka, Rock'n'roll Survivor: The Inside Story Of His Incredible Comeback Rich Podolsky

Touched By Grace: My Time With Jeff Buckley Gary Lucas

A Sense Of Wonder: Van Morrison's Ireland David Burke

What's Exactly The Matter With Me? Memoirs Of A Life In Music P.F. Sloan and S.E. Feinberg

Who Killed Mister Moonlight? Bauhaus, Black Magick, And Benediction David J. Haskins

Lee, Myself & I: Inside The Very Special World Of Lee Hazlewood Wyndham Wallace

Seeing The Real You At Last: Life And Love On The Road With Bob Dylan Britta Lee Shain

Long Promised Road: Carl Wilson, Soul Of The Beach Boys Kent Crowley

Throwing Frisbees At The Sun: A Book About Beck Rob Jovanovic

The Monkees, Head, And The 60s Peter Mills

Complicated Game: Inside The Songs Of XTC Andy Partridge and Todd Bernhardt

Confessions Of A Heretic: The Sacred & The Profane, Behemoth & Beyond Adam Nergal Darski with Mark Eglinton

Perfect Day: An Intimate Portrait Of Life With Lou Reed Bettye Kronstad

Adventures Of A Waterboy Mike Scott

Becoming Elektra: The Incredible True Story Of Jac Holzman's Visionary Record Label Mick Houghton

I Scare Myself: A Memoir Dan Hicks

Shredders! The Oral History Of Speed Guitar (And More) Greg Prato

Fearless: The Making Of Post-Rock Jeanette Leech

Tragedy: The Ballad Of The Bee Gees Jeff Apter

Shadows Across The Moon: Outlaws, Freaks, Shamans And The Making Of Ibiza Clubland Helen Donlon

Staying Alive: The Disco Inferno Of The Bee Gees Simon Spence

The Yacht Rock Book: The Oral History Of The Soft, Smooth Sounds Of The 70s And 80s Greg Prato

Earthbound: David Bowie and The Man Who Fell To Earth Susan Compo

What's Big And Purple And Lives In The Ocean? The Moby Grape Story Cam Cobb

Swans: Sacrifice And Transcendence: The Oral History Nick Soulsby

Small Victories: The True Story Of Faith No More Adrian Harte

AC/DC 1973–1980: The Bon Scott Years Jeff Apter

King's X: The Oral History Greg Prato

Keep Music Evil: The Brian Jonestown Massacre Story Jesse Valencia

Lunch With The Wild Frontiers: A History Of Britpop And Excess In 13½ Chapters Phill Savidge

More Life With Deth David Ellefson with Thom Hazaert

Wilcopedia: A Comprehensive Guide To The Music Of America's Best Band Daniel Cook Johnson

Take It Off: KISS Truly Unmasked Greg Prato

I Am Morbid: Ten Lessons Learned From Extreme Metal, Outlaw Country, And The Power Of Self-Determination David Vincent with Joel McIver

Lydia Lunch: The War Is Never Over: A Companion To The Film By Beth B. Nick Soulsby

Zeppelin Over Dayton: Guided By Voices Album By Album Jeff Gomez

What Makes The Monkey Dance: The Life And Music Of Chuck Prophet And Green On Red Stevie Simkin

So Much For The 30 Year Plan: Therapy? The Authorised Biography Simon Young

She Bop: The Definitive History Of Women In Popular Music Lucy O'Brien

Relax Baby Be Cool: The Artistry And Audacity Of Serge Gainsbourg Jeremy Allen

Seeing Sideways: A Memoir Of Music And Motherhood Kristin Hersh

Two Steps Forward, One Step Back: My Life In The Music Business Miles A. Copeland III

It Ain't Retro: Daptone Records & The 21st-Century Soul Revolution Jessica Lipsky

Renegade Snares: The Resistance & Resilience Of Drum & Bass Ben Murphy and Carl Loben

Southern Man: Music And Mayhem In The American South Alan Walden with S.E. Feinberg

Frank & Co: Conversations With Frank Zappa 1977–1993 Co de Kloet

All I Ever Wanted: A Rock 'n' Roll Memoir Kathy Valentine

Here They Come With Their Make-Up On: Suede, Coming Up ... And More Adventures Beyond The Wild Frontiers Jane Savidge

My Bloody Roots: From Sepultua To Soulfly And Beyond: The Autobiography Max Cavalera with Joel McIver

This Band Has No Past: How Cheap Trick Became Cheap Trick Brian J. Kramp

Gary Moore: The Official Biography Harry Shapiro

Holy Ghost: The Life & Death Of Free Jazz Pioneer Albert Ayler Richard Koloda

Conform To Deform: The Weird & Wonderful World Of Some Bizzare Wesley Doyle

Happy Forever: My Musical Adventures With The Turtles, Frank Zappa, T. Rex, Flo & Eddie, And More Mark Volman with John Cody

Johnny Thunders: In Cold Blood—The Official Biography, Revised & Updated Edition Nina Antonia

Absolute Beginner: Memoirs Of The World's Best Least-Known Guitarist Kevin Armstrong

Turn It Up! My Time Making Hit Records In The Glory Days Of Rock Music Tom Werman

Revolutionary Spirit: A Post-Punk Exorcism Paul Simpson

Don't Dream It's Over: The Remarkable Life Of Neil Finn Jeff Apter

Chopping Wood: Thoughts & Stories Of A Legendary American Folksinger Pete Seeger with David Bernz

Through The Crack In The Wall: The Secret History Of Josef K Johnnie Johnstone

Forever Changes: The Authorized Biography Of Arthur Lee & Love John Einarson

I Wouldn't Say It If It Wasn't True: A Memoir Of Life, Music, And The Dream Syndicate Steve Wynn

Jazz Revolutionary: The Life & Music Of Eric Dolphy Jonathon Grasse

Down On The Corner: Adventures In Busking & Street Music Cary Baker

Gliders Over Hollywood: Airships, Airplay, And The Art Of Rock Promotion Paul Rappaport

Decade Of Dissent: How 1960s Bob Dylan Changed The World Sean Egan

Doing Time: Comedians Talk Stand-Up JT Habersaat

Down River: In Search Of David Ackles Mark Brend